T0295802

Theoretical Foundations of Macroeconomic Policy

The recent economic events driven by the great financial crisis of 2007–2008 have challenged some 'dogma', highlighting various limits and drawbacks of current paradigms. The crisis showed the limitations of monetary policy and led to a revaluation of what levels of public debt could be considered safe. This volume aims to refresh the debate on some important long-run macroeconomic issues from new and fresh perspectives.

Theoretical Foundations of Macroeconomic Policy raises a number of questions relating to the challenges faced by macroeconomic theory and policies. The common themes are the long-run and policy perspectives. The first part of the book is devoted to the theory of growth and productivity. The second part concentrates on the long-run effects of fiscal and monetary policy. Specifically, the topics investigated by the international range of authors are the theory of optimal growth, the productivity policies and production function estimations, demand- vs. supply-driven growth, optimal debt default and the incompleteness of financial markets, the long-run optimal inflation target and its relationship with public finance, the long-term effects of government budget constraints on growth, and the effect on optimal policies in the non-market clearing environment.

The book will be of interest to postgraduates, researchers, and academics studying macroeconomics and fiscal policies.

Giovanni Di Bartolomeo teaches economic policy and monetary economics at the Sapienza University of Rome, Italy.

Enrico Saltari teaches economics and financial economics at the Sapienza University of Rome, Italy.

Routledge Frontiers of Political Economy

For a full list of titles in this series please visit
www.routledge.com/books/series/SE0345

Theoretical Foundations of Macroeconomic Policy

Growth, productivity and public finance

Edited by Giovanni Di Bartolomeo
and Enrico Saltari

Routledge
Taylor & Francis Group

LONDON AND NEW YORK

First published 2017
by Routledge
2 Park Square, Milton Park, Abingdon, Oxon OX14 4RN

and by Routledge
711 Third Avenue, New York, NY 10017

Routledge is an imprint of the Taylor & Francis Group, an informa business

British Library Cataloguing in Publication Data
A catalogue record for this book is available from the British Library

Library of Congress Cataloging in Publication Data
    Names: Di Bartolomeo, Giovanni, 1969- editor. |
    Saltari, Enrico, 1948- editor. Title: Theoretical foundations of macroeconomic
    policy : growth, productivity and public finance / edited by
    Giovanni Di Bartolomeo and Enrico Saltari.
    Description: New York : Routledge, 2016.
    Identifiers: LCCN 2016008458 | ISBN 9781138645844 (hardback) |
    ISBN 9781315627892 (ebook)Subjects: LCSH: Economic development. |
    Fiscal policy. | Inflation (Finance)–Effect of productivity on. | Labor policy.
    Classification: LCC HD75.T496 2016 | DDC 339.5–dc23LC
    record available at http://lccn.loc.gov/2016008458

ISBN: 978-1-138-64584-4 (hbk)
ISBN: 978-1-315-62789-2 (ebk)

Typeset in Times New Roman
by Sunrise Setting Ltd, Brixham, UK

MIX
Paper from
responsible sources
FSC
www.fsc.org   FSC® C013604

Printed and bound by CPI Group (UK) Ltd, Croydon, CR0 4YY

Contents

vi *Contents*

Figures

Tables

Contributors

Bas van Aarle obtained a PhD in economics from Tilburg University in 1997 and has been working as a macroeconomist in various positions since then, including at the universities of Nijmegen, Munich, Hasselt, Maastricht, and the research institutes Institute for Advanced Studies (IHS) Vienna, Zentrum für Europäische Wirtschaftsforschung (ZEW) Mannheim, and the Federaal Planbureau Brussels. Currently, he is working at the University of Leuven, Belgium (Centre for Irish Studies and Vlaams Instituut voor Economie en Samenleving (VIVES)). His research interests concern macroeconomic analysis and European integration in general and macroeconomic adjustment in the euro area in particular. Various studies on euro area monetary and fiscal policy design, macroeconomic adjustment, and structural reforms have been carried out by him in cooperation with other researchers.

Elton Beqiraj is Research Assistant at Sapienza University of Rome. His research interests include labor markets, public debt dynamics, and open economy models. He collaborates with different institutions at the Italian Ministry of Economics and Finance (where he worked on the extension of Italian General Equilibrium Model to financial frictions) and the Fondazione Brodolini.

Giuseppe Ciccarone, MPhil and PhD in Economics at the University of Cambridge and Post Doctoral Fellow at Harvard University, is Full Professor of Economic Policy at the Department of Economics and Law, and Dean of the Faculty of Economics at Sapienza University of Rome, where he is also Senior Fellow of the School of Advanced Studies and a member of the Academic Board of the Doctoral School of Economics. He is the Italian member of the European Employment Policy Observatory of the European Commission. His main contributions, which are mainly in the fields of economic theory, monetary policy and behavioral economics, have been published in books and in leading national and international academic journals.

Giovanni Di Bartolomeo teaches economic policy and monetary economics at the Sapienza University of Rome. He studied at the Universitat Pompeu Fabra (UPF) (Barcelona) and Sapienza. Previously, he worked at the University of

Teramo and Antwerp. He was also visiting at the University of Crete (Marie Curie Fellow), Center for Operations Research and Econometrics (CORE) (Louvain), and Center for Public Sector Research (CEFOS) (Gothenburg). He is active in the fields of monetary and fiscal policy, macroeconomics, and experimental economics. He has also published two research monographs with Cambridge University Press and one with Springer. He is policy advisor for several institutions.

Marco Di Pietro is Research Assistant at Sapienza University of Rome. His research and teaching interests include monetary economics and policy and heterogeneous expectation formation models. He collaborates with the Italian Ministry of Economics and Finance in developing and estimating the Italian General Equilibrium Model.

Silvia Fedeli is Full Professor of Public Finance at Sapienza University of Rome, where she has been Director of the Department of Economics and Law since 2013. She studied in Florence and York. She is a fellow of the International Institute of Public Finance, European Public Choice Society, American Public Choice Society, European Economic Association, and Società Italiana di Economia Pubblica (SIEP). She regularly publishes in refereed international journals. Her research and teaching interests include the theory of public finance, tax evasion, corruption, and voting systems.

Daniela Federici is Associate Professor of International Economics at University of Cassino and Southern Lazio. Federici's broad research interests are in exchange-rate dynamics, international trade, and productivity growth. She has published in journals including *Journal of Economic Dynamics & Control*, *Journal of International Money and Finance*, *Macroeconomic Dynamics*, and *Economics of Innovation and New Technology*.

Francesco Forte is Emeritus Professor of Public Finance at Sapienza University of Rome. He is one of the founders and Past President of the Public Choice Society and Honorary President of the International Institute of Public Finance. He has written on many fields in welfare economics, public economic theory, monetary and fiscal policy, and the theory of public finance, including some applied econometric topics and industrial economics. He has been visiting professor of several UK and US universities and of the Brooking Institution and the International Monetary Fund. He has been Vice President of Ente Nazionale Idrocarburi (ENI), member of the Italian Parliament from 1979 to 1994, Minister of the Italian Government from 1982 to 1987, and president of the Industry Committee of the Chamber and of the Finance and Treasury Committee of the Senate. He was policy advisor for the Italian Government, the Organization for Economic Co-operation and Development, the European Union, the United Nations, and the World Bank.

Francesco Giuli is Assistant Professor of Economic Policy at the Department of Economics of University of Rome III. Born in 1976, he is Doctor of

Philosophy (PhD) in Economics (Sapienza University of Rome, Italy). His main working experience is in economic policy modeling and his fields of study are economic theory, macroeconomic dynamics, and economic policy. He has published in highly ranked international journals such as *Economic Theory*, *Economic Letters*, *Journal of Economic Dynamics and Control*, *Macroeconomic Dynamics*, and *European Journal of Political Economy*.

Andrew Hughes Hallett is Professor of Economics and Public Policy at George Mason University, and Professor of Economics at the University of St Andrews. He is Fellow of the Royal Society of Edinburgh. He has written on many fields of economic theory, monetary and fiscal policy, the theory of economic policy, and policy coordination, including some applied econometric topics and optimization techniques. He is an active policy advisor for the World Bank, Scottish Government, European Central Bank, European Parliament and many others.

Olivier de La Grandville is Senior Professor at Frankfurt University and Visiting Professor in the Management Science and Engineering Department at Stanford University, a position he has held since 1988. He was Professor of Economics at the University of Geneva between 1978 and 2007 and is the author of seven books on a wide range of topics in microeconomics, macroeconomics, and finance.

Enrico Marchetti is Associate Professor of Economic Policy at the Parthenope University of Naples. He received his PhD from Sapienza University of Rome, where he has been assistant professor in economics and where he is a member of the academic board of the Doctoral School of Economics. His main research interests are macroeconomic policy, labor market analysis, and behavioral macroeconomics.

Lebogang Mateane received his PhD from the New School for Social Research, New York in 2015. His research and teaching interests are macroeconomics, international finance, econometrics, and portfolio optimization models. He was an Associate Lecturer at the University of the Witwatersrand, Johannesburg, South Africa, and is currently a Senior Lecturer at the University of Cape Town, South Africa.

Renato Paniccià is Senior Economist at IRPET (Regional Institute for Economic Planning of Tuscany). He has many years of experience in regional macroeconometrics, Multiregional Input–Output Database (MRIO) modeling, and MRIO tables estimation. His research is focused on macroeconomic of growth, regional disparities analysis, and convergence/divergence processes.

Stefano Prezioso is Senior Researcher at SVIMEZ (Association for the Development of Industry in Southern Italy), Rome, Italy. He has been working with a bi-regional econometric model (NMODS). His research is focused on industrial organization and economic development.

Enrico Saltari has been Full Professor of Economia Politica, Facoltà di Economia, Sapienza University of Rome since 2001 (previously at the University of Urbino and Bari). His research is published in *Journal of Monetary Economics*, *Journal of Evolutionary Economics*, *Journal of Economic Behavior and Organization*, *Resource and Energy Economics*, and many other academic journals and books. He has been the editor and coauthored a chapter in *The Economics of Imperfect Markets* (Springer). He has been the editor of special issues for *Economic Modelling*, *Macroeconomic Dynamics*, and *Studies in Nonlinear Dynamics & Econometrics*. His main research interests are currently labor market structure and institutions, and its links with goods and financial markets. He has also applied continuous-time econometric modeling to study the impact of information and communication technologies on the evolution of Italian dynamic productivity.

Willi Semmler is Henry Arnhold Professor of Economics at the New School for Social Research and member of the New York Academy of Sciences. He received his PhD from the Free University of Berlin. He regularly publishes in refereed international journals and he is author of many books. His research and teaching interests are: empirical macroeconomics, macroeconomics of the United States and European Union, financial markets, economics of climate change, business cycles, and macro dynamics. He evaluates research projects for the European Union and he has served as a consultant for the World Bank on fiscal policy projects.

Patrizio Tirelli is Professor of Economics at the Department of Economics, Management and Statistics at the University of Milano-Bicocca. He was the director of the same department until October 2015 and the coordinator of the European Union project RASTANEWS. He regularly publishes in refereed international journals. His current research interests cover the economics and politics of central banking, the interdependency between monetary and fiscal policies, and European Monetary Union (EMU) institutional design.

Introduction

The recent economic events driven by the great financial crisis of 2007–2008 have challenged some 'dogma', highlighting various limits and drawbacks of current paradigms. Some books have been written already, and many conferences and debates have been organized to cast doubts on some of the tenets of the intellectual foundations of the pre-crisis framework. For instance, the dangers associated with financial-sector imbalances and the need for different policies have been emphasized; the crisis showed the limitations of monetary policy and led to a revaluation of what levels of public debt could be considered safe. With this in mind, this volume aims to refresh the debate on some important long-run macroeconomic issues bringing new and fresh perspectives.

The book is not aimed at providing a comprehensive survey on the current state of progress in rethinking a new theory for macroeconomics as a legacy of the financial crisis. It is rather a selective investigation of the developments of some specific topics that seem to be of greater interest to the problems emerging or that will emerge in the coming decades. As the Great Crisis has been characterized by an unprecedented decline in gross domestic product, the common line is the long-run macroeconomic performance. The core of the book is thus growth and productivity, and related theoretical and policy issues.

Using an open-mind approach, traditional and new theoretical approaches are critically discussed and integrated. Specific issues, such as the weak impact of information and communication technology (ICT) on the total factor productivity experienced by some countries are considered, as well as global issues such as the Secular Stagnation hypothesis. The impact of big social transitions on growth and productivity, such as demographic changes, are also taken into account.

The book also attempts to link the theoretical analysis with those developments in terms of policy implications. For instance, on the one hand, we aim to understand how much and under what conditions the forces of demand or public investments are relevant in supporting economic growth; on the other, we ask ourselves how long-run performance is related to financial regulation, labor markets, and the long-run management of fiscal and monetary policies. Complementary policy issues are introduced, e.g., the long-run optimal inflation target and its relationship with public finance and the long-term effects of government budget constraints on growth.

The book is divided into two parts. The first is devoted to the theory. The second concentrates on the long-run effects of policies. Chapters are written by different authors, all internationally renowned. The rest of this introduction summarizes the details of the individual chapters.

The first chapter by Olivier de La Grandville (Stanford University) points out some drawbacks of the optimal growth theory as it stands today. Olivier illustrates how using strictly concave utility functions systematically inflicts distortions on the economy that are either historically unobserved or unacceptable to society. Moreover, he shows that the traditional approach is incompatible with competitive equilibrium: any economy initially in such an equilibrium will always veer toward unwanted trajectories if its investment is planned on the basis of a concave utility function.

In the second chapter, Daniela Federici (University of Cassino and Southern Lazio) and Enrico Saltari (Sapienza University of Rome) specify and estimate two dynamic disequilibrium models of the Italian economy to explore the stagnant labor productivity, the decline of the wage share, and the weak impact of ICT on the total factor productivity. They also review the advantages of continuous time modeling in the specification of macroeconomic models.

Stefano Prezioso (Swimez, Rome) and Renato Paniccià (IRPET, Florence) focus on demand-side factors in determining long-run growth. In the third chapter, they reconsider the relevance of the traditional supply-side approach to potential growth analysis. Their approach draws upon a Kaldorian inspiration for a supply-side norm (the so-called Technical Production Function). They model and empirically validate a framework for different countries where Kaldorian productivity function and aggregate demand simultaneously interact in determining economic growth outcomes.

Elton Beqiraj, Giovanni Di Bartolomeo, and Marco Di Pietro (Sapienza University of Rome) are the authors of Chapter 4, which focuses on the effects of financial imperfections. They consider the interaction between long-run limited-asset market participation and banks' balance sheet constraints in an otherwise simple medium-scale New Keynesian economy, characterized by nominal price and wage frictions, habits, and capital adjustment costs. The key question is whether the assumption that only a fraction of households can access the credit market through financial intermediaries (limited-asset market participation) worsens the negative effects of banks' balance sheet constraints on credit.

In the last chapter of the first part, Bas van Aarle (KU Leuven) introduces the Secular Stagnation hypothesis. Bas considers the effects of hysteresis on potential output in a New Keynesian model. He shows that such an extension has a number of crucial implications for macroeconomic adjustments and policies and discusses how it can help us to better understand Secular Stagnation.

The second part begins with a study of public finance and trend inflation. Giovanni Di Bartolomeo (Sapienza University of Rome) and Patrizio Tirelli (University of Milan, Bicocca) illustrate how inflation can be used to finance public expenditure. In general, they use a rich framework to investigate how commonly used features of New Keynesian models affect the incentive to use different instruments to finance public transfers and the optimal long-run inflation rate. The inclusion of public transfers into New Keynesian models can solve the puzzling result of optimal zero inflation, which is at odds with both empirical evidence and monetary authorities' targets. The effect is due to the different incentives to finance public expenditure through taxes or seigniorage deriving from transfers and public consumption.

In Chapter 7, Silvia Fedeli and Francesco Forte (Sapienza University of Rome) study the long-term effects of Government budget constraints on gross domestic product growth. They apply co-integration analysis to a panel dataset for 20 OECD (Organization for Economic and Co-operative Development) countries from 1980 to 2009, rigorously taking into account the issues of heterogeneous panel and cross sectional dependence. They suggest that the long-term growth effects of a budget deficit and high tax burden are negative. A reduction of budget deficit via expenditure cuts is more effective, from a long-term perspective, than that obtained via a tax increase. Budgetary rules in tending to balance the budget, to be effective for long-term growth, should be completed with limits on the tax burden. In their analysis, by considering the differences in labor markets, Silvia Fedeli and Francesco Forte also show a much greater negative impact of high deficits and taxes on long-term growth rates in less flexible European Union economies.

Chapter 8, written by Andrew Hughes Hallett (University of St Andrews and George Mason University), focuses on the use (and need for) productivity policy to stimulate long-term increases in growth. The chapter reviews the role of productivity from the policy making point of view. His approach is twofold. He first considers the productivity of the private sector. Second, he looks at the key role played by public sector productivity, which is an aspect that is often underestimated in policy discussions.

As long as financial crises can be characterized as unprecedented declines in real activity, policies designed to account for them are as crucial as those designed to recover from their negative effects. Willi Semmler (New School) and Lebogang Mateane (University of Cape Town) propose a unifying framework for the evaluation of the composition of foreign exchange reserves for emerging economies. They propose incorporating the risk–return characteristics of foreign exchange reserves with the idea that a proportion of the total portfolio is motivated by the currency composition of foreign liabilities independently of adverse exchange-rate movements and/or a currency crisis. Thus, they account for the two main motives proposed in the literature in a consistent manner using unique central-bank constraints.

In the last contribution, Giuseppe Ciccarone (Sapienza University of Rome), Francesco Giuli (Roma Tre University), and Enrico Marchetti (University of Naples Parthenope), by calibrating a dynamic model on the United States, study the long-term effects of selected policy measures on long-run income when the economy is characterized by search frictions in the labor market and undeclared work. Specifically, they focus on policies affecting the efficiency of the matching technology, the productivity of regular hours worked, the fiscal burden on employment, the cost of job-vacancy posting, and the penalty rate the state applies to firms caught using underground workers. Special attention is also placed on the long-term response of employment/unemployment, hours worked, wages, and labor-market tightness to these policy changes. The main conclusion they reach is that the most effective reforms are those affecting the efficiency of matching technology and the productivity of regular work.

Part I
Theories

1 Optimal growth theory revisited

Olivier de La Grandville[1]

Introduction

When Frank Ramsey asked his famous question "How much should a nation save?" he faced a huge, fascinating challenge: molding for society both the present and the future of its economy in an optimal way. With his essay "A mathematical theory of saving," he founded nothing less than the theory of optimal economic growth. However, as soon as he tried to add numbers to his theoretical results, he was dumbfounded: he obtained an "optimal" savings rate equal to 60 percent; in his own words "The rate of saving which the rule requires is greatly in excess of that which anyone would suggest," adding that the utility function he used was "put forward merely as an illustration." Not to be discouraged, he attributed this odd result to the special utility function he had chosen—implying that some other function might well give a more meaningful result, a conclusion that certainly was shared by all his readers. At this point, we may conjecture that the alternative functions that Ramsey had in mind were akin to what all his successors would come up with much later: strictly concave utility functions, for instance the immensely popular power function.

Unfortunately, it turned out that whichever functions were chosen, disaster loomed: if the savings rate fell to a more reasonable level—say 10 percent to 20 percent—at least one central variable of the economy went astray, be it the marginal productivity of capital, the growth rate of income per person, or the capital–output ratio.

Our purpose in this chapter is fourfold: (i) to indicate why such a central subject was completely forgotten for such a long time; (ii) to recall the various (failed) attempts to obtain savings rates and optimal time paths for the economy that would be meaningful; (iii) to show that not a single strictly concave utility function is capable of preventing over-investment and over-saving if the economy is initially in competitive equilibrium and to explain why this is so; and (iv) to offer a solution to the problem of optimal economic growth that systematically yields acceptable, observed time paths for all central variables of the economy, while bringing three intertemporal optima—not just one—for society.

A fundamental, long-neglected quest

For many years, the quest for optimal trajectories of the economy remained in the realm of theory. Why was this? The reason is simple and rests upon the very nature of the problem at stake: in its most basic form, it consists in finding the optimal time path of capital $K(t)$ or its derivative $\dot{K}(t)$ by maximizing the integral

$$I = \int_0^\infty U(C_t)e^{-it}\,dt \tag{1.1}$$

subject to

$$C_t = F(K_t, L_t, t) - \dot{K}_t \tag{1.2}$$

where the dependency of the production function on t reflects the possibility that K and L are enhanced by some time-dependent technical progress factors. Even in such a simple model, if neither $U(\cdot)$ nor $F(\cdot)$ are affine functions of their arguments, the resulting Euler equation will unfailingly turn up as a non-linear second-order differential equation, which does not allow for an analytic solution. Numerical methods will be required.

In Ramsey's days, those calculations would have had to be made by hand. Even until the heroic times of main-frame computers and punched cards of the 1960s and 1970s, it would still remain a very cumbersome exercise to determine the initial point of the optimal trajectory that would lead—asymptotically only—to the highly unstable equilibrium implied by the model.

The consequence was that for an exceedingly long time research on optimal growth was pursued on purely theoretical lines, the literature flourishing with more and more elaborate models; a good example is the multi-sector by Samuelson and Solow (1956). Needless to say, your obedient servant did not mind joining the pack of happy campers (1980). As far as numerical applications, they were nowhere to be seen. For their part, until the 1980s, textbooks were content to draw in two-dimensional space phase diagrams to simply outline the stable arm that would lead asymptotically toward an equilibrium—although they usually gave short shrift to the extraordinarily unstable character this saddle point equilibrium exhibited; and the readers were left on their own to calculate or most often just speculate on the exact position of this stable arm, the required starting point of the economy, as well as the associated time paths of its main variables.

A quest that failed when it was finally pursued

Not surprisingly, a third of a century elapsed after Ramsey had written his essay before Richard Goodwin (1961) took up the challenge of determining savings rates that would maximize discounted utility flows. We detailed elsewhere (2016) his methods and results; here we present a brief summary only.

We reported earlier that unfailingly, Goodwin's "optimal" savings rate grew to an order of magnitude of 60 percent and the marginal savings rate easily reached

75 percent and, in one case exceeded 95 percent! Very surprisingly, and contrary to Ramsey's quite understandable reaction, Goodwin did not find anything strange with his results. He justified them by the fact that future generations might reap such big rewards that it would be worth the sacrifices made by the present generation: "So great are the gains that we are fully justified in robbing the poor to give to the rich!" (p. 765), and further: "Some violent process of capital accumulation of the type illustrated is the ideal. The simplifications of the model give an unduly sharp outline of the ideal policy, but its general character is surely a sound guide to policy" (pp. 772, 773). Note here that both Ramsey and Goodwin thought that some simplification of the model gave what Goodwin called "an unduly sharp outline of the ideal policy," implying that a more sophisticated model would lead to more acceptable results. We will see here, in the next section, that this is not the case.

It would another 30 more years to put the traditional theory to the test. King and Rebelo (1993) tried to replicate the evolution of the US economy, supposing that investment had conformed optimal decisions based on the traditional model and adopting, like Goodwin, three different utility functions. Whichever extreme hypotheses they considered regarding either the utility function, or the values of the parameters or the production process itself, at least one variable of the economy took some unwanted course. For instance, in their quest to obtain sensible results, they went as far as having recourse to the utility function $(C^{-9} - 1)/(-1/9)$. This function can be qualified as "extreme" for two reasons. First, it is very close to its limit $\lim_{\alpha \to -\infty}(C^{\alpha} - 1)/\alpha$ represented by a vertical in negative space at $C = 1$, followed by the horizontal abscissa. Second, the marginal utility is $U'(C) = C^{-10}$, a function homogeneous of degree -10. This implies that multiplying C by $\lambda > 0$, the marginal utility is divided by λ^{10}. Suppose for instance that $\lambda = 10^{9/10} \approx 7.943$. This is the coefficient that multiplied real income per person in the United States over a little more than a century. Adopting such a utility function implies that the marginal utility of consumption a century ago was one billion times higher than it is today; certainly an indefensible proposition. Such an extreme hypothesis did not prevent the marginal productivity of capital to start at 105 percent(!) and to stay above 50 percent for about eight years. To obtain a real interest rate more in the range of long-term observations of real returns, King and Rebelo considered a capital share equal to 90 percent(!); it did bring down the marginal productivity of capital but at the expense of a nearly constant investment savings rate equal to 68 percent, a "wildly counterfactual level" in their own words (p. 918).

For our part, we carried out the following tests. First, in 2009, we put to the test *all* utility functions of the families

$$U(C) = (C^{\alpha} - 1)/\alpha, \ \alpha < 1$$

as well as those belonging to the exponential form

$$U(C) = (-1/\beta)e^{-\beta C}, \ \beta > 0$$

(we had never seen any applications of the latter, but since it was declared fit for service—see for instance Blanchard and Fisher (1989)—we tried it out as well). Our results were as follows. With the utility function $U(C)=(C^\alpha-1)/\alpha$, in order to have a chance of being on the stable arm leading to the saddle point equilibrium, the initial savings rate had to be extremely high (in the order of 50 to 60 percent). If we wanted the initial savings rate to be reduced to more acceptable levels, α had to become negative in such a way that the utility function made little sense: it was converging very rapidly toward the limiting position we just mentioned. As to the negative exponential function, it did not even allow a saddle point equilibrium; there was no equilibrium point any more. What at first sight might appear to the experimenter as a stable arm, would lead in fact to a cusp point from where the "optimal" trajectory would veer off toward zero consumption and a huge amount of capital (see La Grandville (2009), pp. 224–230 and 239–256).

Then, in 2016, we went further. We considered all possible power functions and examined what would be the consequences of stable-arm time paths on the marginal productivity of capital and on the growth rate of real income per person. We showed that whenever the savings rate fell into acceptable ranges—at the expense of strange-looking utility functions—it did so while the marginal productivity of capital climbed to never-before-seen levels.

The dire consequences of investing in a competitive economy on the basis of strictly concave utility functions

We should now ask a crucial question: what would happen to an economy that was initially in competitive equilibrium and where agents would be saving and investing according to the traditional lines described above? In that initial situation, the stock of capital in existence is such that its marginal productivity is equal to a long-term interest rate that could carry a risk premium. We suppose that the production function is of constant elasticity of substitution (CES) form, with capital and labor augmenting progress.

Our first task is to determine what would be the initial conditions corresponding to competitive equilibrium, and to check that all implied variables of the economy make perfect sense, i.e. that they are in ranges that have been observed or which definitely seem feasible.

Determining the initial conditions corresponding to competitive equilibrium

The production function is the general mean of order p of the enhanced inputs $G_t K_t$ and $H_t L_t$, leading to a net income (net of depreciation)

$$Y_t = F(G_t K_t, H_t L_t) = Y_0\{\delta[G_t K_t/K_0]^p + (1-\delta)[H_t L_t/L_0]^p\}^{1/p}, \quad p\neq 0 \quad (1.3)$$

where the order p is the increasing function of the elasticity of substitution σ: $p=1-1/\sigma$; here $0<\sigma<1$ and therefore $p<0$. L_t is exogenous. In applications, we will suppose that L_t, G_t, and H_t are exponential, but since we are concerned about very long horizons, we will also suppose in a second phase that they are S-shaped, each of them tending toward an asymptote.

Consider now the competitive equilibrium characterized by the equality between the marginal productivity of capital and the real rate of interest $i(t)$ (that may include a risk premium)

$$F_K(G_t K_t, H_t L_t) = i(t). \tag{1.4}$$

This equation, in all its simplicity, is nothing but the Euler equation ensuring the maximization of the integral of the discounted consumption flows

$$\int_0^\infty C(t) e^{-\int_0^t i(z)dz} dt = \int_0^\infty [F(G_t K_t, H_t L_t) - \dot{K}] e^{-it} dt; \tag{1.5}$$

indeed, the general mean (1.3) is concave with respect to its arguments and the transversality conditions at infinity are met (see La Grandville, 2016).

Applied to (1.3), this competitive equilibrium condition $F_K(G_t K_t, H_t L_t) = i$, where i is taken as constant for simplicity, leads to the following equation in K_t

$$F_{K_t}(G_t K_t, H_t L_t) = Y_0\{\delta[G_t K_t/K_0]^p$$
$$+ (1-\delta)[H_t L_t/L_0]^p\}^{(1/p)-1} \delta K_t^{p-1}(G_t/K_0)^p = i$$

which can be solved to yield the optimal time path K_t^*

$$K_t^* = \frac{K_0}{L_0}\left(\frac{1-\delta}{\delta}\right)^{\sigma/(\sigma-1)} \frac{L_t H_t G_t^{-1}}{\left[i^{\sigma-1}\delta^{-\sigma}(Y_0/K_0)^{1-\sigma} G_t^{1-\sigma} - 1\right]^{\sigma/(\sigma-1)}} \tag{1.6}$$

—for derivation details, see La Grandville (2016). Normalizing L_0 to 1 gives an initial competitive capital–output ratio equal to $K_0/Y_0 = \delta/i$. Normalizing in turn Y_0 to 1 yields $K_0 = \delta/i$ and the optimal trajectory

$$K_t^* = \frac{\delta}{i}\left(\frac{1-\delta}{G_t^{1-\sigma} - \delta}\right)^{\sigma/(\sigma-1)} L_t H_t G_t^{-1}. \tag{1.7}$$

Replacing (1.7) into (1.3) gives the optimal time-path for output and net income

$$Y_t^* = L_t H_t \left[\delta\left(\frac{1-\delta}{G_t^{1-\sigma} - \delta}\right) + 1 - \delta\right]^{1/p} = L_t H_t \left(\frac{1-\delta G_t^{\sigma-1}}{1-\delta}\right)^{\sigma/(1-\sigma)} \tag{1.8}$$

with its growth rate being

$$\frac{\dot{Y}_t^*}{Y_t^*} = n_t + h_t + \sigma\delta\left(G_t^{1-\sigma} - \delta\right)^{-1} g_t. \tag{1.9}$$

From (1.7) and (1.8) the capital–output ratio can be deduced as

$$\frac{K_t^*}{Y_t^*} = \frac{\delta}{i} G_t^{-(1-\sigma)}. \tag{1.10}$$

Finally, the all-important, crucial optimal savings ratio can be determined by $\dot{K}_t^*/Y_t^*$, more conveniently calculated as $s_t^* = (\dot{K}_t^*/K_t^*)(K_t^*/Y_t^*)$. Denoting the growth rates of G_t, H_t and L_t by g_t, h_t and n_t respectively, we obtain

$$s_t^* = \frac{\delta}{i}\left\{ n_t + h_t + g_t\left[\frac{\sigma}{1-\delta G_t^{\sigma-1}} - 1\right]\right\} G_t^{-(1-\sigma)}. \tag{1.11}$$

The crucial test comes with putting numbers into these formulas and ensuring the results make good sense. To this end, we suppose that the capital and labor-enhancing factors grow at the rates observed by Sato (2006) in the United States over a very long period (1909–1989). Those rates are $g = 0.004$ and $h = 0.02$, respectively. We consider an initial capital share $\delta = 0.025$, an exogenous growth rate of population equal to $n = 0.01$ and an elasticity of substitution in the range where it has most often been observed: $0.5 \leq \sigma \leq 0.8$.[2] We have also supposed that the real interest rate, including a risk premium, is between 0.04 and 0.06.

The initial values for the optimal savings rate s_0^* do make sense: their order of magnitude is between 12 percent (for $i = 6$ percent and $\sigma = 0.5$) and 19 percent (for $i = 4$ percent and $\sigma = 0.8$)—see Table 16.3 in La Grandville (2016).

The initial values of the growth rate of income per person $\dot{y}_0^*/y_0^*$ are also in observed ranges and make good sense (they are slightly above 2 percent, and increasing with the elasticity of substitution; see Table 16.3 in La Grandville, 2016). The same can be said about the initial capital–output ratio, which turns out to be in the range 5 to 6.25.

Thus, equipped with initial conditions corresponding to competitive equilibrium, we can describe what will happen to the economy if investment is carried out on the basis not just of one, but *all* possible concave power utility functions. As could have been foreseen from all precedent experiments, the results are disastrous. Not one utility function is able to avoid the economy from over-investing.

The inability of strictly concave functions to prevent the savings rate from shooting into unwanted territory

Given the above-defined initial conditions reflecting competitive equilibrium, we now maximize $\int_0^{\infty} U(C_t)e^{-it}\,dt$ under the constraint $C_t = F(K_t, L_t, t) - \dot{K}_t$ where $F(.)$ is defined by (1.3) and $U(C) = (C^{\alpha} - 1)/\alpha$. Writing $U\left[F(K_t, L_t, t) - \dot{K}_t C_t\right] e^{-it} \equiv \varphi(K, \dot{K}, t)$, the Euler equation

$$\frac{\partial \varphi(K, \dot{K}, t)}{\partial K} - \frac{d}{dt}\frac{\partial \varphi(K, \dot{K}, t)}{\partial \dot{K}} = 0 \tag{1.12}$$

together with the constraint, lead to the following pair of first-order, non-linear differential equations

$$\dot{C} = \frac{C}{1-\alpha} \left\{ [\delta(e^{gK^t}K)^p + (1-\delta)e^{p(n+gL)^t}]^{(1/p)-1} \, \delta e^{pgK^t} K^{p-1} - i \right\} \quad (1.13)$$

$$\dot{K} = \{\delta[e^{gK}K]^p + (1-\delta)[e^{(n+gL)^t}]^p\}^{1/p} - C \quad (1.14)$$

with initial conditions set at $C_0 = (1 - s_0^*) Y_0$, equal to $1 - s_0^*$ since $Y_0 = 1$. The concavity of the integrand with respect to K and $\dot{K}$ and the transversality conditions at infinity enable us to apply Takayama's theorem to ensure that this system of equations leads to a unique maximum of the integral. The transversality conditions at infinity are the following

$$\int_0^\infty U[F(K_t, L_t, t) - \dot{K}]e^{-it} \, dt = \int_0^\infty \varphi(K, \dot{K}, t)e^{-it} \, dt \quad (1.15)$$

with the first condition $\lim_{t\to\infty} \partial\varphi/\partial\dot{K} = \lim_{t\to\infty} -U'(C)e^{-it} = 0$ always met. The second one is $\lim_{t\to\infty} V = 0$ and it is enforced by the convergence of the integral. This last condition is met by the fact that the integrand is positive and e^{-it} converges to zero faster than U^{-1}.

We used the same parameters as above: $n = 0.01$; $\delta = 0.25$; $i = 0.04$; $\sigma = 0.8$; $H = 0.02$; $g = 0.004$; as well as 25 values of α in the utility function $(C^\alpha - 1)/\alpha$ ranging from $\alpha = 0.8$ to $\alpha = -8.8$ in steps of -0.4.

The evolution of the "optimal" savings rate is obtained by numerically solving the above system for K_t^* and C_t^*, replacing K_t^* into $Y_t^* = F(G_t K_t^*, H_t L_t)$. By so doing, we can finally determine either $s_t^* = \dot{K}_t^*/F(G_t K_t^*, H_t L_t)$, or $s_t^* = 1 - C_t^*/F(G_t K_t^*, H_t L_t)$. The reader can find this evolution, as well as those of the growth rate and the capital–labor ratio, in La Grandville (2016). *For all alpha values, the savings rate becomes equal to or larger than 50 percent up to 14 years, before tending toward 100 percent.* As to the capital–output ratio, it increases permanently and is ultimately multiplied by a factor 6. One would expect, of course, that technical progress enhancing capital would *reduce*, not increase, fixed capital's requirement for one unit of net output. On the other hand, in the competitive equilibrium model we suggest later on, we will see that the capital–output ratio decreases, albeit slowly.

The incompatibility of the traditional approach and competitive equilibrium: an analytic explanation

The reason why the traditional approach is not compatible with competitive equilibrium is quite fundamental. It comes from the fact that the equation $i = F_K(K, L, t)$ will never yield the same solution as the equation $i = F_K(K, L, t) + \dot{U}_C'/U_C' = F_K(K, L, t) + U_C''\dot{C}/U_C'$ unless either U_C'' or $\dot{C}$ are both equal to zero. Furthermore, we can see why, from an initial equilibrium characterized by $i = F_K(K, L, t)$, consumption will have to fall and savings rise: investment will increase the stock of capital, whose marginal productivity will fall; in order to maintain equilibrium, a positive number will have to be added to the right-hand side of the equality, and, since U_C'' is negative, $\dot{C}$ must be negative as well, which implies a decrease in consumption.

A suggested solution

We therefore suggest that optimal growth should be sought by investing in saving and investing in such a way as to conform to the competitive equation $i = F_K(K, L, t)$. We should point out how appropriate the adjective "optimal" is in this context, since all time paths described hereafter correspond to no fewer than *five* simultaneous optima—and not just one, as in the traditional approach—in addition to the minimization of production costs.

The intertemporal optimality of competitive equilibrium: its multiple facets in one theorem

We will show how investing in such a way that the marginal productivity of capital stays equal to the rate of interest generates five benefits of considerable importance for society; those benefits may be very surprising in the sense that they can be—and most probably are—far removed from the initial objective of investors, which might simply have been the minimization of their production costs. We will prove the following.

THEOREM 1.1 *Let the production function $F(K_t, L_t, t)$ be concave and homogeneous of degree one in K, L; technical progress may be labor- and capital-augmenting. If investment is carried out over time in such a way that the marginal productivity of capital is maintained equal to the rate of interest $i(t)$, and if capital is remunerated by $i(t)K(t)$, society simultaneously maximizes five magnitudes:*

1   *the sum of the discounted consumption flows society can acquire from now to infinity $\int_0^\infty C(t)e^{-\int_0^t i(z)dz}\,dt$;*
2   *the value of society's activity at any point in time t, defined by the consumption flow received at time t plus the rate of increase in the value of the capital stock at that time (the present value of this sum is equal to $C_t e^{-\int_0^t i(z)dz} + \frac{d}{dt}[\lambda(t)K(t)]$, where $\lambda(t)$ is the discounted price of capital);*
3   *the total value of society's activity over an infinite time span $\int_0^\infty \{C_t e^{-\int_0^t i(z)dz}\,dt + \frac{d}{dt}[\lambda(t)K(t)]\}\,dt$;*
4   *the remuneration of labor at any point in time $F(K_t, L_t, t) - i(t)K(t)$;*
5   *the total remuneration of labor over an infinite time span $\int_0^\infty e^{-\int_0^t i(z)dz}[F(K_t, L_t, t) - i(t)K(t)]\,dt$.*

A detailed proof of each part of this theorem can be found in La Grandville (2016). Here we simply mention that it rests upon Euler's equation and on the modified Hamiltonian that Robert Dorfman had introduced in 1969, which we called a Dorfmanian to honor Professor Dorfman's memory. It turns out that the value of society's activity at any point in time t, defined by the consumption flow received at time t plus the rate of increase in the value of the capital stock at that time, is equal to the Dorfmanian and that, most surprisingly, it is also equal to the remuneration of labor at any point in time.

The optimal evolution of the economy under competitive equilibrium

The crucial questions are now the following. We know that the initial conditions defined by competitive equilibrium are close to what has been observed in the past, but what about future evolutions? Will we encounter at some point or another an unwanted, or even an absurd evolution such as those that have marred the traditional approach? Or will they be similar to those just evidenced by starting from a competitive equilibrium and then planning investing on the basis of a strictly concave utility function? Only in the case of the capital–output ratio do we already have some kind of reinsurance in the sense that a casual look at its formula given by

$$K_t^*/Y_t^* = \frac{\delta}{i} G_t^{-(1-\sigma)} \tag{1.8b}$$

$K_t^*/Y_t^* = \frac{\delta}{i} G_t^{-(1-\sigma)}$, $0 \leq \sigma \leq 1$ tells us two pieces of good news: first it decreases through time; and second it will do this relatively slowly since its relative rate of decrease will be small, equal to $(1-\sigma)g$, and thus in the range of what has been observed and what is quite conceivable in the future. But what about the optimal growth rate of real income per person and the optimal savings rate, given by

$$\dot{Y}_t^*/Y_t^* = n + h + \sigma\delta\left(e^{(1-\sigma)gt} - \delta\right)^{-1} g \tag{1.9b}$$

and

$$s_t^* = \frac{\delta}{i}\left\{n + h + g\left[\frac{\sigma}{1 - \delta e^{-(1-\sigma)gt}} - 1\right]\right\} e^{-(1-\sigma)gt}. \tag{1.10b}$$

Will these lead us into unwanted territory? We have no way of assessing their future outcome except by putting numbers on the relevant parameters.

In a first approach, we assume constant growth rates for L_t, G_t and H_t, denoted as n, g and h (in the next section we will assume very different time paths for those variables). We choose $n = 0.01$; for g, h and σ we took the estimates made by Sato (2006) for the US economy over an 80-year time-span, i.e., $\sigma = 0.8$; $h = 0.02$ and $g = 0.004$ as a first series of values for those parameters.

The optimal time path of the savings rate

We are now in a position to undertake the comparative dynamics of the optimal savings rate, and answer in particular the nagging question asked by Frank Ramsey and certainly by anybody who would take up the subject of optimal growth: will

Table 1.1 The optimal savings rate $s^*(t, i)$ as a function of the rate of preference for the present, and as a slowly decreasing function of time ($\sigma = 0.8$; $n = 0.01$; $\delta = 0.25$; $g = 0.004$; $h = 0.02$)

t	i				
	0.04	0.045	0.05	0.055	0.06
0	18.9	16.8	15.1	13.8	12.6
30	18.5	16.4	14.8	13.4	12.3
60	18.0	16.0	14.4	13.1	12.0

Table 1.2 The optimal growth rate of income per person $r^*(t, i) = \dot{y}_t^* / y_t^*$ as a function of the elasticity of substitution ($n = 0.01$; $\delta = 0.25$; $g = 0.004$; $h = 0.02$)

t	σ						
	0.5	0.55	0.6	0.65	0.7	0.75	0.8
0	2.07	2.07	2.08	2.09	2.09	2.10	2.11
30	2.06	2.07	2.08	2.08	2.08	2.09	2.10
60	2.06	2.06	2.07	2.08	2.08	2.09	2.10

technical progress increase or decrease the optimal savings rate? We will now use our central equation (1.11) not only as we did before to determine the initial conditions prevailing in a competitive economy but also to study its whole time-path. Examination of (1.11) immediately reveals that s_t^* *decreases through time for any given value of the parameters.* This sharply contrasts with many traditional approaches and in particular with what we just witnessed when the economy was planned with strictly concave utility functions from an initial situation of competitive equilibrium. It makes a lot of sense: indeed, such a (welcome) decrease is due to the technological progress incorporated into capital through coefficient g. Table 1.1 presents first results.

The optimal growth rate of income per person

From (1.9b), it immediately appears that the growth rate of real income per person $\dot{y}_t^* / y_t^*$, an increasing function of the elasticity of substitution, is higher than h and very slowly decreases asymptotically toward h, as illustrated in Table 1.2. (Notice once more that the ultimate growth rate of income per person may converge toward the rate of labor-augmenting technical progress even in the presence of capital-augmenting progress—this is due to a property of general means when the order of the mean is negative; see La Grandville (2011).)

The optimal time path of the capital–output ratio

In a reassuring way, as mentioned earlier, the capital–output ratio K^*/Y^*, determined from (1.10), is a slowly decreasing function of time. It would indeed

Table 1.3 The capital–output ratio K^*/Y^* as a function of time and the rate of preference for the present ($n = 0.01$; $\delta = 0.25$; $g = 0.004$; $h = 0.02$)

t	i					
	$\sigma = 0.5$			$\sigma = 0.8$		
	0.04	0.05	0.06	0.04	0.05	0.06
0	6.25	5.00	4.17	6.25	5	4.17
30	5.89	4.71	3.92	6.10	4.88	4.07
60	5.54	4.43	3.70	5.96	4.76	3.97

Table 1.4 The evolution of θ_t^* as a function of the initial capital share δ and the elasticity of substitution

t	δ					
	$\sigma = 0.5$			$\sigma = 0.8$		
	0.25	0.30	$0.\overline{3}$	0.25	0.30	$0.\overline{3}$
0	0.75	0.7	$0.\overline{6}$	0.75	0.7	$0.\overline{6}$
30	0.764	0.717	0.686	0.756	0.707	0.675
60	0.778	0.734	0.704	0.762	0.714	0.682

be bad news if this ratio were to stay constant (the Cobb–Douglas case $\sigma = 1$, with $K^*/Y^* = \delta/i$), meaning that society would have to match any growth rate in its standard of living by the same growth in fixed capital. Table 1.3 indicates how it slowly decreases in time, this decrease being less pronounced if the elasticity of substitution is larger, which makes good sense. And of course, the degree of capitalization of the economy is smaller whenever the rate of interest is higher.

The optimal evolution of the labor share in competitive equilibrium

From Theorem 1.1, we know that the remuneration of labor, equal to the value of society's activity, is maximized at any point of time, and is therefore intertemporal. But what is the evolution of the share of labor through time? From (1.10), we can determine the share of capital as $i K^*/Y^* = \delta e^{-(1-\sigma)gt}$. Therefore, the share of labor, denoted by θ_t^*, is equal to

$$\theta_t^* = 1 - \delta e^{-(1-\sigma)gt}. \tag{1.16}$$

Table 1.4 presents this evolution as a function of the initial capital share δ and the elasticity of substitution. The increase is very gradual, and slightly less pronounced when the elasticity of substitution is higher.

The robustness of the optimal trajectories of the economy to non-exponential scenarios of population and technical progress

Any model of long-term growth should take into account the fact that no exponential evolution can be sustained with the hypothesis of an infinite horizon. We may even add that such evolutions do not make sense even with horizons in the order of magnitude of a few hundred years. We definitely have to suppose that population in some distant time will have a stationary value and that if it is observed today as having an exponential evolution, its whole time path will be S-shaped. We have made such a change in our 2016 study and supposed that not only population but also technical progress coefficients $G(t)$ and $H(t)$ would follow sigmoid evolutions.

We proceeded as follows: let $G(t)$ designate a generic function of time whose growth rate $g(t)$ is also a function of time. Suppose that $G(0) = G_0$ and that the growth rate $g(t)$, with an initial value g_0 (observed today), is *decreasing* at a rate $(1/g)dg/dt = \gamma$ $(\gamma < 0)$. We thus have $g(t) = g_0 e^{\gamma t}$, $\gamma < 0$; this implies $(1/G)dG/dt = g(t) = g_0 e^{\gamma t}$ and therefore

$$G(t, \gamma) = G_0 e^{\int_0^t g(z)\,dz} = G_0 \exp \int_0^t g_0 e^{\gamma z}\,dz = G_0 \exp\left(\frac{g_0(e^{\gamma t}-1)}{\gamma}\right). \quad (1.17)$$

If we let A designate the asymptotic factor defined by the ratio $G(\infty)/G_0$, we have, setting $G_0 = 1$

$$A \equiv G(\infty) = e^{-g_0/\gamma}. \quad (1.18)$$

It is convenient to express it by reference to the asymptote A rather than γ, the (negative) growth rate of $g(t)$. So we have

$$\gamma = -g_0/\ln A \quad (1.19)$$

and therefore

$$G(t, A) = A^{[1-\exp(-g_0 t/\ln A)]} \quad (1.20)$$

as a function of A. If $A > e$, $G(t, A)$ is S-shaped with an inflection point at

$$\hat{t} = (1/\gamma)\ln(-\gamma/g_0) = (1/g_0)\ln A \ln(\ln A).$$

If $1 < A \le e$, then $G(t)$ is strictly concave throughout, with the same asymptote $A = e^{-g_0/\gamma}$.

We have supposed that $L(t)$ and factors reflecting technical progress $G(t)$ and $H(t)$ share the properties of that generic function. Their growth rates $n(t)$, $g(t)$ and $h(t)$ are declining at constant rates $\dot{n}(t)/n(t) = \nu < 0$, $\dot{g}(t)/g(t) = \gamma_K < 0$ and $\dot{h}(t)/h(t) = \gamma_L < 0$; their initial values are the observed n, g and h previously mentioned.

What we wanted to know was what the optimal trajectories would be under those new hypotheses. We chose very strong assumptions: the asymptotic factors would be either 5 or 10.

The competitive equilibrium condition $F_K(K_t, L_t, t) = i$ now implies new optimal trajectories: indeed, all equations (1.7) to (1.13) now incorporate the S-shaped curves $L(t)$, $H(t)$ and $G(t)$

$$L(t) = A_L^{[1-\exp(-n_0 t / \ln A_L)]} \tag{1.21}$$

$$H(t) = A_H^{[1-\exp(-h_0 t / \ln A_H)]} \tag{1.22}$$

$$G(t) = A_G^{[1-\exp(-g_0 t / \ln A_G)]} \tag{1.23}$$

as well as their growth rates

$$n(t) = n_0 \exp(-n_0 t / \ln A_L) \tag{1.24}$$

$$h(t) = h_0 \exp(-h_0 t / \ln A_H) \tag{1.25}$$

$$g(t) = g_0 \exp(-g_0 t / \ln A_G). \tag{1.26}$$

We first tested what would be the asymptotic factors of the main variables to make sure they made sense. Those asymptotic factors of consumption per person, income per person and capital–output ratio are given by

$$c_\infty^*/c_0^* = \frac{(1-s_\infty^*)y_\infty^*}{(1-s_0^*)y_0^*} = \frac{A_H \left[\frac{1-\delta A_G^{\sigma-1}}{1-\delta} \right]^{\sigma/(1-\sigma)}}{1 - \frac{\delta}{i} \left\{ n_0 + h_0 + g_0 \left[\frac{\sigma}{1-\delta} - 1 \right) \right] \right\}}, \tag{1.27}$$

$$y_\infty^*/y_0^* = A_H \left[\frac{1 - \delta A_G^{\sigma-1}}{1-\delta} \right]^{\sigma/(1-\sigma)}, \tag{1.28}$$

and

$$(K_\infty^*/Y_\infty^*)/(K_0^*/Y_0^*) = A_G^{-(1-\sigma)} \tag{1.29}$$

respectively. For example, with $A = 5$ and $\sigma = 0.8$, we get $c_\infty^*/c_0^* = 8.8$; $y_\infty^*/y_0^* = 7.1$ and $(K_\infty^*/Y_\infty^*)/(K_0^*/Y_0^*) = 0.63$.

We could already, just by considering these numbers, predict that the optimal trajectories of our main variables will not go into unwanted territory. Indeed, as can Tables 8 and 9 from La Grandville (2016) attest, they remain within reasonable, predictable ranges. For instance, with a very low asymptotic factor $A = 5$, the optimal savings rate after 60 years became 10 percent against 18 percent in the exponential scenario; the optimal growth rate of real income per person became 1 percent instead of 2.06 percent; and the capital–output coefficient decreased to 5.54 as opposed to 5.63. We are justified in concluding that the optimal time-paths of an economy driven by competitive equilibrium are highly robust to extremely diverse hypotheses about the future evolution of population and the technical progress that may enhance its factors of production.

Conclusion

Even if traditional optimal growth theory had come up with sensible time-paths for the economy, it would still have had to face serious, overwhelming difficulties: first, the necessity to define for a whole society what should be its utility function, not only at the present time but also in the future as well; the second hurdle would be the fact—which we demonstrated—that it would systematically lead to time-paths that would differ from those of competitive equilibrium.

For our part, we suggest that optimal growth be founded on the Euler equation that defines competitive equilibrium. This provides society with the intertemporal maximization of three fundamental magnitudes, not just one:

1   the sum of the discounted consumption flows society can acquire from now to infinity;
2   the total value of society's activity over an infinite time span;
3   the total remuneration of labor over an infinite time span.

The problem now for societies is to come closer to such an equilibrium. In recent decades, there have been signs that, on the contrary, we are moving away from it. Two of them are the decrease in the share of labor in national income, and the fast increasing share taken by the financial sector, both in terms of remuneration and in terms of profits. For instance, in the United States, the percentage of profits from the financial sector in the total profits of the economy grew from 8 percent in 1947 to 28 percent in 2014.[3] In many other countries, the private and public monopolies, from the energy sector to retail distribution, have never been as powerful.

Competitive equilibrium is an ideal that may never be achieved, and democratic institutions that are required to get closer to it have their own failings. History shows that democracy, as well as ideas and values that translate into principles at the core of civilization look akin to fractal processes, with sudden, unexpected downfalls. But their evolution is not entirely random: they definitely exhibit an upward trend in the long run, which, despite all the downfalls we have witnessed, is of our own making.

Notes

1 It is with great pleasure that I want to express my gratitude to a number of individuals. First I want to acknowledge the invaluable help given to me by my colleague Ernst Hairer; without his mastery at solving numerically differential equations, I would not have been able to put the utility functions to the test of competitive equilibrium. And of course I want to heartily thank Robert Solow who for so many years provided me with continuous, highly helpful advice. I am also indebted to Kenneth Arrow, Giuseppe De Archangelis, Giovanni Di Bartolomeo, Robert Chirinko, Daniela Federici, Robert Feicht, Giancarlo Gandolfo, Jean-Marie Grether, Erich Gundlach, Andreas

Irmen, Bjarne Jensen, Anastasia Litina, Miguel Leon-Ledesma, Hing-Man Leung, Rainer Klump, Peter McAdam, Bernardo Maggi, Elisabeth Paté-Cornell, Enrico Saltari, Wolfgang Stummer, Jim Sweeney, Alpo Wilman, Juerg Weber, and Milad Zarin-Nejadan as well as to participants in seminars at Stanford, Frankfurt, Luxembourg, and Rome (La Sapienza) for their highly constructive remarks.

2 The size of the elasticity of substitution is important. On the one hand, it is a powerful engine of growth. In La Grandville (1989) we made the conjecture that the spectacular rise of East Asian economies was due less to technical progress than to a higher elasticity of substitution. The conjecture was successfully tested by Ky Hyang Yuhn (1991) in the case of South Korea. The reason for the sensitivity of income per person y to σ on the fact that income per person is also a general mean of order $p = 1 - 1/\sigma$; a general mean of two arguments, as an increasing function of p, has a unique point of inflection (this was conjectured in La Grandville and Solow (2006) and proven by Thanh and Minh (2008)). It turns out that when $\sigma \in (0.5, 0.8)$, we are very close to this inflection point. But, on the other hand, σ cannot be too high either: La Grandville showed in 2016 (chapter 6) that $\sigma > 1$ is incompatible with competitive equilibrium in the following sense: at some point in time the easily determined equality $F_K(G_t K_t, H_t L_t) = i$ cannot be enforced any more for the following reason: as time passes, the elasticity of substitution increases the marginal productivity so much that capital should be growing extremely fast for the equality to be maintained, until the equation does not have a solution any more (this corresponds to the denominator $G_t^{1-\sigma} - \delta$ in (1.7) becoming equal to zero). Note also that considering a production function with $\sigma > 1$ makes very little sense, since it implies that any amount of output can be produced with one factor only, the other factor being equal to zero.

3 See Bureau of Economic Analysis, National Data, Income and Employment by Industry, Tables 6-16a–6-16.d.

References

Blanchard, O. and S. Fisher (1989), *Lectures on Macroeconomics*, MIT Press, Cambridge, MA.

Dorfman, R. (1969), "An Economic Interpretation of Optimal Control Theory," *American Economic Review*, December 1969, Vol. 59, No 5, pp. 817–831.

Goodwin, R. M. (1961), "The Optimal Growth Path for an Underdeveloped Economy," *The Economic Journal*, Vol. 71, No 284, 756–774.

King, R. G. and S. T. Rebelo (1993), "Transitional Dynamics and Economic Growth in the Neoclassical Model," *The American Economic Review*, Vol. 83, No 4, pp. 908–931.

La Grandville, O. de (1989), "In Quest of the Slutsky Diamond," *The American Economic Review*, Vol. 79, No 3, pp. 468–481.

La Grandville, O. de (2009), *Economic Growth – A Unified Approach*, with two special contributions by R. M. Solow, Cambridge University Press, Cambridge, UK.

La Grandville, O. de (2011), "A New Property of General Means of Order p, with Applications to Economic Growth," *The Australian Journal of Mathematical Analysis with Applications*, Vol. 8, Issue 1, Article 3.

La Grandville, O. de (2016), *Economic Growth – A Unified Approach*, second edition, Cambridge University Press, Cambridge, UK.

La Grandville, O. de and R. M. Solow (2006), "A Conjecture on General Means," *Journal of Inequalities in Pure and Applied Mathematics*, Vol. 7, No 1, Article 3.

Samuelson, P. and R. M. Solow (1956), "A Complete Capital Model Involving Heterogeneous Capital Goods," *The Quarterly Journal of Economics*, Vol. 70, No 4, pp. 537–562.

Sato, R. (2006), *Biased Technical Change and Economic Conservation Laws*, Springer, New York, NY.

Thanh, N. P. and M. N. Minh (2008), "Proof of a Conjecture on General Means," *Journal of Inequalities in Pure and Applied Mathematics*, Vol. 9, No 3, Article 86.

Yuhn, K. H. (1991), "Economic Growth, Technical Change Biases, and the Elasticity of Substitution: A Test of the de La Grandville Hypothesis," *The Review of Economics and Statistics*, Vol. LXIII, No 2, pp. 340–346.

2 The continuous-time approach to macroeconomic modelling with an application to the Italian economy

Daniela Federici and Enrico Saltari

Introduction

This contribution is made up of two parts. The first is devoted to a short review of the advantages of continuous-time modelling over discrete-time modelling in the specification of macroeconomic models. A basic issue concerning the specification of macroeconomic models is whether they should be specified in continuous or discrete time. Although it is likely that an economy might be best represented by a set of non-linear mixed difference/differential equations, the analysis of such a system is at present intractable. If a choice has to be made, we think that a continuous rather than a discrete model gives a better representation. A number of advantages that we briefly summarize motivates this choice. In the second part, we estimate two dynamic-disequilibrium models of the Italian economy to explore some relevant features characterizing its evolution over the last three decades, such as the stagnant labour productivity, the decline of the wage share and the weak impact of ICT on the total factor productivity (TFP). The first model focuses on the effects of the technological change. It investigates the rate and the effects of ICT introduction on capital and production in the Italian economy and the extent to which that is being affected by skills in the labour force. While the first model examines the role of ICT in enhancing general production in the Italian economy, by assuming that the ICT contribution is exogenous, in the second model, the process of innovation is endogenous, employing a nested approach based on a two-level constant elasticity of substitution (CES) aggregate production function. The models behave quite well in replicating the dynamics of the Italian economy. However, they also show that there remain some structural inefficiencies that have worsened in recent years. In fact, the main finding of both models is the existence of a permanent gap between 'optimal' and actual output, which increased in the latter part of the sample period. While a fraction of this gap can be attributed to unavoidable (market and non-market) adjustment costs, part is also associated with efficiency losses.

Advantages of continuous-time modelling

A basic issue concerning the specification of macroeconomic models is whether they should be specified in continuous or discrete time. Although it is likely that an economy might be best represented by a set of non-linear mixed difference/differential equations, the analysis of such a system is, at present, almost intractable. If a choice has to be made, we think that a continuous rather than a discrete model gives a better representation. A number of advantages that we briefly summarize motivates this choice (for a review, see Gandolfo (1993), and Bergstrom and Nowman (2007)).

Synchronization

The first advantage, which is a very general one, is that a continuous-time model can take account of a matching problem between the unit observation period and the moment individual economic decisions are made. Discrete-time models are constrained, by their true nature, to match the decision making structure with that of the observation period. That is, the discrete-time approach assumes that individual decisions are so perfectly synchronized as to be made at same moment and with reference to the same interval of the observation period. Conversely, in continuous time, no such problem exists. Indeed, within the observation data period, economic agents are continuously taking individual decisions, and this makes the working of economic systems a continuous process. Thus, a continuous-time approach is more realistic and consistent with the macroeconomic process, independently from the unit observation period. The independence from the unit observation period is also important for forecasting purposes, and thus essential for governments and central banks' policy making.

Partial adjustment and dynamic disequilibrium

Second, a specification in continuous time is useful for modelling dynamic-disequilibrium partial-adjustment processes of variables to their equilibrium levels, the main reason being the presence of adjustment costs. This way, the dynamic model incorporates frictions and market rigidities that, while exerting a major influence in the short run, do not affect its long-run behaviour. This implies that the models used are *nontâtonnement*, so that there is no assumption that prices or quantities are in equilibrium at any point in time. Much of the current theoretical literature follows the Walrasian assumption that markets continuously 'clear'. It seems to us that such assumptions are too restrictive to give a realistic representation of an economic system. The continuous-time models are more general than those incorporating such Walrasian assumption, but their *long-run* properties are consistent with rational expectations. They are dynamic-disequilibrium models in that they specify the transition from one long-run equilibrium to another. Since in the second part of this contribution we will make use of the partial-adjustment approach in specifying and estimating two models of the Italian economy, we give a brief summary of their formal derivation.

A formal derivation of the partial-adjustment equations

We now briefly describe how to derive the partial-adjustment equations (for a detailed treatment, see Bergstrom and Nowman (2007)). They are the solutions to an intertemporal dynamic minimization problem whose functional depends on adjustment costs. We begin with the simplest case of the first-order partial-adjustment equations, where the adjustment costs depend only on the derivative of the adjusting variables.

Assume that the economic agent has control over a variable $x(t)$, where t is time. This variable changes in response to a vector $z(t)$, which includes both exogenous and other endogenous variables. The partial-equilibrium level of $x(t)$ is defined by the function $f(z(t))$, which could be the outcome of some optimization process (such as utility or profit). If there were no adjustment costs, at all points in time we would have $x(t) = f(z(t))$.

A more realistic representation of the individual behaviour takes into account the existence of adjustment costs, related to frictions, rigidities and uncertainty. For simplicity, we assume that these costs are a quadratic function of the deviation of $x(t)$ from its expected level (defined below) and the rate of change of $x(t)$, i.e. on $\frac{dx(t)}{dt}$. It is the presence of such costs that gives rise to the partial-adjustment functions. If $x(t)$ is not at its expected equilibrium level, the agent plans to move gradually along an optimal path determined by the intertemporal minimization of the integral of adjustment costs.

The expected equilibrium level is defined in such a way as to be consistent with the long-run expectations assumption. To simplify, let us assume that the equilibrium level of $x(t)$ grows at a constant rate λ. Consequently, the expected equilibrium level of the variable at a future time $t + r$, with $r > 0$, is given by

$$E\left(f\left(z\left(t+r\right)\right)\right) = f\left(z(t)\right) + \lambda r$$

Taking into account assumptions about expectations and the form of adjustment costs, the optimal planned path is obtained by the following integral minimization

$$\int_0^\infty \left(x\left(t+r\right) - E\left(f\left(z\left(t+r\right)\right)\right)\right)^2 + a \left(\frac{dx\left(t+r\right)}{dr}\right)^2 \right) dr$$

where a is given by the weight of the adjustment costs deviation.

Minimizing the above objective functional gives rise to a second-order differential equation. Discarding the positive solution, the actual path of $x(t)$ satisfies the following differential equation

$$\frac{dx(t)}{dt} = \lambda + \gamma\left(f\left(z\left(t\right)\right) - x(t)\right). \tag{2.1}$$

To put it into words, $x(t)$ increases at a velocity equal to the long-rate expected rate λ plus the deviation from its equilibrium at an adjustment speed equal to γ.

We turn now to the second-order partial-adjustment functions. In its formulation, we assume that the adjustment costs depend not only on the deviation between the actual and expected level of $x(t)$ but also on its acceleration, that is $\frac{d^2x(t)}{dt^2}$. In this case the integral objective function to be minimized is

$$\int_0^\infty \left(x(t+r) - E\left(f\left(z(t+r)\right)\right)^2 + a\left(\frac{dx(t+r)}{dr}\right)^2 + b\left(\frac{d^2x(t)}{dt^2}\right)^2 \right) dr$$

where a and b reflect the weights of first- and second-order adjustment costs. Following a procedure similar to that seen above, we can derive the second-order partial-adjustment function, which takes the following form

$$\frac{d^2x(t)}{dt^2} = \gamma_1\left(\lambda - \frac{dx(t)}{dt}\right) + \gamma_2\left(f\left(z(t)\right) - x(t)\right). \tag{2.2}$$

In this case, $x(t)$ accelerates at a rate equal to the sum of two deviations: the excess of the expected rate of increase of $x(t)$ over its actual rate of change with a speed of adjustment equal to γ_1; and the excess of partial-equilibrium level over its actual level with a speed of adjustment γ_2.

Adjustment speed and distributed lags

A third advantage, which is related to the previous one, is that the disequilibrium approach allows us to estimate the adjustment speeds in goods and services markets without making any a priori assumption about adjustment processes in goods and asset markets. For instance, it is usual to assume that asset markets have an adjustment speed to equilibrium which is much faster than goods and services markets. The continuous-time econometrics allows us not only to test these assumptions but also to estimate precisely the speed of adjustment.

A formal derivation of the distributed-lag relations

The partial-adjustment equations seen above imply that the current value of the dependent variable $x(t)$ depends on all its past values $x(t-r)$, with $r > 0$, or, in other words, on all past values of the explanatory variables $z(t-r)$. This is simply the result of solving the previous differential (partial-adjustment) equations in reverse (for a detailed treatment, see Bergstrom and Nowman, 2007). For obvious reasons, these expressions are called distributed-lag relations and always take the following form

$$y(t) = \int_0^\infty \left[h(r)g(z(t-r))\right] dr, \text{ with } \int_0^\infty h(r)dr = 1 \text{ and } \lim_{r\to\infty} h(r) = 0, \tag{2.3}$$

where $f(r)$ is the time weighting function and is usually interpreted as a density.

Let us begin with the first-order partial-adjustment equation. First we define two new variables

$$y(t) = x(t) - \lambda t \quad \text{and}$$

$$g(z(t)) = f(z(t)) - \lambda t.$$

In other words, $x(t)$ and $f(z(t))$ fluctuate around the trend λ, and $y(t)$ and $g(z(t))$ represent their deviations from the trend. Differentiating the first equation we get

$$\frac{dy(t)}{dt} = \frac{dx(t)}{dt} - \lambda,$$

so that (2.1) can be rewritten as

$$\frac{dy(t)}{dt} = \gamma (g(z(t)) - y(t)). \tag{2.4}$$

We now show that the solution to this differential equation is

$$y(t) = \int_0^\infty \gamma \exp(-\gamma r)\, g\,(z\,(t-r))\, dr \tag{2.5}$$

where the density in this case is $\int_0^\infty \gamma \exp(-r\gamma)\, dr$.

Let us perform a change of variable from r to s, where $s = t - r$. We obtain

$$y(t) = \int_{-\infty}^t \gamma \exp\left[-\gamma\,(t-s)\right] g\,(z\,(s))\, ds$$

$$= \gamma \exp(-\gamma t) \int_{-\infty}^t \exp\left[\gamma\,(s)\right] g\,(z\,(s))\, ds.$$

Differentiating this last expression with respect to t and by applying Leibniz's rule we get

$$\frac{dy(t)}{dt} = -\gamma^2 \exp(-\gamma t) \int_{-\infty}^t \exp\left[\gamma\,(s)\right] g\,(z\,(s))\, ds$$

$$+ \gamma \exp(-\gamma t) \exp(\gamma t)\, g\,(z(t))$$

$$= \gamma\,(g\,(z(t)) - y(t)).$$

This proves that (2.5) is indeed the solution to the differential (2.4). From the density function we can also calculate the mean time lag (MTL), that is the time necessary for the discrepancy between $y(t)$ and $g\,(z(t))$ to be eliminated by changes in $y(t)$, defined as

$$\int_0^\infty r h_1\,(r)\, dr = \int_0^\infty r\gamma \exp(-\gamma r)\, dr.$$

Integrating by parts, we obtain

$$\int_0^\infty r\gamma \exp(-\gamma r)\, dr = -\left[r \exp(-\gamma r)\,\big|_0^\infty - \int_0^\infty \exp(-\gamma r)\, dr\right] = \frac{1}{\gamma}.$$

That is, for first-order partial adjustment the MTL is the reciprocal of the adjustment speed.

The distributed-lag relations implied by the second-order adjustment equation are derived in a similar way. Again using the definitions of $y(t)$ and $g(z(t))$ given above, the second-order differential (2.2) becomes

$$\frac{d^2 y(t)}{dt^2} = -\gamma_1 \frac{dy(t)}{dt} + \gamma_2 (g(z(t)) - y(t)). \qquad (2.6)$$

The characteristic equation of (2.6) involves two roots, which we shall assume are both negative, implying that $y(t)$ converges monotonically to $g(z(t))$. Let us denote the two roots by $-\alpha$ and $-\beta$, with $\beta < \alpha > 0$, so that $\alpha + \beta = \gamma_1$ and $\alpha\beta = \gamma_2$. Then, (2.6) can be written as

$$\frac{d^2 y(t)}{dt^2} + (\alpha + \beta) \frac{dy(t)}{dt} + \alpha\beta\gamma y(t) = \alpha\beta g(z(t)). \qquad (2.7)$$

Following a procedure similar to the one seen above, it can be shown that the solution to (2.7) is

$$y(t) = \int_0^\infty h_2(r) g(z(t-r)) \, dr$$

where the density is

$$h_2(r) = \frac{\alpha\beta}{\beta - \alpha} \left[\exp(-\alpha r) - \exp(-\beta r) \right]. \qquad (2.8)$$

The MTL of this distribution is given by

$$\int_0^\infty r h_2(r) \, dr = \frac{1}{\beta - \alpha} \left\{ \beta \int_0^\infty r\alpha \exp(-\alpha r) \, dr - \alpha \int_0^\infty r\beta \exp(-\beta r) \, dr \right\}$$

$$= \frac{1}{\beta - \alpha} \left[\frac{\beta}{\alpha} - \frac{\alpha}{\beta} \right] = \frac{\alpha\beta}{\beta - \alpha}.$$

The modal time lag (MDTL), which is the lag to the peak of the distribution, is given by

$$\arg\max h_2(r) = \frac{\log \beta - \log \alpha}{\beta - \alpha}. \qquad (2.9)$$

Since $\arg\max h_2(r)$ is the value of r for which

$$\frac{dh_2(r)}{dr} = \frac{d \frac{\alpha\beta}{\beta - \alpha} (\exp(-\alpha r) - \exp(-\beta r))}{dr} = 0,$$

it follows that it satisfies the condition

$$\alpha \exp(-\alpha r) = \beta \exp(-\beta r).$$

Solving for r, we obtain (2.9).

Stocks and flows

Continuous time econometrics permits a correct treatment of stock and flow variables as it solves the temporal aggregation bias that occurs in discrete-time models where no distinction is made between these variable. Indeed, stock variables can be observed instantaneously, while flow variables can be measured only as aggregation over an observation period, thus inducing a misspecification bias.

Structural approach

Finally, the continuous-time equation system typically derives from optimization processes and hence provides an estimation of 'deep' parameters, i.e. parameters which are independent of other parameters in the system. It is thus appropriate for considering parameter changes that are relevant for policy purposes.

The role of ICT in Italian economic growth

In this part of our contribution, we adopt the continuous-time approach to specify and estimate two continuous-time general disequilibrium models of the Italian economy. In an attempt to explain the slowdown of the Italian productivity growth rate in the last three decades, the literature has emphasized the role of three shocks: two are related to international factors: globalization and the adoption of the euro; the third has to do with the technological shock caused by the introduction of ICT.

In the first model we focus on the effects of the technological changes. In particular, we investigate the rate and the effects of ICT introduction on capital and production in the Italian economy and the extent to which it is being affected by skills in the labour force. Consequently, this model is based, on the one hand, on the distinction between traditional and innovative, i.e. ICT capital and, on the other, on the difference between skilled and unskilled labour.

While the first model examines the role of ICT in enhancing general production in the Italian economy, by assuming that ICT contribution is exogenous, in the second model, the process of innovation is endogenous and more complex. The process of endogenization is based on the following modelling structure. We model and estimate a two-level CES aggregate production function – that nests two CES production functions into another CES function – with four inputs. Hence, we introduce a specific factor setup with two different kinds of capital and two different types of labour used in the production of the two intermediate goods (ICT and traditional). Thus, ICT enters as a factor of production through a nested CES production function allowing us to analyse mechanisms for ICT to influence productivity growth.

Notice that, in both models, for estimation purposes we consider ICT producing industries only. The mechanism linking technological progress in ICT to these industries is direct. Technological progress that enables the ICT producing industries to produce greater aggregate output per unit of input is a direct potential contributor to productivity dynamics. We choose to leave out ICT-using industries since, in their case, ICT mostly affects the way they operate and organize their businesses. Clearly, the way ICT impacts on productivity growth is an open issue.

The assumption underlying both models is that the market environment is one of imperfect competition, where firms have similar production functions but different endowments, and their products are sufficiently differentiated, implying they are monopolistic competitors in the short run, setting their own prices. Thus, they may set prices according to their marginal costs plus some mark-up or margin which will vary according to the elasticity of demand for their specific product. Each firm will be assumed to be a 'quantity-taker' aiming to supply the amount demanded. Also, it is assumed, at least in aggregate, that firms can vary the amount of unskilled labour to produce the required output relatively easily, but with some costs such as those imposed by rigidities in the labour market or by regulation. Firms vary their skilled workforce more slowly, particularly where such labour must be more highly trained or educated. The capital stocks adjust more slowly to their marginal products. These rates of adjustment reflect the costs and risks of firms changing their capital stock.

The theoretical basis for this is the maximization of an intertemporal value function for the firm which incorporates these costs and risks of investment and changing technology. The model allows the marginal product of ICT capital and skilled labour to differ between an all-purpose output and an ICT output so it helps determine whether such differences exist and, if so, whether they are relevant and whether they are being reduced by factor movements. As marginal products depend on the output/capital ratio and on parameters of the production functions, they will change over time but should converge to some differential representing a relative risk premium.

Although both models have a traditional structure in that the resource endowments play a fundamental part in explaining technological choice, they feature three main distinguishing characteristics.

1   They analyse the effects of the introduction of ICT technology on the Italian economy not in a partial-equilibrium context of a single market (e.g. labour market) but from a macro point of view where capital (both of the traditional and the innovative type) and (skilled and unskilled) labour markets interact.

2   The model does not assume that input markets instantaneously clear but rather that there are imperfections and frictions – such as those measured by the Employment Protection Legislation (EPL) index. In other words, the economic representation of the model is one of disequilibrium dynamics. Similarly, prices are not determined by demand and supply but by price setting through a mark-up on marginal labour cost.

3 The models do not impose the condition that the economy necessarily converges into a steady state, as does much of the existing literature; in fact, the requirement that the system has a steady state would imply, for instance, that the distinction between skilled and unskilled labour vanishes in the long run. Rather, we do not introduce such a condition from the start, but rather let the estimates tell us what kind of dynamics the economy has. Note that even if the model economy may not have a steady state or be stable in a classical sense, it may still have an attractor and be stable.

ICT as an exogenous input

The first model gives a stylized representation of the main characteristics of the Italian economy. In the model, firms produce two goods (one traditional and one innovative) using four inputs (traditional and innovative capital, skilled and unskilled labour). Specifically, the model considers two production sectors: the output of the total economy (Y) and the ICT output (Y_I), both specified as CES technologies. The output of the total economy Y is obtained through a combination of capital (both traditional and innovative, K and C), and labour, where the latter is defined as a geometric average with weights (γ_s, γ_u) of skilled (L_s) and unskilled labour (L_u). The ICT production function considers ICT capital (C) and only skilled labour with a specific labour augmenting factor with growth rate λ_C.

The two production functions are as follows.

1 The general production function:

$$Y = f(K, C, L_s, L_u) = \beta_3 \left[(C^{\gamma_1} K)^{-\beta_1} + \left(\beta_2 e^{(\lambda_K + \gamma_1 \lambda_C)t} L_s^{\gamma_s} L_u^{\gamma_u}\right)^{-\beta_1} \right]^{-\frac{1}{\beta_1}}.$$

(2.10)

In (2.10) λ_K, λ_C are the rates of technical progress in the use of standard capital stock K and ICT capital C. Their linear combination $\lambda_K + \gamma_1 \lambda_C$ is the growth rate of labour efficiency, β_2 is the labour augmenting technical progress, while β_3 is a measure of the total factor productivity. The efficiency of traditional fixed capital stock is augmented by ICT capital, C, with a weighting factor equal to γ_1; the elasticity of substitution is given by $e_1 = \frac{1}{1+\beta_1}$.

2 The ICT production function is

$$Y_I = f_I(C, L_{Is}) = \beta_6 \left[C^{-\beta_4} + \left(\beta_5 e^{\lambda_C t} L_{Is}\right)^{-\beta_4} \right]^{-1/\beta_4}.$$

(2.11)

In this equation, β_5 is labour augmenting technical progress, while β_6 is a measure of TFP. The elasticity of substitution is $e_4 = \frac{1}{1+\beta_4}$.

The dynamic part of the model, in its deterministic form, is set out below. It is a system of seven second-order nonlinear differential (partial-adjustment) equations with 40 structural parameters, including a vector β of 13 parameters, a vector γ of three weight parameters, a vector λ of four trend parameters and a vector α of 20 speed of adjustment parameters. In what follows, we give a brief description of the derivation of the partial-adjustment equations.

The two investment equations can be obtained from the intertemporal optimization of a profit function leading implicitly to a second-order distributed lag in the capital stock to a first-order function in investment; α_2 and α_4 are the rates of adjustment of the two capital marginal productivities ($\frac{\partial f}{\partial K}$, $\frac{\partial f_I}{\partial C}$) to the respective user costs, while α_1 and α_3 describe the adjustment to the long-run equilibrium growth rates (μ_K, μ_C) of the two capital stocks. A similar specification is used in the determination of the employment of skilled labour (with a long-run growth rate λ_s), as well as in that of unskilled wages (whose long-run growth rate in efficiency units is the same as the general production function, $\lambda_K + \gamma_1 \lambda_C$, the long-run capital accumulation rate). Notice that, while skilled employment is assumed to be determined by the demand for labour, unskilled employment is ready to fill any shortfall in producing the required output, so that the pool of unskilled labour acts as a buffer. Finally, prices are determined according to marginal (labour) cost per unit of output, $w\,(\partial L / \partial Y)$, derived from the inverse of the production function multiplied by indirect taxes τ and with a mark-up β_{13}. The price dynamics reflect the competitive process and the way in which prices are likely to be affected by the rates of change of real wages adjusted for increases in efficiency. The marginal cost of labour is obtained in the usual way as a ratio between the mean wage and the marginal product of labour, where labour is defined (as seen above) as a geometric average between skilled and unskilled labour.

These equations lead to the specification of a structural model of general and ICT investments, the skilled and unskilled labour sectors, and price determination.

1   Investment functions.

    a   Traditional capital:

$$\dot{k} = \alpha_1 \left[\alpha_2 \left(\frac{\partial f}{\partial K} - (r - \beta_7 D \ln p + \beta_8) \right) - (k - \mu_K) \right]. \tag{2.12}$$

    b   ICT capital:

$$\dot{c} = \alpha_3 \left[\alpha_4 \left(\frac{\partial f_I}{\partial C} - (r - \beta_9 D \ln p + \beta_{10}) \right) - (c - \mu_C) \right] \tag{2.13}$$

    where in (2.12), $\mu_K = \lambda_K + (\gamma_S - \gamma_1)\lambda_S + \gamma_u \lambda_u$ and in (2.13), $\mu_C = \lambda_s + \lambda_c.$[1]

2   Skilled labour.

a   Demand for skilled labour:

$$\dot{\ell}_s = \alpha_5 \left[\alpha_6 \ln \left(\frac{\partial f}{\partial L_s} \Big/ \frac{w_s}{p} \right) + \alpha'_6 \ln \left(\frac{\partial f_I}{\partial L_{Is}} \Big/ \frac{w_s}{p} \right) - (\ell_s - \lambda_s) \right].$$

(2.14)

b   Determination of skilled nominal wages:

$$D^2 \ln w_s = \alpha_7 [\alpha_8 \ln \left(\frac{\partial f / \partial L_s}{p / w_s} \right) + \alpha'_8 \ln \left(\frac{\partial f_I / \partial L_{Is}}{p / w_s} \right) +$$
$$- (\alpha_7 + \alpha_8 + \alpha'_8)(D \ln w_s - \beta_{11} D \ln p - \lambda_K - \gamma_1 \lambda_C)]$$

(2.15)

where β_{11} measures money illusion.[2]

3   Unskilled labour.

a   Employment:

$$\dot{\ell}_u = \alpha_9 \alpha_{10} \ln \left(L_u^d / L_u \right) - (\alpha_9 + \alpha_{10})(\ell_u - \lambda_u).$$

(2.16)

b   Determination of unskilled wages:

$$D^2 \ln w_u = \alpha_{11} \left[\alpha_{12} \ln \left(\frac{L_u^d}{L_u^s} \right) - (D \ln \frac{w_u}{p} - \lambda_K - \gamma_1 \lambda_C) \right]$$

(2.17)

where $L_u^s = L_{u0} \left(\frac{w_u}{p} \right)^{\beta_{12}} e^{\lambda_u t}$. In the model, changes in the unskilled labour supply depend on the real wage, with elasticity β_{12}. Thus, the effect on labour supply will be largely symmetrical at the margin for increases and decreases of real wages. However, this is only one side of the labour market. We should also take into account the demand side. Unless the elasticity of real wages in the supply function is one, changes in nominal wages have a differing effect on prices and hence on real wages. The price effect then feeds back into investment, capital and thus on the demand for labour via its marginal product. The effect on the capital stock is not symmetrical, but this is slow acting.[3]

4   Price determination:

$$D^2 \ln p = \alpha_{13} \alpha_{14} \ln \left(\frac{\beta_{13} \times \tau \times mc \left(\frac{\partial L}{\partial Y} \right)}{p} \right) - (\alpha_{13} + \alpha_{14}) D \ln p$$
$$+ \alpha_{15} \left\{ \left\{ D \ln \left(\frac{w_s}{p} \right) - \lambda_C \right\} + \alpha_{16} \left\{ D \ln \left(\frac{w_u}{p} \right) - (\lambda_K + \gamma_1 \lambda_C) \right\} \right\}$$
$$+ \alpha_{17} \left\{ \ln \left(\frac{M}{pY} \right) + \upsilon + \lambda_\upsilon t \right\}$$

(2.18)

where β_{13} is the mark-up and $mc\left(\frac{\partial L}{\partial Y}\right)$ is the marginal cost determined as follows:

$$mc\left(\frac{\partial L}{\partial Y}\right) = \left(\frac{w_s L_s}{\gamma_s} + \frac{w_u L_u}{\gamma_u}\right) L_s^{-\gamma_u} L_u^{-\gamma_u} (\beta_2 \beta_3)^{-1} e^{-(\lambda_K + \gamma_1 \lambda_C)t}$$

$$\times \left[1 - \left(\frac{Y}{\beta_3 K C^{\gamma_1}}\right)^{\beta_1}\right]^{\frac{1+\beta_1}{\beta_1}}.$$

Further, $\upsilon = \overline{\ln p} + \overline{\ln Y} - \overline{\ln M}$ is the mean velocity over the sample and is assumed to vary at a rate λ_υ with more efficient transactions and an increase in the use of electronic money.

For brevity, we will not give all the estimated parameters (for a complete list, see Saltari *et al.*, 2012), but we will limit ourselves to discussing the main findings.

We begin our discussion with the parameters of the two production functions, and in particular of the elasticities of substitution. The elasticity of substitution of the general production function is about 0.65 while that of the ICT sector is 0.57. These estimates imply that the inputs are complements in both sectors. As a matter of definition, this means that a fall in the wage–rental ratio leads to a lower decrease in the capital–labour (in a broad sense) ratio. As expected, the ICT sector has a lower elasticity. This result agrees with economic intuition according to which the more technologically advanced sector, that of ICT, should have a lower elasticity of substitution because of the stricter complementarity between capital and labour.

We will now look at the estimates of net domestic product (NDP) and restrict our attention to the analysis of the core of the model, in order to compare the dynamics of theoretical net output to the observed one. The former is determined by the production function specified in (2.10) with the estimated values of parameters. This procedure implies that there are no adjustment costs, or in other words, that the adjustment speeds are infinite so that this level of output can be considered 'optimal'. The theoretical evolution of this variable is then compared with the actual evolution of NDP. Figure 2.1 reports the levels of estimated and actual NDP for the whole period 1980–2005, and for the two sub-periods, 1980–1992 and 1992–2005.

The production function (2.10) gives an estimate of output value of €955 billion, while the observed NDP is €893 billion for the period 1980–2005 (see Table 2.1). Thus, there exists a gap between the 'optimal' and the actual value of about 6.5 per cent over the whole period. It suggests that there are structural inefficiencies or at least long-term costs, some of which are costs of adjustment. Of course, some of these will always exist, but others may really be unnecessary or excessive but may have become institutionalized. These adjustment costs, be they avoidable or not, are represented in the model through the alphas.

Looking at Table 2.1, two observations emerge. First of all, the model replicates quite well the dynamics of the Italian economy. Besides the first part of the

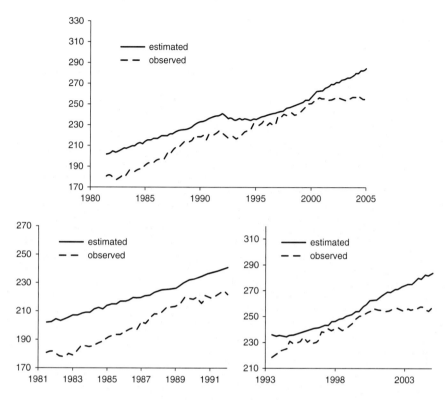

Figure 2.1 The dynamics of observed and estimated NDP.

Table 2.1 Estimated and observed NDP

Period	Net national product (in bn. of € , yearly values)	
	Observed	Estimated
1980–2005	893	955
1980–1992	810	887
1992–2005	976	1024

sample, the only period in which the estimation diverges from the observed path is concentrated in the last 20 quarters, when the discrepancy between observed and 'optimal' output increases markedly. It also increased, but to a lesser extent, during the downturn in the early 1990s. One explanation is that in a downturn, capital stock will still exist and will not be written down (i.e. depreciated) quickly so capital utilization will fall, which may show up more clearly as a fall in actual output. Presumably net investment will fall, but the effect of that on the capital stock is not immediate. The model does not include depreciation so that if depreciation were increased in the recession that would be picked up by the model. Investment in ICT fell heavily in the early 1990s and again towards the end of the sample, but the effect of that on the ICT capital stock is much less pronounced.

ICT as an intermediate input

The aim of the second model is to endogenize the ICT contribution, which is different from the first model where ICT is exogenous. As said in the introductory section, the endogenization is realized through a nested approach. To this end, we specify and estimate a two-level CES aggregate production function – that nests two CES production functions into another CES function – with four inputs. Hence, we introduce two different kinds of capital, K and C, and two different types of labour, L and L_I, used in the production of the two intermediate goods (ICT and traditional).

The two lower level CES production functions yield two outputs that enter into the global function as intermediate inputs. The upper level production function produces the general output. One of the main contribution, of this chapter is that the lower level CES produces the ICT output, thus making endogenous its contribution to final output. In the following paragraphs, we detail the production structure of the model.

Final output Y is obtained by a production function of labour L and capital K embedded in a CES function extended to allow for ICT goods and services, Y_I, as an additional factor input. Hence, the overall aggregate CES production function is specified as

$$Y = f\left(\varphi, Y_I\right) = \beta_3 \left[\left(e^{\lambda_I I'} \varphi\right)^{-\beta_2} + \left(\beta_5 Y_I\right)^{-\beta_2}\right]^{-\frac{1}{\beta_2}} \tag{2.19}$$

where φ and Y_I are the intermediate outputs of the two lower level CES functions, β_3 is a scaling factor and β_5 is the relative weight of the two sectors. The elasticity of substitution between the two intermediate goods is given by $\sigma_2 = \frac{1}{1+\beta_2}$. Under the assumption that ICT efficiency itself is increasing, an ICT efficiency factor $e^{\lambda_I I'}$ is applied to φ, where λ_I is the rate of decrease in the amount of labour and capital required to produce a given output with the use of ICT goods and services. Although ICT is a factor input in itself, it may also act as a catalyst for change.

Let λ_K and λ_C be the rates of technical progress in the use of standard capital stock K and ICT (and thus the rate of decrease in the amount of labour required to produce a given output with a given capital stock), and λ_L the rate of growth of labour. In addition, any efficiency gains from the use of ICT determine the long-run rate of growth of output Y, which is $\mu_Y = \lambda_K + \lambda_I + \lambda_L$. This is the steady-state rate of growth, should it exist.

The quantity φ represents the 'traditional' input produced with the non-innovative capital (K) and unskilled labour (L). Its production function is

$$\varphi = \left[K^{-\beta_1} + \left(\beta_4 e^{\lambda_K t} L\right)^{-\beta_1}\right]^{-\frac{1}{\beta_1}}. \tag{2.20}$$

In (2.20), $e^{\lambda_K t}$ is the labour augmenting factor, while β_4 is the weight of labour relative to capital. In the long run, the rate of capital accumulation as usual must be equal to the sum of the growth rate of labour efficiency (λ_K) and the growth rate of labour (λ_L), hence the long-run growth rate of φ is $\lambda_K + \lambda_L$. The elasticity of substitution between traditional capital and labour is $\sigma_1 = \frac{1}{1+\beta_1}$.

The other CES production function shows ICT output depending on ICT capital (C) and skilled labour only (L_I)

$$Y_I = f_I(C, L_I) = \beta_7 \left[C^{-\beta_6} + \left(\beta_8 e^{\lambda_C t} L_I \right)^{-\beta_6} \right]^{-\frac{1}{\beta_6}}. \tag{2.21}$$

Similarly to (2.19), β_8 is the weight of labour relative to ICT capital while β_7 is a scaling factor. The elasticity of substitution between ICT capital and skilled labour is $\sigma_3 = \frac{1}{1+\beta_6}$. As seen above, the long-term rate of growth of ICT output and ICT capital C is equal to the sum of growth rates of skilled labour and technical progress, $\mu_{Y_I} = \mu_C = \lambda_C + \lambda_{L_I}$.[4]

The conditions for this model to have a steady state are quite severe and include[5]

$$\mu_Y = \mu_\varphi + \lambda_I = \lambda_K + \lambda_L + \lambda_I$$

and

$$\mu_Y = \mu_{Y_I}.$$

The effect of the introduction of ICT into the production sector of the economy, and thus the general production function, is to change the curvature or the position of the production frontier, so allowing more efficient use of the other factors of production. It is considered that in (2.1) the feedback of ICT on general production is a better and more general representation than the one provided by the previous model.

What we have just described is the long-run equilibrium of the system or what is usually called the balanced growth path. Most of the literature proposes that in the short run the input user cost is equal to its marginal productivity. In our theoretical framework, there are imperfections and frictions that hinder short-run instantaneous adjustment. In other words, the model does not assume that input markets instantaneously clear, i.e. the economic representation of the model is one of disequilibrium dynamics.

In what follows, we give a brief description of the derivation of the partial-adjustment equations.

As before, the model is set out below in its deterministic form. It is a system of nine mixed first- and second-order nonlinear differential (partial-adjustment) equations. It includes a vector β of 12 parameters, a vector γ of 2 weight parameters, a vector λ of 4 trend parameters, and a vector α of 20 speed of adjustment parameters. In what follows, we give a brief description of the derivation of the partial-adjustment equations.

1   In our disequilibrium framework, the adjustment of the traditional capital to its short- and long-run equilibrium determines the investment decisions of the firm. Formally, the partial derivative with respect to capital and the real interest rate, or the marginal user cost of capital, defines the investment function in terms of the second-order (time) derivative of $\ln(K)$

$$\dot{k} = \alpha_1 \left[\alpha_2 \left(\frac{\partial f}{\partial K} - (r - D \ln(p) + \beta_{10}) \right) - (k - \mu_K) \right],$$ (2.22)

where $k = D \ln(K)$ and $\mu_K = \lambda_K + \lambda_L$, the average long-run rate of growth of K, and $\frac{\partial f}{\partial K}$ is the marginal product of traditional capital. Owing to the effect of efficiency gains in the application of ICT to the production frontier, the long-run rate of growth of capital is not equal to that of output.

In (2.22), α_1 is the speed at which the capital growth rate approximates its long-run value; in other words, α_1 can be interpreted as the speed of the accumulation process. For its part, α_2 has the nature of an investment adjustment cost to the desired capital stock. It gives a measure of the frictions and constraints found by the firms in profit maximization. The second term in parentheses in (2.22) is a measure of the real interest rate plus a risk premium, β_{10}. As a whole, (2.22) can be seen as the medium-run adjustment process of investment.

2   Similarly to general capital K, ICT capital input C adjusts according to its own marginal product

$$\dot{c} = \alpha_3 \left[\alpha_4 \left(\frac{\partial f_{Y_I}}{\partial C} - r - D \ln(p) + \beta_{11} \right) - (c - \mu_C) \right]$$ (2.23)

where $c = D \ln(C)$ and β_{11} is the risk premium for ICT capital. We can interpret α_3 and α_4 in the same way as in the partial-adjustment investment function of the traditional sector, and $\frac{\partial f_{Y_I}}{\partial C}$ is the marginal product of ICT capital in the ICT sector.

3   Considering some stickiness in increasing employment, or reducing it, the employment equation is

$$\dot{l} = \alpha_5 \alpha_6 \ln \left(\frac{L^d}{L} \right) - (\alpha_5 + \alpha_6)(l - \lambda_L)$$ (2.24)

where $l = D \ln(L)$ and L is actual employment deriving from the adjustment by firms towards the demand function, and L^d is obtained by inverting the general production function. If demand is expected to be satisfied quickly, α_6 will be high. In this equation, α_5 may be assumed to be a variable function of adjustment costs present in the labour market, as for instance the costs of firing someone proxied by the EPL index.

4   Wages in the general sector are determined by demand and supply. The supply
     function for labour L^s is

$$L^s = L_0 \left(\frac{w}{p}\right)^{\beta_{12}} e^{\lambda L^t}. \tag{2.25}$$

The labour force is assumed to grow (or decline) at a rate λ_L and vary according to the real-wage rate with elasticity β_{12}. L_0 is a parameter representing the
base labour force (at $t = 0$). The determination of wages is specified as

$$D^2 \ln(w) = \alpha_7 \ln\left(\frac{L^d}{L^s}\right) - \alpha_8 \left(D \ln\left(\frac{w}{p}\right) - \lambda_K\right) \tag{2.26}$$

where the numerator is the demand for labour defined as the inverse of the
production function.

Although wages are defined in nominal terms in (2.26) and in units corresponding to the definition of L, the function determining wages is in real
terms such that the long-term real-wage rate in efficiency units is expected to
grow at a rate λ_K. Thus, prices feed back into the nominal wage determination equation, but in equilibrium the real-wage rate would equal the marginal
product of labour.

5   Prices are determined according to marginal (labour) cost per unit output,
     $w (\partial L/\partial Y)$, derived from the inverse of the production function multiplied
     by indirect taxes rate τ, and with a mark-up γ_1 to give a partial-equilibrium
     price $\gamma_1 \tau w (\partial L/\partial Y)$. The price dynamics of the model reflect the competitive
     process and the way in which prices are likely to be affected by the rates
     of change of real wages adjusted for increases in efficiency. The dynamics
     of price determination are described by a second-order process in which the
     acceleration of prices, or the rate of change of the inflation rate, is specified as

$$D^2 \ln(p) = \alpha_{13}\alpha_{14} \ln\left(\frac{\gamma_1 \tau mc\,(\partial L/\partial Y)}{p}\right) - (\alpha_{13} + \alpha_{14})(D \ln(p) - \mu_P)$$

$$+ \alpha_{15}\left[D \ln\left(\frac{w}{p}\right) - \lambda_K\right] + \alpha_{16} \ln\left(\frac{vM}{pY}\right). \tag{2.27}$$

The first two terms represent a second-order adjustment of prices to short-run
marginal cost, the next term that prices are likely to rise faster if there is an
expectation that real wages will increase faster than some long-run average,
and the last term is a monetary effect that prices will be expected to rise faster
if the ratio of the volume of money M to nominal output is high relative to
some long-run measure of the velocity of money $\frac{1}{v}$. λ_M is the long-run rate
of growth of the volume of money, adjusted for changes in velocity and the
long-run expected rate of growth of prices $\mu_P = \lambda_M - \mu_Y$.

6   Employment in the ICT sector is defined as

$$\dot{i}_I = \alpha_9 \left[\alpha_{10} \ln \left(\frac{\partial f_{Y_I}}{\partial L_I} \Big/ \frac{w_I}{p_I} \right) - \left(l_I - \lambda_{L_I} \right) \right].$$
(2.28)

7   Nominal wages are specified to allow for stickiness:

$$D^2 \ln (w_I) = \alpha_{11} \alpha_{12} \ln \left(\frac{\partial f_{Y_I}}{\partial L_I} \Big/ \frac{w_I}{p_I} \right) - (\alpha_{11} + \alpha_{12}) \left(D \ln (w_I) - D \ln (p) - \lambda_C \right).$$
(2.29)

8   As in the general sector, it is assumed that ICT prices are determined according to marginal (labour) cost per unit output, $w_I \, (\partial L_I / \partial Y_I)$, derived from the inverse of the production function multiplied by indirect taxes τ_I and with a mark-up γ_2 to give a partial-equilibrium price $\gamma_2 \tau_I w_I \, (\partial L_I / \partial Y_I)$. The price dynamics of the model reflect the competitive process and the way in which prices are likely to be affected by the rates of change of real wages adjusted for increases in efficiency. Thus, if necessary, providing the supply of labour in the ICT sector is fully elastic such that the supply of labour equals the marginal product, the model can be specified without the use of employment data and (2.28) becomes superfluous.

Again, the dynamics of price determination are described by a second-order process in which the acceleration of ICT prices is specified as

$$D^2 \ln (p_I) = \alpha_{17} \alpha_{18} \ln \left(\frac{\gamma_2 \tau_I mc \, (\partial L_I / \partial Y_I)}{p_I} \right) - (\alpha_{17} + \alpha_{18}) \left(D \ln (p_I) - \mu_{p_I} \right)$$

$$+ \alpha_{19} \left[D \ln \left(\frac{w_I}{p_I} \right) - \lambda_C \right].$$
(2.30)

The long-run rate of growth of ICT prices is $\mu_{P_I} = \lambda_M - \mu_I.$[6]

9   In partial equilibrium, the marginal product of Y with respect to Y_I in the general production function will equal the real price of ICT inputs, or in terms of the usual equality between marginal cost and output price

$$p = \frac{p_I}{\partial f / \partial Y_I}.$$

Thus, it is assumed that the demand for ICT is a function of the discrepancy between the marginal product of the final good with respect to ICT input and its real price, $\frac{p_I}{p}$. The price of ICT inputs, p_I, is determined by its marginal cost plus a mark-up.

The equation which links the ICT sector with the general sector is the demand and supply of ICT goods and services which may be represented by the difference, in logarithmic terms, of the marginal product of ICT inputs in the general production function and the relative cost of those inputs. This is specified as

$$D \ln (Y_I) = \alpha_{20} \ln \left(\frac{\partial f}{\partial Y_I} \bigg/ \frac{p_I}{p} \right). \tag{2.31}$$

We will now look at the estimates of NDP and restrict our attention to the analysis of the core of the model in order to compare the dynamics of theoretical net output to the observed one. The former is determined by the production function specified in (2.19). This estimation procedure implies that there are no adjustment costs or, in other words, that the adjustment speeds are infinite so that this level of output can be considered 'optimal'. The theoretical evolution of this variable is then compared with the actual evolution of NDP.

The general production function (2.19) gives an estimate of average output value of €1100 billion per year, while the average observed NDP is €1076 billion for the period 1981–2011. Thus, there exists an average gap between the 'optimal' and the actual value of 2 per cent over the whole period. It suggests that there are structural inefficiencies or at least long-term costs, some of which are costs of adjustment. Of course, some of these will always exist, but others may really be unnecessary or excessive but may have become institutionalized. These adjustment costs, be they avoidable or not, are represented in the model through the alphas. It seems that the model replicates quite well the dynamics of the Italian economy. For a more detailed discussion of the empirical results, see Federici *et al.* (2015).

The adjustment dynamics

We now turn to the partial-adjustment processes of capital and labour markets, wages and prices. By partial, we mean that each of these variables adjusts, with a distributed time lag, to its partial-equilibrium value, which is a function of a subset of other variables of the model. We will not discuss the adjustment speed in all the markets, but will limit ourselves to the capital and labour markets.

Adjustment in capital markets

The adjustment process of the aggregate capital stock, (2.22), does not assume the standard form. Indeed, a more general lag is used since the difference between the desired and actual values is implicitly defined in terms of the marginal product of capital. Log-linearizing about the sample mean, we get a coefficient for $\ln (K)$, call it $\alpha_K = 0.046$, which multiplied by α_2 gives the MTL for traditional capital adjustment

$$MTL_K = \frac{1}{b'} = \frac{1}{\alpha_2 \alpha_K} \simeq 126$$

that is over 30 years. This time length must be interpreted as the MTL needed for changes in investment to bring the marginal product of capital into line with the real interest rate. As for the modal time lag, we have

$$\text{MDTL}_K = \frac{\ln\left(\frac{\alpha_1 + \sqrt{\alpha_1^2 - 4\alpha_1\alpha_2\alpha_K}}{\alpha_1 - \sqrt{\alpha_1^2 - 4\alpha_1\alpha_2\alpha_K}}\right)}{\sqrt{\alpha_1^2 - 4\alpha_1\alpha_2\alpha_K}} \simeq 34.$$

MTLs not too dissimilar were obtained for the UK economy (Bergstrom and Nowman, 2007). These values suggest that the speed at which firms adjust the existing capital stock to its desired level is very slow.

Similarly, considering the adjustment of ICT capital stock, (2.23), we follow the same procedure obtaining an MTL of more than six years since

$$\text{MTL}_C = \frac{1}{\alpha_4\alpha_C} \simeq 24$$

where $\alpha_C = 0.2$ is the result of log-linearizing the ICT marginal product about the sample mean. Thus, perhaps not surprisingly, the capital adjustment in the ICT sector is much shorter than in the traditional goods sector.

Adjustment in labour markets

Equation (2.24) specifies the time required by firms in the aggregate sector to adjust the actual level of employment to the desired or demanded one. The MTL in this case is given by

$$\text{MTL}_E = \frac{1}{\alpha_5} + \frac{1}{\alpha_6} \simeq 38.$$

This means that, other things being equal, it takes about 38 quarters – more than nine years – for the labour market to close the gap. The presence of rigidities in the labour market in Italy may justify such very slow adjustment. Note, however, that the mode in the labour market is much shorter and equal to

$$\text{MDTL}_E \simeq 4.$$

Following the same procedure seen above for the adjustment of capital stocks, the adjustment process in the labour market of the ICT sector, which involves demand and supply, is given by

$$\text{MTL}_{E_I} = \frac{1}{\alpha_{10}\alpha_{L_I}} \simeq 20$$

where, as above, $\alpha_{L_I} = 1 + \beta_6$ is the result of log-linearizing the labour marginal product in the ICT sector about the sample mean. This period is longer than expected and seems to suggest a shortage of skilled labour in the Italian labour market.

Conclusions

In this chapter we discussed the advantages of the continuous-time disequilibrium modelling, which in our opinion represents a coherent framework for macroeconomic specification and estimation. We then applied this approach to two different models of the Italian economy, focussing on the role of the ICT sector. Although this approach appears more complex than the standard discrete one, it results in better hypotheses testing and dynamic properties. These characteristics are confirmed by our estimation results, which on the whole appear quite satisfactory.

Notes

1 While the investment equations allow for money illusion in specifying the real interest rate, estimates showed that β_7 and β_9 were not significantly different from 1 and in the final estimates they were set to 1.
2 Estimates of β_{11} were not significantly different from 1 showing there is no money illusion in the determination of real wages. In the final model β_{11} was set to 1.
3 Behind (2.17), there is the idea that real wages react to labour demand and supply discrepancies. Empirically, this implies the existence of a relationship between wages and employment – the so-called 'wage curve'. This topic is much debated in the literature. With reference to our sample period, we can distinguish two subperiods. In the first half, which goes up to the early 1990s, empirical estimates do not find evidence of such a wage curve. In the second half, beginning after the July Income Policy Agreement, there is a clear empirical evidence supporting the wage curve relationship (see Devicienti *et al.*, 2008).
4 To see this, assume that in the long run the variables, such as C and L_I, grow at constant rates

$$C = C^* e^{\mu_C t}, L_I = L_I^* e^{\lambda_{LI} t}$$

where μ_j is the generic growth rate of the endogenous variables and λ_j is the generic growth rate of the exogenous variables. Substitute these expressions into (2.17) and denote by μ_I the long-run growth rate of ICT output. Determine this rate by taking the time derivative of the log of Y_I. The result is that stated in the main text. By definition, Y_I is the accumulation rate of the ICT capital stock, so that their long-run growth rates are the same.
5 The steady states may not exist, but these terms may be interpreted as an indication of the expected long-run term rates of growth, providing the system is stable. The (constant) rates of growth in efficiency in the use of labour in the ICT production function λ_C and in the use of ICT on general production function λ_I need not be the same. Although the same linear function of the rate of technical progress λ_K and the ICT efficiency factor λ_I appears in many places in the model, the rate of technical progress appears separately in the investment function for general capital K, so the efficiency rates are identified uniquely.
6 The parameters for the rates of growth in the volume of money, the ICT labour force and for technical progress in the ICT sector are all identified, the latter from the equations for employment and wages in the ICT sector and the former from both price equations.

References

Bergstrom, A. R. and K. B. Nowman (2007), *A Continuous Time Econometric Model of the United Kingdom with Stochastic Trends*. Cambridge, UK: Cambridge University Press.

Devicienti F., A. Maida and L. Pacelli (2008), 'The resurrection of the Italian wage curve', *Economics Letters*, 98, 335–341.

Federici, D., E. Saltari and C. Wymer (2015), 'Endogenizing the ICT sector: A multi-sector approach', MPRA Paper No 66723.

Gandolfo, G. (1993), *Continuous Time Econometrics*, London: Chapman and Hall.

Saltari, E., C. Wymer, D. Federici and M. Giannetti (2012), 'Technological adoption with imperfect markets in the Italian economy', *Studies in Nonlinear Dynamics & Econometrics*, 16, 2.

3 The role of demand factors in the determination of the GDP growth rate

Renato Paniccià and Stefano Prezioso[1]

Introduction

The world financial crash at the end of 2008 resulted in the longest and deepest crisis since the Second World War. An extensive literature, both from academia and economic institutions, has underlined that the prolonged drop in demand has significantly affected potential output (Ball, 2014; Hall, 2014; International Monetary Fund, 2015).

Although these contributions produced helpful insights into the consequences that a prolonged fall in activity levels has on potential output, demand is still considered the aggregate from which an exogenous shock could originate. As a result, any possible feedback between the cycle and the path of potential output is ignored. This *modus operandi* reflects the mainstream thought on growth: the growth of gross domestic product (GDP) in a medium to long period is determined solely by supply factors, while in the short term deviations from the growth path can also be determined by fluctuations in demand. In any case, it has been noted even by *mainstream* economists that this logical separation between the two sides of the economy leaves a wide margin for uncertainty, although less so in the medium term. Precisely, 'At the five to ten years time scale, we have to piece things [supply and demand] together as best as we can, and look for an hybrid model that will do the job' (Solow, 2000, p. 158). The specification of causal linkages of GDP growth implying the interactions between [supply and demand] determinants of growth is the main aim of this chapter.

Theoretical framework: technical progress function and demand

In the models that explicitly formalize the interaction between supply and demand in the determination of the output growth (Pasinetti, 1981, 1993), the technical process (supply side) embedded in product/process is identified as the most important factor: a role that, from the demand side, is played by the different income elasticities of the (main) groups of products and services. The interaction over time of these two elements determines the so-called 'structural change' of an economy. The breadth and direction of this phenomenon is reflected in the intensity of the growth process experienced by the economy itself.[2]

Empirically, a notable volume of analysis has been conducted:[3] these, however, have mainly concentrated on one of the two aforementioned elements as the
drivers of change and growth.

In this contribution, a causal relationship in which the two sides of the economic
system – supply and demand – effectively interact in the determination of the GDP
growth, will be specified and tested. In consideration of the entirely preliminary
characteristic of this analysis, both the supply and the demand are identified in
their essential features.

The relationship (3.1) can be considered a *consensus* approximation in identifying the elements relating to the supply side of the economic system:

$$\pi = Ak \qquad\qquad\qquad (3.1)$$

where, π is labour productivity and k is the capital/labour ratio. This is indeed
the functional form from which practically all the standard supply functions are
derived (total factor productivity, TFP). The same 'ingredients', however, can be
used in different theoretical contexts. In this contribution, (3.1) is created following the original definition by Kaldor (1957), renewed by Thirlwall (2002). The
theoretical and empirical fundamentals of (3.1) were developed by the authors
in different essays; among these we refer you to Paniccià *et al.* (2013). The
importance, in any case, of this specific supply function, even for some important
implications explained later, becomes relevant in the theoretical context adopted
here and warrants additional explanation. Figure 3.1 helps to clarify the main
features of Equation (3.1).

The 45° line is the locus of points in which capital and product are growing at
the same rate. The gradient of the technical progress function (TPF) expresses
the elasticity of labour productivity to the accumulation process. A shift from

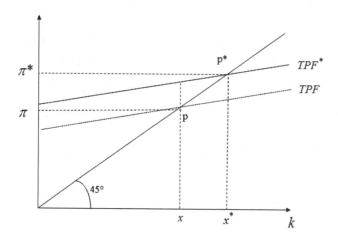

Figure 3.1 Technical progress function.

point x to point x^* – originating, essentially, from an upward movement of the TPF – implies that the accumulation of capital is adequate to make use of the current flow of product and process innovations. A tendency, over time, to move to the right (or vice versa, to the left), compared with the 45° line, shows an accumulation path comparatively less (or more) effective with regard to the capacity to absorb the flow of potentially available innovations and, therefore, similarly the internal activation – the 'creation' – of additional value will be less (or greater). More generally, if the economic system is able to redistribute employment from declining sectors, in relative terms, to others in expansion – positive structural change – the time profile of the TPF will tend to be similar, in the medium to long term, to the 'virtuous' evolution postulated in Figure 3.1. In this case, constant/increasing returns will prevail in that economic system. In the opposite scenario, the process of accumulation will in any case guarantee the progressive reduction of the labour technical coefficients through the continuous improvements embodied in the investment goods, but will not be the driving force associated with the realization of new products/acquisition of new markets.

The implicit hypothesis in this supply function, as with the *mainstream* functions and derived from the production function in its standard version, is that the acquisition of technical progress originating in the system is the driver of development.

The statement that TFP should be considered the engine for growth is a difficult point to argue, when even more recent applications have confirmed that it accounts for almost 90 per cent of the variability in the growth rates of output per worker, with reference to a wide set of countries (Helpman, 2004).

If this point is widely shared, the linkages between productivity and investment are conditioned by the ways, *in primis* the institutional setting, of the effective absorption of technical progress. Actual relationships between factor accumulation and growth appear conditioned by a stock of accumulated knowledge, in particular within the empirical and experimental sciences. The capability to effectively exploit this pool of knowledge would provide the background to the prevailing role of TFP in differential growth. The following quotation may thus be assumed to be a valid approximation of the reality: 'It is the growth of the knowledge about how to get things done that has been the central phenomenon of economic evolution' (Loasby, 1999).

The relevant knowledge from which technical progress emanates cannot simply be embodied in a set of machinery purchasable on the market, but must refer to the overall capability of the economy to innovate its productive assets and to develop supply for new goods and services. These conditions may hardly be proxied by a single variable (education, research and development, etc.) but extend to the whole set of institutional and relational norms, which all frame the collective action together. As recent economic researches have clearly shown, the division of labour brought forth by specialization in particular productive applications will entail parallel effects on overall potential knowledge (*à la Young*). Then the capability to coordinate this potentiality, spread through society, will assume a key role.

To exploit and make use of this potentiality, the standard costs of investment and production will surely be incurred, but other factors – which may, in a broad sense, be assimilated to notions of transaction costs – are also implied. For example, the state of knowledge on the potential applications of goods and services, which are outside the bounds of an agent, may become decisive for competitiveness. The efficient integration of material and immaterial items, dispersed throughout the complex structures of modern economies, requires something more than efficient information given by prices and the market mechanism. Institutions and organizations, allowing the agent to learn about externalities, overcoming asymmetric information, contrasting opportunistic behaviour, etc., are also involved. The latter are precisely the factors that impact on differences in transaction costs. The diverse set of knowledge within complex systems needs to be coordinated and mobilized by institutions and by the use of symbolical systems for knowledge storage and transmission, allowing lower transaction costs. 'Indeed [. . .] the failure to achieve such an integration is at the heart of development problems' (North, 2005, p. 73).

The institutional characteristics of the system are thus deeply connected to the absorption capability of technical progress. So, each country or specific area does not start from homogeneous conditions, but rather from the specific conditionings of their development history. As it has been observed, growth differentials amongst countries with structurally different characteristics arise from the fact that '[. . .] rich and poor countries are simply not on the same production function' (Thirlwall, 2002, p. 37).

Summing up, the parameter A in (3.1) can be assumed to be a rough approximation of the 'technological capability' of the economic system. Our choice can be led back to a theoretical framework in which: (a) the technological frontier *is not* equally accessible to all countries; and (b) *ad hoc* hypotheses, such as those related to production factor contribution to the output, are not involved.

Once the supply-side conditions have been defined, then its linkages and interaction with the other side of the aggregate macroeconomic system should be outlined.

Since the original intuition by Harrod and Domar,[4] the common denominator linking macro variables on the demand and the supply side of economy is given, *in primis*, by the accumulation process, i.e. investment dynamics, the demand component most sensible to cyclical fluctuations in the economy. In the short run, indeed, the fluctuations of actual output follow impulses from the demand side: we have summarized in Figure 3.2[5] the causal circuit amongst the main macro-variables.

The demand fluctuations impact on investments, affecting the numerator of capital/labour ratio. The variation in the level of k in our case will determine the capability of absorption of technical progress, modifying the parameters in (3.1) and thereby affecting the rate of *potential* growth of output, as determined from capital and technology on the supply side. The demand side, in its turn, commands the *actual* variations of output, given technology, according to the usual Keynesian relationships.

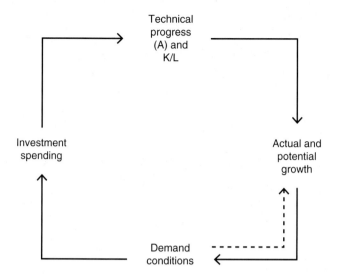

Figure 3.2 The link between demand conditions and output growth.

The expressions listed below allow for further clarification of this point, which is of crucial importance within our scheme:

$$I = z(g_d^e, E) \tag{3.2}$$

$$E = D/Y^p \tag{3.3}$$

$$\dot{E} = g_d^e - g_y^p \tag{3.4}$$

$$D \equiv DD + E_w/M_w \tag{3.5}$$

$$K = K_{(t-1)} + I \tag{3.6}$$

$$L = 1/\pi \tag{3.7}$$

$$k = K/L \tag{3.8}$$

$$g_y^p = a(A, I) \tag{3.9}$$

$$\dot{g}_d^e = G(g_y^p/g_d^e) \quad G' > 0 \tag{3.10}$$

where I is gross investment, g_d^e is the growth of effective demand, E is the level of excess capacity utilization, D is the level of effective demand, Y^p is potential capacity, DD is domestic demand, E_w/M_w is net export, g_y^p denotes the rate of growth of potential output, K is the capital stock, L is labour stock, π is labour productivity and Y is the actual output.

Equation (3.2) is a simple specification of the accelerator principle. Investments are positively affected by growth of demand and level of capacity utilization. Equations (3.3) and (3.4) are the definitions for levels and rates of variations of this excess capacity utilization. The relationships at (3.6) and (3.7) introduce capital and labour and the ratio between them, k, which is our key variable.

Equation (3.9) is consequential to (3.1) and states that the growth of potential product is influenced by the parameters A and I. The parameter A is the reciprocal of the incremental capital/output ratio (or ICOR). Its number provides the increase, in terms of GDP, associated with accumulation of capital. It can be estimated as an empirical parameter, as the ratio of value-added increase, associated with positive change in the mix of productive resources. The inclusion of investments in (3.9) allows us to partly endogenize the rate of technical progress. In the meantime, in (3.10), the growth of effective demand appears as positively driven by growth in the potential output. As a possible path, a positive 'jump' in technological capability may, *in primis*, enhance exports. Otherwise, when increases in productivity are implied, these will result in increases in the income of workers, thereby positively affecting consumption, or increases in the profits of firms, thereby increasing capacity for investment.

In the following section, we verify the actual relevance of this demand–supply interaction through empirical estimates for a group of countries.

The demand and supply interaction: an econometric test

In order to test the interaction hypotheses explained in the previous paragraph, we have specified and tested Error Correction Model (ECM) equations of GDP growth, which aim to identify the long-run cointegration norm and the short-run coefficients for the dependent variable, $\Delta \log(Y)$. The following specification has been adopted for the ECM in the countries[6] included in the analysis:

$$\Delta \log(Y) = a + b\Delta \log(DD) + c\Delta \log(E_w/M_w) + d\text{Lrun}(-1) \qquad (3.11)$$

where Y is the GDP, DD is domestic demand, E_w/M_w foreign export over foreign import, and Lrun are the residuals of the long-run relation

$$\log(Y) = \alpha + \beta \log(k). \qquad (3.12)$$

The last term represents the effect of a short-run adjustment of a long-term norm, given the linkage between growth of output and the capital/labour ratio (k). The parameters and significance of this component, derived from cointegration analysis, reflect their different capacities to absorb potential technical progress. The preliminary step in the quantitative exercise consists in controlling for the cointegration relationship linking Y and k. The results of ADF tests, as reported in Table 3.1, confirm the unit-root hypothesis for both variables and that the countries and the residuals produced from the cointegrating regression are stationary (see Table 3.2).

Table 3.3 reports the estimates of long-run cointegration relationships for the countries. The results, while preliminary, suggest that the United States retains the highest parameter A in (3.9) proxied by the β coefficient in (3.12). In the sample estimate the United States is the country with the highest average

Table 3.1 Augmented Dickey–Fuller (ADF) test for unit roots log(Y) and log(k)

Dependent variable: log(I)	Germany	France	Italy	USA
C	−5.60636	−2.56992	−2.87634	−6.08079
	(1.8752)*	(0.3720)**	(1.3385)*	(0.9670)**
MovAv[2,(Δ log(D^*)]	2.20611	2.52208	2.29004	7.78354
	(0.4819)**	(0.5326)**	(1.0276)*	(1.1385)**
(1 − E(−1))	−0.38292	−3.41710	−4.01393	−1.20348
	(−0.4714)	(0.3324)**	(1.0625)**	(0.5376)*
log(K(−1))	0.61291	1.03164	1.06902	1.34343
	(0.1175)**	(0.0421)**	(0.1584)**	(0.0907)**
Dummy = 2002				0.09620
				(0.0386)*
Dummy = 2005	−0.07639			
	(0.0305)*			
Dummy >= 2013	0.0522	0.07612	−0.14315	−0.11203
	(0.0240)*	(0.0271)*	(0.0601)*	(0.0267)**
R-squared	0.8293	0.9769	0.9235	0.9535
Sample	1995–2014	1995–2014	1995–2014	1995–2014

Source: Our calculation on data-set AMECO release 2014.

Note: D^* stands for final demand net of investments.
* for 5% significancy level. ** for 10% significancy level.
The p-values are given in brackets.

Table 3.2 Stationary tests for cointegration residuals

Countries	t-statistics	P-values
Germany	−2.787	0.008
France	−2.092	0.036
Italy	−2.404	0.017
USA	−1.975	0.047

Source: Our calculation on data-set AMECO release 2014.

Table 3.3 Cointegration estimation log(Y) and log(k)

		Coefficient	t-statistics	Observations	R-squared	Sample
Germany	Constant	10.26	(0.33)**	24	0.72	1991–2014
	log (k)	1.51	(0.19)**			
France	Constant	9.30	(0.04)**	55	0.99	1960–2014
	log (k)	1.23	(0.02)**			
Italy	Constant	8.84	(0.04)**	45	0.97	1970–2014
	log (k)	1.04	(0.02)**			
USA	Constant	12.44	(0.15)**	45	0.91	1970–2014
	log (k)	2.04	(0.09)**			

Source: Our calculation on data-set AMECO release 2014.

GDP growth.[7] In comparative terms the Italian A is almost half that of the United States. Germany and France are in between, with Germany closer to the US value and France more similar to Italy. The gap between Italy and the United States is consistent with the evidences on the labour productivity distances, indeed in 2014 the Italian GDP per unit of labour was 54.6 per cent of the same ratio in the United States.

Table 3.4 shows the result of the whole (3.11) model. As a whole Table 3.4 shows that the model holds. Furthermore, we have some insights from the econometric estimates: (i) the Lrun variable is significant across countries (when thinking that the dependent variable is the year difference in log of GDP, it is not a trivial result) and (ii) the coefficients of both components of the demand, domestic and foreign, are fully consistent. For instance, the net foreign demand parameter is, as expected, higher in Germany, in the biggest export-led economy worldwide. On the contrary, the same coefficient is relatively lower in the United States, where domestic demand plays a crucial role.

In Figure 3.3 the absolute contribution of the long term (supply) to GDP growth, derived from (3.12), is shown. The graph shows a clear divergence across the countries. In France, and above all in Italy, from 2005, and in particular during the Great Recession, a *decalage* in the supply contribution to GDP increase could be recorded. Indeed in those years, the aggregate demand and in particular investments have been affected by a significant demand gap. On the opposite side, we have the case of Germany where the absolute contribution of supply to GDP growth has risen steadily over the last decade, pushed by investment dynamics and then by variables (k, A) of our model.[8]

To close the causal relationship expressed in (3.2), in Table 3.5 an accelerator-type model is reported. Despite its relative parsimony, even in this case the model holds up in its main relationships.

Table 3.4 ECM equation on GDP growth

Dependent variable $\Delta \log(Y)$ Method: least squares	Germany	France	Italy	USA
Constant	−0.00036	−0.00154	0.00085	−0.00471
	(−0.0021)	(−0.0018)	(−0.001)	(−0.003)
$\Delta \log(DD)$	1.08	1.12	1.08	1.15
	(0.1148)**	(0.0905)**	(0.0512)**	(0.1015)**
$\Delta \log(E_w/M_w)$	0.31	0.14	0.23	0.09
	(0.0553)**	(0.0599)*	(0.0223)**	(0.0288)**
Lrun(−1)	−0.054	−0.041	−0.054	−0.023
	(0.0221)*	(0.0202)*	(0.0220)*	(0.0131)*
Observations	23	25	30	30
R-squared	0.94	0.90	0.95	0.96
DW	1.929	2.81	2.464	1.892
Sample	1992–2014	1990–2014	1985–2014	1985–2014

Source: Our calculation on data-set AMECO release 2014.

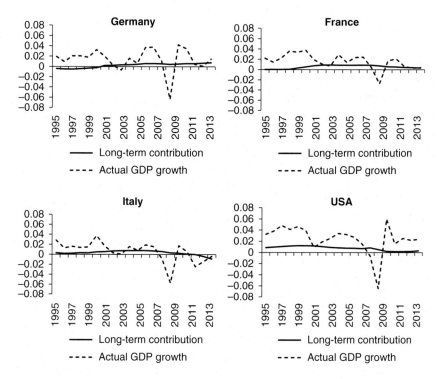

Figure 3.3 Supply determinant of GDP growth.

Table 3.5 Estimate of accelerator-type equations

Dependent variable: log(I)	Germany	France	Italy	USA
C	−5.60636	−2.56992	−2.87634	−6.08079
	(1.8752)*	(0.3720)**	(1.3385)*	(0.9670)**
MovAv[2,(Δ log(D*)]	2.20611	2.52208	2.29004	7.78354
	(0.4819)**	(0.5326)**	(1.0276)*	(1.1385)**
(1 − E(−1))	−0.38292	−3.41710	−4.01393	−1.20348
	(−0.4714)	(0.3324)**	(1.0625)**	(0.5376)*
log(K(−1))	0.61291	1.03164	1.06902	1.34343
	(0.1175)**	(0.0421)**	(0.1584)**	(0.0907)**
Dummy = 2002				0.09620
				(0.0386)*
Dummy = 2005	−0.07639			
	(0.0305)*			
Dummy >= 2013	0.0522	0.07612	−0.14315	−0.11203
	(0.0240)*	(0.0271)*	(0.0601)*	(0.0267)**
R-squared	0.8293	0.9769	0.9235	0.9535
Sample	1995–2014	1995–2014	1995–2014	1995–2014

Source: Our calculation on data-set AMECO release 2014.

Note: D* stands for final demand net of investments.

Concluding remarks

The first step of the analysis proposed in this chapter has been the adoption of a notion of 'TPF', as the main description of the supply-side of the economy, in lieu of the traditional aggregate production function multiplied by 'TFP'.

This framework allows for an explicit linkage between productivity growth and rate of capital accumulation, which avoids unnecessary or restrictive hypotheses upon marginal returns and factor remunerations. This relation has been inspired by a delimited frame for 'stylized facts' accounting for interaction between supply and demand in the path of actual output. These intuitive frames have been verified through empirical estimations. For a group of countries, we have estimated a relationship in which technology parameter, A, is included in the determination of the growth path as experienced, year after year, by a particular country.

In terms of policy, our frame of analysis implies significant consequences. Following the Great Recession, the policies followed in the United States, on one side, and the EU (or more narrowly, in the *Euro zone*) on the other, have been divergent: expansionary in the first and strongly restrictive in the second. Our point is that, beyond the short run, different policies also impact on the supply potentials for the medium term. The time profile of the stock of capital in Italy has indeed become wholly flat, an evidence observed only in rare circumstances. This fall in investment has a negative impact on the capital/labour ratio, implying in our framework a reduction in the capability of technological absorption in the economy. Moreover, this trend has affected two European countries – France and Italy – in which, in our estimations, the values for the parameter A were already relatively lower. The so-called 'structural reform policies' – deregulating the labour market and increasing competition in the market sectors – have been stressed, in particular in the European Policy context, as the only path to help a process of catching up. We do not wish to deny the relevance of the path to reform; however, without a significant recovery in investment and accumulation processes, it is unlikely that a persistent improvement in the supply potential will follow.

Notes

1 The authors have the sole responsibility for the views and results presented in this chapter, which do not necessarily reflect those of the institutions to which they belong. The authors would like to thank Professor Paolo Piacentini (University La Sapienza, Rome) who provided helpful insights into dealing with post-Keynesian thought and Stefano Rosignoli (IRPET) for his valuable statistical assistance.
2 It is interesting to note that, after the crisis of 2008, even institutions such as the European Commission recognized the importance of the mechanisms of interaction between supply and demand in their analyses for accelerating growth (EC, 2013).
3 By way of example, Baumol *et al.* (1989) and Nordhaus (2008) emphasized the role of technical progress as the primary cause of structural change. The same phenomenon is explained by Rowthorn and Ramaswamy (1999) and Peneder *et al.* (2003) with the different income elasticities between industry and services.
4 Even the pioneering models proposed by Harrod and Domar establish a relationship between the evolution of demand and supply. In any case, in these approaches, unlike the

supply function proposed here, investments influence levels of the productive capacity of the economic system but not its steady growth rate.

5 Figure 3.2 marginally modifies the original frame in Palley (2002). The same source has inspired the formalization which follows, and our theoretical background essentially follows this inspiration.

6 France, Germany, Italy and the United States.

7 From 1980 to 2014, the average GDP growth in the United States was 2.5 per cent, 1.8 per cent in France and Germany and 1.2 per cent in Italy.

8 To provide some figures, over the period 2008–2014, the rates of growth of gross fixed investments were, in the United States and Germany, respectively 0.4 per cent and 0.6 per cent per year. In France, and more so in Italy, the impact of restrictive budget policies has given rise to negative rates of investment: 1.3 per cent in the case of France and 5.2 per cent in Italy.

References

Ball, L. M. (2014), *Long-Term Damage from the Great Recession in OECD Countries*, NBER Working Papers 20185.

Baumol, W. J., S. A. B. Blackman and E. N. Wolff (1989), *Productivity and American Leadership: The Long View*. Cambridge, MA: MIT Press.

European Commission (2013), 'Towards knowledge-driven reindustrialization', *Commission Staff Working Document*, Brussels.

Hall, R. E. (2014), *Quantifying the Lasting Harm to the U.S. Economy from the Financial Crisis,* NBER Working Papers 20183.

Helpman, H. (2004), *The Mystery of Economic Growth*, Cambridge, MA: Harvard University Press.

International Monetary Fund (2015), *Where Are WE Headed? Perspectives On Potential Output*, World Economic Outlook, April 2015.

Kaldor, N. (1957), 'A model of economic growth', *The Economic Journal*, LXVII(268), 591–624.

Loasby, B. J. (1999), *Knowledge, Institutions, and Evolution in Economics*, London: Routledge.

Nordhaus, W. D. (2008), 'Baumol's diseases: A macroeconomic perspective', *The B.E. Journal of Macroeconomics*, 8(1), 1–37.

North, D. C. (2005), *Understanding the Process of Economic Change*, Princeton, NJ: Princeton University Press.

Palley, T. I. (2002), 'Longer-run aspects of Kaleckian macroeconomics', in Setterfield M. (ed.), *The Economics of Demand-Led Growth*, Cheltenham, UK: Edward Elgar Publishing.

Paniccià R., P. Piacentini and S. Prezioso (2013), 'Total factor productivity or technical progress function? Post-Keynesian insights for the empirical analysis of productivity differentials in mature economies', *Review of Political Economy*, 25(3), 476–495.

Pasinetti, L. L. (1981), *Structural Change and Economic Growth: A Theoretical Essay on the Wealth of Nations*, Cambridge, UK: Cambridge University Press.

Pasinetti, L. L., (1993), *Structural Economic Dynamics: A Theory of the Economic Consequences of Human Learning*, Cambridge, UK: Cambridge University Press.

Peneder, M., S. Kaniovski and B. Dachs (2003), 'What follows tertiarisation? Structural change and the role of knowledge based services', *The Service Industries Journal*, 23(2), 47–66.

Rowthorn, R. and R. Ramaswamy (1999), 'Growth, trade and deindustrialization', *IMF Staff Papers*, 46(1), 18–41.

Solow, R. M. (2000), 'Towards a macroeconomics of the medium-run', *Journal of Economic Perspectives*, 14(1), 151–158.

Thirlwall, A. P. (2002), *The Nature of Economic Growth*, Cheltenham, UK: Edward Elgar Publishing.

4 Financial crises, limited-asset market participation, and banks' balance-sheet constraints

Elton Beqiraj, Giovanni Di Bartolomeo, and Marco Di Pietro

Introduction

After a phenomenal increase, within a year, between 2007 and 2008, stock prices dropped by 30 percent. The economy experienced a sudden sharp reduction in the availability of credit from banks and other lenders, and trade and industrial activity reduced dramatically. At the time, the credit crunch induced an unprecedented decline in real activity. The legacy of the financial crisis was in fact a depressed economy characterized by a persistent decline in economic activity. Almost 12 million workers had lost their jobs in the OECD (Organization for Economic Co-operation and Development) countries by mid-2014. Many more saw their retirement and education investments dwindle in value.

The events driven by the financial crisis have stimulated a new wave of models of economies with financial frictions, where a formal bank channel is specifically introduced; understanding phenomena such as the recent financial crisis and policy responses "requires the use of a macroeconomic framework in which financial intermediation matters for the allocation of resources" (see Woodford, 2010, p. 21). The idea that imperfections in the financial sphere amplify the business cycle was developed in the 1930s and it was later fully developed in a dynamic stochastic general equilibrium (DSGE) model by Bernanke *et al.* (1996). Then, following the eruption of the financial crisis, the possibility that adverse conditions in the real economy and in financial markets mutually reinforce each other has been revisited by a number of authors.[1]

An appropriate framework was developed by Gertler and Karadi (2011) and Gertler and Kiyotaki (2010), which extends the original mechanism for the financial accelerator based on the cyclical variations of the value of collateral (see Bernanke *et al.*, 1999). Financial frictions are introduced by assuming an agency problem between banks and depositors. The amplification provided by the moral hazard problem in the bank–depositor relationship results in bankers being constrained in the amount of credit they can provide. Disturbances in the quality of capital induce a reduction in credit and a significant downturn by creating capital losses in the financial sector.

Our chapter contributes to this literature by jointly considering the above banks' balance-sheet constraints with the limited-asset market participation (LAMP) assumption in an otherwise simple medium-scale New Keynesian economy.[2] In other words, our key question is whether the assumption that only a fraction of households can access the credit market via financial intermediaries worsens the negative effects of banks' balance-sheet constraints on credit.

As the behavior of liquidity-constrained agents crucially depends on their capacity to supply labor (e.g., Colciago, 2011), we also fully model labor market imperfections. We assume the existence of differentiated workers organized in unions that are allowed to set their wage-facing nominal rigidities.

Finally, it is worth noticing that in a different line of research, by considering the presence of endogenous search frictions *à la* Pissarides (2000) in both labor and credit markets, Wasmer and Weil (2004) show that credit-market imperfections exacerbate labor-market frictions by restricting firms' entry, with both short- and long-run effects on unemployment. More recently, Chugh (2013) and Petrosky-Nadeau and Wasmer (2013) find similar results in more complex frameworks.

The rest of the chapter is structured as follows. The next section briefly introduces the model. Then we discuss our main results. Finally, we present the conclusions.

The model

We consider a simple medium-scale New Keynesian economy characterized by nominal price and wage rigidities, consumption habits, and investment adjustment costs. The economy is augmented with an imperfect banking sector by assuming that firms borrow indirectly from households via the banking sector that operates in an imperfect financial market. Financial frictions are twofold: (i) only a fraction of households can access the credit market by financial intermediaries (limited-asset market participation assumption, LAMP henceforth);[3] and (ii) an agency problem between banks and their depositors implies that financial intermediaries are subject to endogenously determined balance-sheet constraints that could limit the ability of non-financial firms to obtain investment funds (see Gertler and Karadi, 2011).

Production

The supply side of the economy is characterized by a retail competitive sector that combines intermediate goods produced by labor with capital to obtain the final consumption good. The final sector operates under imperfect competition and is subject to price stickiness. By contrast, intermediate goods and capital-producing firms operate in competitive markets. Intermediate firms borrow from the banks to acquire physical capital.

The intermediate goods sector is composed of a continuum of competitive producers. The typical firm uses labor inputs and capital to produce intermediate goods Y_t sold to retail firms, according to the following Cobb–Douglas technology

$$Y_t = A_t L_t^\alpha \left(u_t^k K_t \right)^{1-\alpha} \tag{4.1}$$

where $\alpha \in (0, 1)$ is the labor share, A_t represents the total factor productivity, L_t denotes labor inputs hired, K_t is the capital stock, and u_t^k is the utilization rate of the capital. Capital acquisition is financed by borrowing from a financial intermediary.

Introducing the real wage (W_t), real marginal cost (MC_t), and the capital depreciation function ($\delta\left(u_t^k\right)$), the firm's first-order conditions are

$$W_t = \alpha MC_t \frac{Y_t}{L_t} \tag{4.2}$$

$$u_t^k = MC_t (1 - \alpha) \frac{Y_t}{\delta'\left(u_t^k\right) K_t}, \tag{4.3}$$

which implicitly define a labor and capital demand (utilization rate of the physical capital).

Capital-producing firms act in an environment characterized by perfect competition. In particular, at the end of period t, they buy capital from the intermediate sector, repairing the depreciated capital and building new capital stock. Both the repaired and the new capital are then sold. A typical capital-producing firm maximizes discounted profits, i.e.,

$$\max E_t \sum_{\tau=t}^{\infty} \beta^{\tau-t} \Lambda_{t,\tau} \left\{ (Q_\tau - 1) I_{N\tau}^O - \mathcal{F}\left(\frac{I_{N\tau}^O + I_{SS}^O}{I_{N\tau-1}^O + I_{SS}^O} \right) \left(I_{N\tau}^O + I_{SS}^O \right) \right\} \tag{4.4}$$

where $\mathcal{F}(1) = \mathcal{F}'(1) = 0$ and $\mathcal{F}''(1) > 0$, $\beta \in (0, 1)$ is the discount factor, $\Lambda_{t,\tau}$ denotes the stochastic discount factor between t and τ, $I_{Nt}^O \equiv I_t^O - \delta\left(u_t^k\right) K_t^O$ is the net capital created (I_t^O and I_{SS}^O are gross capital and its steady state), and Q_t should be interpreted as the Tobin's Q. As we will explain in the next section, we denote capital and investment by a superscript "O" to take account of the limited-asset market participation assumption. Then, $K_t = (1 - \lambda) K_t^O$ and $I_t = (1 - \lambda) I_t^O$, where λ is the fraction of agents who cannot access the financial markets (recall that these agents do not own either assets or firm's equity capital).

The first-order condition for investment is then

$$Q_t = 1 + \mathcal{F}\left(\frac{I_{Nt}^O + I_{SS}^O}{I_{Nt-1}^O + I_{SS}^O} \right) + \left(\frac{I_{Nt}^O + I_{SS}^O}{I_{Nt-1}^O + I_{SS}^O} \right) \mathcal{F}'\left(\frac{I_{Nt}^O + I_{SS}^O}{I_{Nt-1}^O + I_{SS}^O} \right) +$$

$$- \beta E_t \Lambda_{t,t+1} \left(\frac{I_{Nt+1}^O + I_{SS}^O}{I_{Nt}^O + I_{SS}^O} \right)^2 \mathcal{F}'\left(\frac{I_{Nt}^O + I_{SS}^O}{I_{Nt-1}^O + I_{SS}^O} \right)$$

where the above expression describes the Q relation for net investment.

Retail firms operate in imperfect competition. Aggregation is obtained as follows

$$Y_t = \left[\int_0^1 Y_t(j)^{\frac{\varepsilon_p-1}{\varepsilon_p}} dj \right]^{\frac{\varepsilon_p}{\varepsilon_p-1}} \tag{4.5}$$

where $Y_t(j)$ is the output by retailer j, and ε_p is the elasticity of substitution between differentiated goods.

In this setup, prices are sticky according to a Calvo mechanism (we denote by $1 - \gamma_p$ the probability of being able to reset prices). The corresponding optimal price adjustment and aggregate inflation are then described by the following expressions[4]

$$\pi_t^* = \frac{\varepsilon_p}{\varepsilon_p - 1} \frac{\Upsilon_t^p}{\Xi_t^p} \pi_t \tag{4.6}$$

$$\pi_t = \left[\gamma_p \pi_{t-1}^{\gamma_{ind}(1-\varepsilon_p)} + (1 - \gamma_p)(\pi_t^*)^{1-\varepsilon_p} \right]^{\frac{1}{1-\varepsilon_p}} \tag{4.7}$$

where γ_{ind} indicates the degree of indexation to past inflation.

The auxiliary variables Υ_t^p and Ξ_t^p evolve as

$$\Upsilon_t^p = Y_t M C_t + \beta \gamma_p E_t \Lambda_{t,t+1} \pi_{t+1}^{\varepsilon_p} \pi_t^{-\gamma_{ind}\varepsilon_p} \Upsilon_{t+1}^p \tag{4.8}$$

$$\Xi_t^p = Y_t + \beta \gamma_p E_t \Lambda_{t,t+1} \pi_{t+1}^{\varepsilon_p-1} \pi_t^{\gamma_{ind}(1-\varepsilon_p)} \Xi_{t+1}^p. \tag{4.9}$$

Financial market

Limited-asset market participation

Households can be either liquidity constrained or not. However, apart from their ability to access the financial market, they share the same kind of preferences. Formally, there is a continuum of households in the space [0, 1]. The households' period preferences are defined as

$$\mathcal{U}_t = \frac{(C_{t+i} - h C_{t+i-1})^{1-\sigma}}{1 - \sigma} - \chi \frac{L_{t+i}^{1+\varphi}}{1 + \varphi} \tag{4.10}$$

where C_t is the aggregate consumption, $h \in [0, 1)$ denotes the habits in consumption parameter, χ measures the relative weight of the labor disutility, φ is the inverse Frisch elasticity of labor supply, and σ is the relative risk-aversion coefficient.

Non-liquidity-constrained households ("dynamic-optimizer households" from now on) solve the following intertemporal optimization problem

$$\max_{C_{t+i}^O \cdot L_{t+i} \cdot B_{t+i}} W_t^O = E_t \sum_{i=0}^{\infty} \beta^i \left[\frac{(C_{t+i}^O - h C_{t+i-1}^O)^{1-\sigma}}{1 - \sigma} - \chi \frac{L_{t+i}^{1+\varphi}}{1 + \varphi} \right] \tag{4.11}$$

such that $C_t^O + B_{t+1} = W_t L_t + \Pi_t + T_t + R_t B_t$

where C_t^O is the consumption of the dynamic-optimizer households, R_t is the gross real return of one period real bonds, B_t is the total quantity of short-term debt that the household acquires, Π_t are the net payouts to the household from ownership of both non-financial and financial firms, and T_t is a lump sum net transfer.

The resulting first-order conditions are

$$\varrho_t^O = \left(C_t^O - hC_{t-1}^O\right)^{-\sigma} - \beta h E_t \left(C_{t+1}^O - hC_t^O\right)^{-\sigma} \tag{4.12}$$

$$E_t \beta \Lambda_{t,t+1} R_{t+1} = 1 \tag{4.13}$$

where $\Lambda_{t,t+1} = \dfrac{\varrho_{t+1}^O}{\varrho_t^O}$ denotes the stochastic discount rate.

The first equation denotes the marginal utility of consumption marginal utility of consumption for the dynamic optimizers, the second is the Euler equation.

LAMP households solve

$$\max_{C_{t+i}^L, L_{t+i}} \mathcal{W}_t^L = E_t \sum_{i=0}^{\infty} \beta^i \left[\frac{(C_{t+i}^L - hC_{t+i-1}^L)^{1-\sigma}}{1-\sigma} - \chi \frac{L_{t+i}^{1+\varphi}}{1+\varphi} \right] \tag{4.14}$$

such that $C_t^L = W_t L_t + T_t$.

According to the budget constraint, their optimal consumption is equal to

$$C_t^L = W_t L_t + T_t. \tag{4.15}$$

Moreover, their marginal utility of consumption is

$$\varrho_t^L = \left(C_t^L - hC_{t-1}^L\right)^{-\sigma} - \beta h E_t \left(C_{t+1}^L - hC_t^L\right)^{-\sigma}. \tag{4.16}$$

The banks' balance-sheet constraints

The representation of the banking sector is borrowed from Gertler and Karadi (2011) and Gertler and Kiyotaki (2010).[5] It is assumed that each dynamic-optimizer household is composed of workers and bankers. The workers supply labor and give back their labor income to their household. Each banker manages a financial intermediary and returns its earnings back to its family. Banks are owned by the fraction of households that are dynamic optimizers as well. Each period a fraction θ of bankers survives while a fraction $1 - \theta$ exits and is replaced.

Financial intermediaries obtain B_{jt+1} deposits from households and make loans to non-financial firms. Each bank faces financial claims S_{jt} by the non-financial firms and has an amount of net worth denoted by N_{jt}. Thus, the balance sheet of an intermediary is

$$Q_t S_{jt} = N_{jt} + B_{jt+1} \tag{4.17}$$

where Q_t is the relative price of a financial claim.

The bank pays back a real gross return R_{t+1} on the funds obtained from the household and earns the stochastic return R_{kt+1} on the loans to non-financial firms.

Thus, N_{jt} can be thought of as the intermediaries' equity capital, which is the difference between the earnings on assets $(R_{kt+1}Q_t S_{jt})$ and interest payments on liabilities $(R_{t+1}B_{jt+1})$. Hence

$$N_{jt+1} = (R_{kt+1} - R_{t+1})Q_t S_{jt} + R_{t+1}N_{jt}. \tag{4.18}$$

The term $(R_{kt+1} - R_{t+1})$ represents the premium that the banker earns on their assets.

Each banker's objective is to maximize the expected discounted present value of their future flows of net worth N_t, which is

$$V_t = E_t \sum_{i=0}^{\infty} (1-\theta)\theta^i \beta^{i+1} \Lambda_{t,t+1+i} N_{jt+i}. \tag{4.19}$$

Following Gertler and Karadi (2011), in order to avoid that in the presence of a positive premium the bankers will expand their loans indefinitely, it is assumed that there is a limit to doing this represented by the presence of a moral-hazard problem. In particular, the bank can divert a fraction ζ of funds to its family. Diverting assets can be profitable for a bank, which can then default on its debt and shut down, correspondingly representing a loss for creditors who could only reclaim the fraction $1 - \zeta$ of assets, at best.

As a consequence, depositors would restrict their credit to banks as they realize that the following incentive constraint must hold for the banks in order to prevent them from diverting funds:

$$V_{jt} \geqslant \zeta Q_t S_{jt} \tag{4.20}$$

i.e., the potential loss of diverting assets (the left-hand side of the above equation) should be greater than the gain from doing so (the right-hand side of the above equation). Moreover, V_{jt} can be expressed as

$$V_{jt} = v_t Q_t S_{jt} + \eta_t N_{jt} \tag{4.21}$$

where η_t is a variable representing the expected discounted value of having an additional unit of net worth and v_t must be interpreted as the expected discounted marginal gain to the banker of expanding assets $Q_t S_{jt}$ by a unit.[6] In this framework, the financial intermediary can acquire assets accordingly on their equity capital

$$Q_t S_{jt} = \frac{\eta_t}{\zeta - v_t} N_{jt} = \phi_t N_{jt} \tag{4.22}$$

where ϕ_t is the private leverage ratio, i.e., the ratio of privately intermediated assets to equity.

Labor market

Labor markets are imperfect: sticky wages are set by monopolistic unions, who represent differentiated labor inputs provided by both dynamic optimizers and LAMP agents. Labor unions set the nominal wages facing nominal rigidities *à la* Calvo. Labor is aggregated by a Dixit–Stiglitz function; we indicated by ε_w the elasticity of substitution between labor inputs.

Formally, a typical union chooses the optimal nominal wage W_t^* to maximize a weighted utility function:

$$\max_{W_t^*} \sum_{j=0}^{\infty} (\gamma_w \beta)^j \left\{ W_t^* \left(\frac{W_t^*}{W_{t+j}} \right)^{-\varepsilon_w} L_{t+j} \left[\lambda \varrho_{t+j}^L + (1-\lambda)\varrho_{t+j}^O \right] \right.$$

$$\left. - \frac{\chi}{1+\varphi} \left[\left(\frac{W_t^*}{W_{t+j}} \right)^{-\varepsilon_w} L_{t+j} \right]^{1+\varphi} \right\}$$

where γ_w is the probability of keeping the wage unchanged in the future.

Solving the above problem we obtain the adjustment dynamics for wage inflation[7]

$$\pi_t^{w*} = \frac{\varepsilon_w}{\varepsilon_w - 1} \frac{\Upsilon_t^w}{\Xi_t^w} \pi_t^w \tag{4.23}$$

$$\pi_t^w = \left[\gamma_w \left(\pi_{t-1}^w \right)^{1-\varepsilon_w} + (1-\gamma_w) \left(\pi_t^{w*} \right)^{1-\varepsilon_w} \right]^{\frac{1}{1-\varepsilon_w}} \tag{4.24}$$

where the auxiliary variables Υ_t^w and Ξ_t^w evolve

$$\Upsilon_t^w = U_{L,t} L_t + \gamma_w \beta E_t \left(\pi_{t+1}^w \right)^{\varepsilon_w} \Upsilon_{t+1}^w \tag{4.25}$$

$$\Xi_t^w = W_t L_t \left[\lambda \varrho_t^L + (1-\lambda)\varrho_t^O \right] + \gamma_w \beta E_t \left(\pi_{t+1}^w \right)^{\varepsilon_w - 1} \Xi_{t+1}^w. \tag{4.26}$$

Aggregation, resource constraint, and government policies

The economy-wide resource constraint is given by

$$Y_t = C_t + I_t + G_t + \frac{\psi}{2} \left(\frac{I_t^N + I_{SS}}{I_{t-1}^N + I_{SS}} - 1 \right)^2 (I_t^N + I_{SS}) \tag{4.27}$$

where ψ indicates the elasticity of investment adjustment cost.

Following Galí *et al.* (2007), aggregate consumption is

$$C_t = (1-\lambda) C_t^O + \lambda C_t^L. \tag{4.28}$$

The total value of intermediated assets is

$$Q_t S_t = \phi_t N_t. \tag{4.29}$$

The law of motion of capital is

$$K_{t+1}^O = K_t^O + I_{Nt}^O.$$ (4.30)

Government expenditures G_t are financed by lump sum taxes

$$G_t = T_t.$$ (4.31)

The nominal interest rate i_t follows a simple Taylor rule

$$i_t = \rho i_{t-1} + (1-\rho)\kappa_\pi \pi_t$$ (4.32)

where ρ denotes the degree of interest-rate smoothing and κ_π measures the response of the monetary authority to inflation.

Results

We simulate the effects of a financial crisis assuming that there is a redistribution of wealth from intermediaries to households. In particular, in what follows, we depict the effects of a 1 percent decrease in the intermediary net worth involving, in turn, an equal transfer of wealth to households. The calibration used in our simulations is the same as that used by Gertler and Karadi (2011) and reported in Table 4.1.

Table 4.1 Model calibration

Households		
β	0.99	Discount factor
h	0.815	Habit formation
χ	3.409	Relative utility weight of labor
σ	1	Relative risk aversion
φ	0.276	Inverse of Frisch elasticity
Financial intermediaries		
ζ	0.381	Fraction of diverted capital
θ	0.972	Bankers' survival rate
Production		
α	0.33	Capital share
$\delta(u^k)$	0.025	Depreciation rate
ψ	1.728	Elasticity of investment adjustment cost
ε_p	4.167	Price elasticity of demand
γ_p	0.779	Calvo parameter (prices)
γ_{ind}	0.241	Price indexation
Taylor rule		
κ_π	1.5	Inflation coefficient Taylor rule
ρ	0.8	Smoothing parameter

Regarding the other parameters that are specific to our model, we assume that LAMP represents 30 percent of the population ($\lambda = 0.3$); the elasticity of substitution between workers (ε_w) is set at 6 (consistent with a 20 percent gross wage markup); and the probability of resetting wages by a union (γ_w) is 25 percent (implying an average duration of wage spell of one year).

The impulse response functions to a negative net-worth shock are plotted in Figure 4.1. When a negative net-worth shock hits the economy, we observe an increase in the premium. As our model incorporates financial frictions, the decline in the intermediaries' wealth, together with the premium increase, result in a recession that is deeper than that arising in a world without a financial sector (see Gertler and Karadi, 2011).

When further frictions are introduced, in the guise of limited-asset market participation, the recession is attenuated. The rationale behind this result is that the presence of a fraction of LAMP, i.e., agents that consume their entire labor income in each period, means that for this share of households the marginal utility of consumption increases during a crisis. Thus, they supply more labor, triggering a fall in the real wage which stimulates, in turn, a recovery. Output downturn is smaller in the LAMP framework and also the decrease of investment is slightly smaller at the beginning of the crisis.

The rise in the premium is almost identical in the two worlds considered and it influences only the investment decision of the dynamic-optimizer households, as liquidity-constrained agents cannot access financial markets. As expected, inflation and the nominal interest rate exhibit a strong decrease as the crisis hits the economy; further, this induces an initial increase in the real rate that contributes to the real fall in the economy.

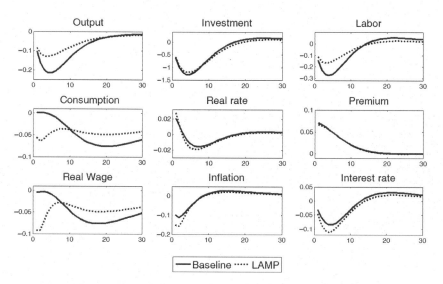

Figure 4.1 The interactions between LAMP and banks' balance-sheet constraints after a financial crisis.

Conclusions

In this chapter we investigated the effects of a financial crisis in a framework similar to that used by Gertler and Karadi (2011). This framework is particularly suitable to evaluate how the presence of asymmetric information between financial intermediaries and non-financial firms gives rise to a deeper recession when negative shocks hit the economy. The main channel that triggers this stronger slump is the increase in the premium that bankers earn on their assets, resulting in firms borrowing less and, consequently, reducing their investment.

The banks' balance-sheet constraint mechanism is enriched by an additional financial imperfection: the assumption that a fraction of households are liquidity constrained, i.e., they do not have access to financial markets. Moreover, as long as the behavior of liquidity-constrained agents crucially depends on their capacity to supply labor, we also represent labor markets in a realistic way by assuming differentiated workers organized in unions that are allowed to set the wage and who face nominal rigidities. In this setup, we find that the negative effects of a crisis are partially alleviated. This attenuation is due to the fact that LAMP households increase their labor supply during a crisis, inducing a small recovery in output.

Notes

1 See, e.g., Goodfriend and McCallum (2007), Angeloni and Faia (2009), Cúrdia and Woodford (2009), Christiano *et al.* (2010), Gertler and Kiyotaki (2010), Gerali *et al.* (2010), Meh and Moran (2010), Jermann and Quadrini (2012), and Iacoviello (2013). See also Woodford (2010) for a survey.
2 The assumption of limited participation in the asset markets and its implications for policies are investigated in, e.g., Galí *et al.* (2007), Di Bartolomeo and Rossi (2007a, 2007b), Bilbiie (2008), Colciago (2011), Motta and Tirelli (2012, 2015), and Albonico *et al.* (2015).
3 See Galí *et al.* (2007).
4 The price inflation is $\pi_t = P_t/P_{t-1}$; $\pi_t^* = P_t^*/P_{t-1}$ is the price inflation of the adjusting firm.
5 We show a short description of the financial intermediaries sector. For a complete derivation, see Gertler and Karadi (2011).
6 See Gertler and Karadi (2011) for the evolution of υ_t and η_t and a wider discussion on the agency problem.
7 The wage inflation is $\pi_t^w = W_t/W_{t-1}$; $\pi_t^{w*} = W_t^*/W_{t-1}$ is the wage inflation of the adjusting union.

References

Albonico, A., A. Paccagnini and P. Tirelli (2015), "In search of the Eurozone fiscal stance," University of Milano Bicocca, Mimeo.

Angeloni, I. and E. Faia (2009), "A tale of two policies: Prudential regulation and monetary policy with fragile banks," *Kiel Working Paper No. 1569*, October 2009.

Bernanke, B., M. Gertler and S. Gilchrist (1996), "The financial accelerator and the flight to quality," *Review of Economics and Statistics*, 78: 1–15.

Bernanke, B., M. Gertler and S. Gilchrist (1999), "The financial accelerator in a quantitative business cycle framework," in *Handbook of Macroeconomics*, vol. 1C, Taylor, J. and M. Woodford (eds), Amsterdam: Elsevier, 1341–1393.

Bilbiie, F. O. (2008), "Limited asset markets participation, monetary policy and (inverted) aggregate demand logic," *Journal of Economic Theory*, 140: 162–196.

Christiano, L., R. Motto and M. Rostagno (2010), "Financial factors in economic fluctuations," *ECB Working Paper No. 1192*.

Chugh, S. K. (2013), "Costly external finance and labor market dynamics," *Journal of Economic Dynamics and Control*, 37: 2882–2912.

Colciago, A. (2011), "Rule of thumb consumers meet sticky wages," *Journal of Money Credit and Banking*, 43: 325–353.

Cúrdia, V. and M. Woodford (2009), "Credit spreads and monetary policy," *Journal of Money, Credit and Banking*, 42: 3–35.

Di Bartolomeo, G. and L. Rossi (2007a), "Efficacy of monetary policy and limited asset market participation," *International Journal of Economic Theory*, 3: 213–218.

Di Bartolomeo, G. and L. Rossi (2007b), "Heterogeneous consumers, demand regimes, monetary policy and equilibrium determinacy," *Rivista Italiana di Politica Economica*, 97: 111–142.

Galí J., J. D. López-Salido and J. Vallés (2007), " Understanding the effects of government spending on consumption," *Journal of the European Economic Association*, 5: 227–270.

Gerali, A., S. Neri, L. Sessa and F. M. Signoretti (2010), "Credit and banking in a DSGE model of the Euro Area," *Journal of Money, Credit and Banking*, 42: 107–141.

Gertler, M. and N. Kiyotaki (2010), "Financial intermediation and credit policy in business cycle analysis," in B. M. Friedman and M. Woodford (eds), *Handbook of Monetary Economics*, vol. 3A, Amsterdam: Elsevier, chapter 11, 547–599.

Gertler, M and P. Karadi (2011), "A model of unconventional monetary policy," *Journal of Monetary Economics*, 58: 17–34.

Goodfriend, M. and B. T. McCallum (2007), "Banking and interest rates in monetary policy analysis: A quantitative exploration," *Journal of Monetary Economics*, 54: 1480–1507.

Iacoviello, M. (2013), "Financial business cycles," *Federal Reserve Board*, mimeo.

Jermann U. and V. Quadrini (2012), "Macroeconomic effects of financial shocks," *American Economic Review*, 102: 238–271.

Meh, C. and K. Moran (2010), "The role of bank capital in the propagation of shock," *Journal of Economic Dynamics and Control*, 34: 555–576.

Motta, G. and P. Tirelli (2012), "Optimal simple monetary and fiscal rules under limited asset market participation," *Journal of Money, Credit and Banking*, 44: 1351–1374.

Motta, G. and P. Tirelli (2015), "Money targeting, heterogeneous agents, and dynamic instability," *Macroeconomic Dynamics*, 19: 288–310.

Petrosky-Nadeau, N. and E. Wasmer (2013), "The cyclical volatility of labor markets under frictional financial markets," *American Economic Journal: Macroeconomics*, 5: 193–221.

Pissarides, C. A. (2000), *"Equilibrium Unemployment Theory,"* 2nd edition, Cambridge, MA: MIT Press.

Wasmer, E. and P. Weil (2004), "The macroeconomics of labor and credit market imperfections," *American Economic Review*, 94: 944–963.

Woodford, M. (2010), "Financial intermediation and macroeconomic analysis," *Journal of Economic Perspectives*, 24: 21–44.

5 Secular Stagnation

Insights from a New Keynesian model with hysteresis effects

Bas van Aarle

Introduction

Europe's economy is recovering only very slowly from the Great Recession that resulted from the global financial crisis of 2008. In most countries output and employment growth have been small if positive at all, and output and employment levels are struggling to reach pre-crisis levels. Policy makers and economists have had a rather difficult time providing a complete explanation for the observed shallowness of recovery and finding the most effective policy responses under these difficult conditions.

A recent debate – 'the Secular Stagnation hypothesis' – seeks to obtain a better understanding of this very slow recovery. Summers (2014) summarizes this debate as follows:

> The new Secular Stagnation hypothesis responds to recent experience and the manifest inadequacy of conventional formulations by raising the possibility that it may be impossible for an economy to achieve full employment, satisfactory growth and financial stability simultaneously simply through the operation of conventional monetary policy. It thus provides a possible explanation for the dismal pace of recovery in the industrial world and also for the emergence of financial stability problems as an increasingly salient concern.

In the Secular Stagnation scenario the output effects of the crisis persist, and actual output levels do not seem to return to (pre-crisis) potential-output levels for a protracted period. One possible explanation for this phenomenon is the hysteresis hypothesis: the observed Secular Stagnation could reflect a permanent drop in potential output and employment as a consequence of the financial crisis. Hysteresis effects of current output (gaps) on future potential output arise as a result of reduced investment on future capital and the effect of unemployment on worker skills and labour-force attachment. Hysteresis is not easy to prove. What adds to the difficulties in the analysis of hysteresis is that potential output is an unobservable variable: it is actually very difficult to pin down in the real world. In fact, it cannot be excluded that potential output had been overestimated in the boom-period before the financial crisis.

An other important feature of the Secular Stagnation debate is the presumed presence of excess savings that would require real interest rates to be low or negative for an extended time. In a recent narrative policy study on Secular Stagnation coordinated by Teulings and Baldwin (2014), a number of crucial demand (adverse demographic trends, fiscal stringency, monetary policy impotence due to a zero lower bound, over-indebtedness causing excess saving and a 'balance-sheet' recession) and supply factors (lack of innovation, slowdown in efficiency, sclerotic factors in the labour market) were identified that could be behind the Secular Stagnation hypothesis.

To analyse the most important aspects of the Secular Stagnation hypothesis, this chapter considers the effects of hysteresis in potential output in a New Keynesian model that is extended with hysteresis in potential output. To do so, a number of simulations of relevant scenarios are undertaken. It is demonstrated that such an extension has a number of crucial implications for macro-economic adjustment and macro-economic management. It is indicated how the model can indeed help us to understand a number of important elements in the Secular Stagnation hypothesis.

This chapter is organized as follows. The next section discusses the Secular Stagnation hypothesis, focusing on the effects of the financial crisis and its aftermath on potential output. The following section provides a New Keynesian analytical framework, extended by hysteresis effects. After that, numerical simulations of a stylized example are used to illustrate the workings of the model and relate the results to the context of Europe's debt crisis and the current discussions about fiscal management in the Euro Area. The final section presents the conclusions.

The financial crisis, (potential) output and the Secular Stagnation hypothesis

The very sluggish output and employment recovery in Europe from the financial crisis and ensuing recession has led economists and policy makers increasingly to consider the possibility that the Great Recession was not an ordinary recession from which the economy could recover relatively quickly. Instead, they argue, this period of very slow growth may actually point to deeper, structural problems that have prevented a quick recovery so far. In several studies on the recent financial crisis and Great Recession, it has been pointed out that in many OECD (Organization for Economic Co-operation and Development) countries a substantial potential output loss (of the order of 5 to 10 per cent of gross domestic product, GDP) occurred as a result of the Great Recession. The European Commission (2009), OECD (2009), Furceri and Mourougane (2012), Ball (2014), Ollivaud and Turner (2014) and Anderton *et al.* (2014) are all detailed empirical studies that seek to estimate the effects of the financial crisis on potential output and employment, finding evidence for such a substantial loss in potential output.

It is important to understand how the financial crisis could lead to such a drop in the (actual and potential) output level and/or growth rate and how persistent such a drop might be. The adverse effects on potential output would result from the impact of the financial crisis on its three main determinants: the stock of capital, the amount of labour and technology reflected in the total factor productivity. The financial crisis and recession have reduced investment in new capital and technology: investment opportunities declined and also credit from the banks became more scarce as they became more concerned with credit risk. The recession has also reduced opportunities in the labour market. There is the accompanying risk that the increase in unemployment as a result of the crisis becomes an increase in structural unemployment.

The hysteresis hypothesis assumes that the economy retains a memory of the shocks associated with recessions, implying path-dependence in macro-economic adjustments. Hysteresis has pervasive implications for macroeconomic adjustment and policy. It opens up the possibility that temporary shocks may have permanent effects on the economy, in particular a permanent drop in the level of potential output and an increase in structural unemployment, subsequently affecting the broader economy. Hysteresis results from capital scrapping and labour market rigidities (including the well-known 'insider/outsider' conflicts) that prevent/discourage many unemployed workers from re-entering employment again after the recession. The high rate and long duration of joblessness discourage workers further and will result in a permanent destruction of human capital when discouraged workers halt their labour-market search.

A significant literature on hysteresis resulted from the experiences of the 1970s and 1980s when, after the first and second oil crises and ensuing recessions, unemployment displayed the 'ratchet-effect' that is characteristic of hysteresis. In both cases, unemployment failed to drop to the level before the recession and stayed stubbornly high.[1] Clearly, countries are likely to differ in the degree to which hysteresis is affecting the economy at a certain moment. These differences reflect the underlying institutional settings, the impact of various shocks and the policy reactions. Some countries were much less affected, for example, by the Great Recession than others for whom hysteresis could be a serious concern.

For some, theoretical literature that is also of some relevance to our analysis studies the effect of output gap uncertainty on monetary and fiscal policy management (see, e.g., Ehrmann and Smets, 2003). This literature takes as a starting point the observation that policy makers face incomplete information about current economic conditions. Potential output is an unobservable variable, resulting in uncertainty about its actual adjustment. As a result, policy makers have to form estimations/expectations about the actual level of potential output (and its growth rate) and consequently of the actual output gap. As a result of this uncertainty, potential output and the output gap are often subject to significant revisions, especially during crisis periods. This uncertainty makes it difficult to evaluate the adequacy of current monetary and fiscal policies from the perspective of business cycle stabilization. This literature concludes that more potential output uncertainty requires more caution in setting policies as the possibility of policy errors increases. This literature, however, focuses on output gap uncertainty and does not consider the possibility of hysteresis as a source of endogenous business-cycle fluctuations.[2]

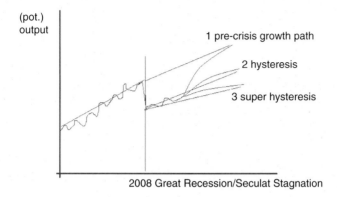

Figure 5.1 Effects of the financial crisis on the level and growth rate of potential output (hypothetical potential and actual output series).

A consequence of the financial crisis and Great Recession is higher uncertainty surrounding estimates of potential output compared to the previous decade of Great Moderation. This uncertainty is evident in the continued downward revision in the estimates of potential output growth for almost all OECD countries during the Great Recession since 2008. It is not therefore clear, in the wake of the observed very weak recovery in output and employment, what the most realistic expectations are concerning output and employment in either the near and more distant future. It also depends on which scenario is the most likely concerning the impact the financial crisis has had on potential output growth. Three possible scenarios concerning the effects of the financial crisis on the potential output level and its growth rate in the long run are distinguished in Figure 5.1. First are one-off changes in the level of GDP without a change in long-run potential output level and its growth rate (upper path). In this scenario, following the Great Recession, economic recovery will eventually bring the economy back to the pre-crisis growth path in the long run. While the recession could be deep and persistent, this scenario would imply that the output loss is eventually recovered. Second is the possibility of a permanent decline in the potential output level without a change in the long-run potential growth rate (middle path). This scenario is equivalent to hysteresis in output and unemployment. Third is a permanent drop in the potential output level *and* long-run potential growth rates, resulting in a form of 'super-hysteresis' (lower path).

Hysteresis is not considered in mainstream macroeconomic models given the complexities it entails in terms of theory, empirical estimation and policy analysis. Hysteresis implies that a temporary shock has permanent effects so that the economy does not return to the initial steady-state but adjusts to a new – endogenous – steady-state, an aspect that we will demonstrate in detail in the numerical analysis. In a similar vein, empirical analysis is also complicated by hysteresis: variables contain a unit root so that the second and higher order moments of variables are not defined. Estimation and measurement errors of the true potential output/output gap will translate into policy errors; in particular policy makers are faced with the uncertainty of whether actual output and inflation adjustment reflects the occurrence of potential shocks or is caused by other shocks, demand shocks, mark-up shocks etc. For example, an overestimation of potential output implies an overestimation of the output gap in times of recession, inducing policy makers to make policies that could be inflationary in the short run, and the fiscal stance is likely to be too lax from the perspective of the true potential output. In a similar manner, in the case of underestimation of potential output, macroeconomic policies could be too restrictive and risk contributing to deflationary pressures.

The analytical framework

Our analytical framework follows the baseline New Keynesian model as a description of the behaviour of macroeconomic variables (see, e.g., Woodford, 2003; Galí, 2008). The adjustment of output, inflation and interest rates is described by the dynamic investment–saving (IS) curve (5.1), the Phillips curve (5.2), and dynamic Taylor rules that characterize monetary policy (5.3) and fiscal policy (5.4). In addition to these standard equations, we add dynamics of potential output (5.5) as we would like to analyse the hysteresis in potential output. The dynamic IS curve summarizes the aggregate goods demand in the economy:

$$y_t = \omega E y_{t+1} + (1 - \omega) y_{t-1} - \sigma (i_t - E\pi_{t+1} - r_t^n) + g_t + \epsilon_t^y \tag{5.1}$$

in which y denotes real output, i the short-term nominal interest rate, π the rate of inflation in the general price level, r^n the equilibrium real interest rate, g net government spending and ϵ^y is an aggregate demand shock. The subscript t refers to time, and E is the expectations operator.

In this reduced form, output depends on past output, expected future output, the real interest rate (expressed as a deviation from the natural rate), net government spending and a demand shock. The backward-looking component in the IS curve results from the fraction of consumers that are backward-looking because of habit formation in consumption decisions (and/or who are subject to credit constraints). The forward-looking part is produced by rational, intertemporally maximizing agents that apply the principles of optimal consumption smoothing. All macroeconomic shocks in the model – demand shocks (ϵ^y), cost-push shocks (ϵ^π), monetary shocks (ϵ^i), fiscal shocks (ϵ^g), potential-output shocks ($\epsilon^{\bar{y}}$) and natural interest rate shocks (ϵ^{rn}) – are assumed to follow stationary $AR(1)$ processes, $\epsilon_t^j = v_j \epsilon_{t-1}^j + v_t^j$ where all innovations are white noise innovations and all innovations are assumed to be contemporaneously uncorrelated.[3]

Inflation adjusts according to a New Keynesian hybrid Phillips curve, which contains elements of both forward and backward-looking price setting. In addition, the output gap as a measure of demand-pull inflation and mark-up shocks ϵ^π affect inflation

$$\pi_t = \beta E\pi_{t+1} + (1 - \beta)\pi_{t-1} + \kappa x_t + \epsilon_t^\pi. \tag{5.2}$$

The output gap $x_t = y_t - \overline{y}_t$ measures the distance between actual output and potential output, $\overline{y}_t$.

A Taylor rule with partial adjustment will be used as an approximation of monetary policy decisions in the economy. The monetary authority is assumed to set the short-term nominal interest rate in response to movements in inflation and the output gap. In the following equation, ρ_i measures inertia in interest rate adjustment, χ_π and χ_x are reaction coefficients to inflation and output gap, $\overline{\pi}$, is the inflation target

$$i_t = \rho_i i_{t-1} + (1 - \rho_i)(r_t^n + \overline{\pi} + \chi_\pi \pi_t + \chi_x x_t) + \epsilon_t^i. \tag{5.3}$$

The feedback on inflation and output gap are standard arguments in the Taylor rule, and the weights given to both objectives are given by the reaction coefficients χ_π and χ_x. The degree of instrument smoothing is measured by ρ_i, where $0 < \rho_i < 1$. If ρ_i goes to zero, the original Taylor rule, which ignores instrument smoothing, is obtained. If ρ_i goes to 1, monetary policy is increasingly smoothed over time.

Fiscal policy also follows a Taylor rule: the fiscal authority is assumed to set net government spending in response to movements in the output gap. In the following equation, ρ_g measures inertia budgetary adjustment, χ_π and χ_x reaction coefficients to inflation and output gap; ϵ^g denotes a budgetary shock

$$g_t = \rho_g g_{t-1} + (1 - \rho_g)(-\mu x_t) + \epsilon_t^g. \tag{5.4}$$

The standard New Keynesian model assumes potential output to be constant (possibly subject to stochastic shocks) in order to focus on short-run fluctuations in output as a result of shocks to consumer preferences, labour-supply shocks, firms' mark-up shocks, technological shocks and policy shocks. For our purpose, it is more useful to consider endogenous adjustment of potential output, reflecting the possibility of hysteresis. The standard New Keynesian model does not consider hysteresis, therefore we introduce endogenous potential output into the model in the following way

$$\overline{y}_t = \rho_{\overline{y}} \overline{y}_{t-1} + \alpha y_{t-1} + \epsilon_t^{\overline{y}}. \tag{5.5}$$

Potential output depends on past potential output, actual output and potential output innovations, $\epsilon^{\overline{y}}$. In the case of $\alpha = 0$, the model reduces to the standard New Keynesian model with exogenous potential output, and, in the case $\alpha = 1$, potential output displays hysteresis. In the intermittent case, $0 < \alpha < 1$, potential output dynamics are consistent. We will consider a value $\alpha = 0.5$ to study this intermittent case. In their analysis on the impact of potential output persistence on optimal monetary policy, Kienzler and Schmid (2014) consider values of α between 0 and 0.5[4] and demonstrate the need for additional monetary policy activism (in terms of reacting to temporary shocks) in the presence of potential output gap persistence. The intuition lies in the shock persistence in potential

Table 5.1 Baseline parameter set

ω	0.5	$\bar{\pi}$	0	$\rho_{\bar{y}}$	0.5	$\nu_{\epsilon\bar{y}}$	0.25
σ	1.0	χ_π	1.5	α	[0,0.5,1]	$\nu_{\epsilon g}$	0.0
β	0.5	χ_x	0.5	$\nu_{\epsilon y}$	0.5	$\nu_{\epsilon r^n}$	0.5
κ	0.1	ρ_g	0.5	$\nu_{\epsilon\pi}$	0.0		
ρ_i	0.5	μ	0.5	$\nu_{\epsilon i}$	0.0		

output, which is transmitted to output and inflation volatility and, therefore, to welfare.

Numerical results

In this section, we simulate a number of relevant scenarios for the New Keynesian hysteresis model (5.1)–(5.5). We consider the effects of: (i) a temporary negative demand shock; (ii) a one-off positive cost-push shock; (iii) a temporary negative shock to the natural interest rate; and (iv) varying the degree of fiscal stabilization. The simulations assume the model parameters summarized in Table 5.1. These parameters were not estimated but chosen based on plausibility and their usefulness as a baseline. Small changes in this baseline will lead to changes in the model's responses.

A temporary demand shock

A crucial implication of hysteresis is the possibility that temporary shocks can have permanent effects on output and unemployment (through the hysteresis effects on potential output): in the long run, output is at a lower level than it would have been in the absence of the shock. We can illustrate the workings of hysteresis in our model by considering the impact and transmission of a temporary demand shock. Figure 5.2 displays the effects of a negative demand shock in period 1 and its subsequent transmission in (potential), output, output gap, inflation, interest rate and net government spending. The "black" line shows the adjustment in the case of the standard New Keynesian model without hysteresis ($\alpha = 0$), the "light gray" line shows the adjustment in the persistent potential-output case ($\alpha = 0.5$), and the "dark gray" line shows the adjustment under hysteresis ($\alpha = 1$).

The implications of hysteresis are quite clearly demonstrated by this example. While in the standard New Keynesian model and in the persistent potential output case, output returns to the initial output level after a temporary recession, it fails to do so in the hysteresis case. The reason that it fails to do so is exactly the permanent drop in potential output in the hysteresis case. Given the New Keynesian Phillips curve, the output gap is closed and inflation disappears once the temporary shock has faded away. Active monetary and fiscal policies in the form of lower interest rates and higher net government spending contribute to the adjustment dynamics, but cannot prevent the long-run drop in (potential) output in the hysteresis cases. It is also clearly demonstrated that where there is more

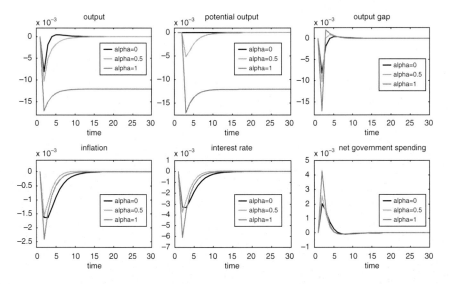

Figure 5.2 Effects of a temporary negative demand shock.

hysteresis in potential output, the more detrimental the temporary shock is in the long run.

A temporary cost-push shock

Mark-up/cost-push like oil price or wage cost shocks are other important sources of macroeconomic fluctuations. Mark-up shocks in the real world and in the New Keynesian model create even more complications for policy makers than demand shocks, since inflation is only indirectly controlled by the influence of active policies on the output gap. In the case where mark-up shocks occur, the monetary policy maker is facing a dilemma between actively stabilizing output by setting lower interest rates (and accepting the higher inflation resulting from expansionary monetary policy) or stabilizing inflation by raising interest rates (and accepting the resulting temporary output loss). Figure 5.3 considers the effects of a one-off 1 per cent positive cost-push shock in period 1.

The mark-up shock creates stagflation: output drops and inflation increases. In the no-hysteresis case, the New Keynesian model displays a convergence to the initial output level over time since potential output is unaffected. Monetary and fiscal stabilization policies are relatively ineffective, they just moderate inflation and/or output during the adjustment to the initial output level. In the case of hysteresis, adjustment is different as the economy would settle for a lower potential and actual output level due to the hysteresis channel. This also increases significantly the potential role for fiscal and monetary stabilization policies: these policies can contribute to moderating the eventual actual and potential output drop as a result of the temporary shock.

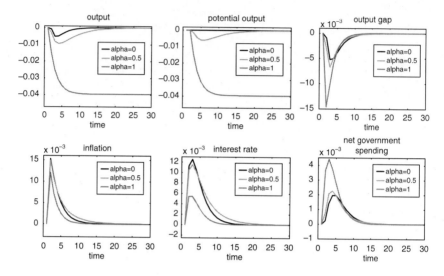

Figure 5.3 Effects of a one-off positive cost-push shock.

A shock to the natural rate of interest

The natural or equilibrium rate of interest is defined as the interest rate that would produce an aggregate demand equal to the natural rate of output, the rate of output that prevails if prices are fully flexible. The natural rate of interest in other words represents a neutral monetary policy stance. According to Summers (2014) and other observers, one factor that has also been connected to the Secular Stagnation hypothesis is a decline in the equilibrium real rate of interest. This drop reflects imbalances between global savings (which have increased) and investment (which has decreased) that resulted from the global financial crisis. In cases like the current one, where there is a natural rate of interest and inflation approaching zero, conventional monetary policy is increasingly impotent to stimulate the economy as that would require setting interest rates below zero. Figure 5.4 demonstrates the effects in the New Keynesian model with hysteresis of a temporary 1 per cent negative shock to the natural rate of interest r_t^n in period 1.

The simulations of the model of this shock are in line with the intuitions by Summers (2014) and other observers. The drop in the natural rate of interest provokes a recessionary and deflationary spiral. In the no-hysteresis regime, the economy recovers quite quickly, also helped by expansionary monetary and fiscal policies; in the persistent potential output case the adjustment is similar but more gradual. In the hysteresis case, outcomes are more problematic as potential output is affected in the long run by this temporary shock. The hysteresis scenario in the model in other words is quite in line with the assertions of Summers and other observers on the Secular Stagnation hypothesis.

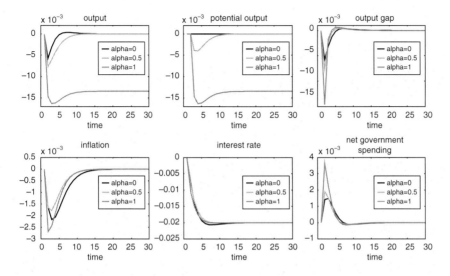

Figure 5.4 Effects of a temporary negative natural interest rate shock.

Effects of changing the strength of fiscal stabilization

The presence of hysteresis would a priori seem to strengthen the case for monetary and/or fiscal stabilization policies. In the no-hysteresis case (and the persistent potential output case with some delay), the economy will return to the original level of output when the shocks have been absorbed. Stabilization policies contribute by speeding the adjustment back to the original output level. In the hysteresis case, the argument for stabilization is much stronger: stabilization policies could contribute in reducing the onset of hysteresis effects. This point has also repeatedly been made in the recent debates about 'self-defeating' fiscal austerity policies (see Delong and Summers, 2012) and about the need for unconventional monetary policies and quantitative easing.

It would also be interesting to consider this debate about the role of fiscal stabilization in the Great Recession in the context of our model. Figure 5.5 displays the effects of the same negative demand shock in period 1 as in Figure 5.1 under three alternative fiscal policy regimes.

We can clearly see that if fiscal stabilization is stronger, hysteresis is less pronounced: in the no-stabilization case the hysteresis effects on (potential) output are roughly double those in the case of the strongest fiscal stabilization.

The presence of hysteresis is also helpful in understanding the possibility of 'self-defeating' fiscal austerity policies that have been attributed to the sovereign debt crisis in the Euro Area. The deterioration in public finances as a result of the financial crisis has led most Member States to adopt sizeable consolidation packages. Such fiscal consolidation strategies may turn out to be self-defeating in the sense that the reduction in government expenditure could lead to an even stronger

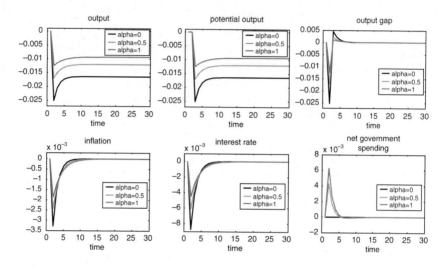

Figure 5.5 Effects of alternative degrees of fiscal stabilization.

fall in activity implying that fiscal performance indicators actually worsen. In the particular case here of our small model, think of a case where an economy is facing recession as a result of, for example, a temporary negative demand shock and policy makers implement fiscal austerity measures at the same time. This austerity policy could contribute to the onset of hysteresis effects. The resulting permanent drop in potential output and unemployment would also aggravate the budgetary position, which may end up worsening rather than improving the fiscal balance.

Counteracting the recession with structural reforms

In response to the crisis, policy makers at the EU and OECD have advocated the implementation of more ambitious structural reform programmes, especially in countries most severely affected by the Great Recession. In the setting of our model we interpret structural reforms as positive potential output shocks.[5] Figure 5.6 displays the case where the initial temporary negative demand shock in period 1 of Figure 5.1 is complemented by a temporary structural reform policy in period 2.

The structural reform effort cushions the recession produced by the negative demand shock, as is clear from a comparison with Figure 5.1. Interestingly, the hysteresis regime now gives the best outcomes in the long run: the negative hysteresis that would be produced from the temporary recession is surpassed in the long run by the positive effects on potential output from structural reform. The presence of hysteresis in other words also raises the importance/possible benefits of structural reforms. Seen in this light, the recommendation of pursuing structural reform programmes like the EU's Horizon2020, even in the presence of recession, seems warranted.

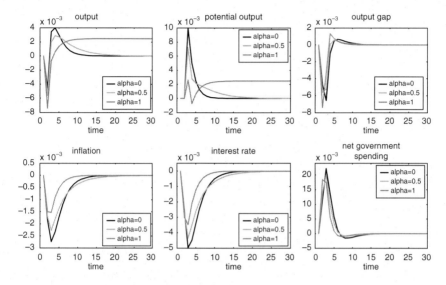

Figure 5.6 Effects of a temporary negative demand shock counteracted by a structural-reform policy.

Conclusion

Policy makers and academics have had a hard time recently in understanding the very shallow economic recovery ('Secular Stagnation') in most OECD countries from the global financial crisis and Great Recession. One of the most radical explanations that has been proposed is the hysteresis hypothesis, whose origin lies in the strong global recession of the early 1980s. Where hysteresis is present, temporary macroeconomic shocks may result in permanent effects. In that scenario, the economy is path-dependent and the case for macroeconomic stabilization policies is strongly enhanced when compared to that of non-hysteresis. In the case of hysteresis, adjustment is different as the economy would settle over time for a lower potential and actual output level due to the hysteresis channel.

Hysteresis also significantly increases the potential role for fiscal and monetary stabilization policies: these policies can contribute to moderating the eventual actual and potential output drop as a result of the temporary shock. In fact the entire logic of stabilization policies is affected: in the standard New Keynesian (DSGE) model without hysteresis, stabilization policies serve to fine-tune macroeconomic adjustment thereby reducing the volatility in the adjustment to the long-run equilibrium that is unaffected by macroeconomic shocks. In the case where hysteresis is added, stabilization policies are needed to reduce the (typically substantial) long-run impact from temporary shocks. In a similar vein, policy errors, like a procyclical fiscal deficit bias, are of greater concern in the case of hysteresis.

Our chapter extended a basic New Keynesian model by inserting hysteresis into potential output. Using the model, a number of simulations of relevant scenarios was undertaken to illustrate the implications of hysteresis in the context of the Secular Stagnation hypothesis. It was demonstrated that such an extension has a number of crucial implications for macro economic adjustment and macro economic management (compared to the standard New Keynesian model with constant potential output and a second case with persistent potential output). The simulations illustrated the central tenet of the hysteresis hypothesis: the possibility that temporary shocks may have permanent effects on the economy; in particular a permanent drop in the level of potential output (and an increase in structural unemployment) is provoked, subsequently affecting the broader economy. The hysteresis hypothesis not only has such implications in the case of temporary demand shocks but our examples also considered temporary mark-up shocks and natural interest rate shocks.

In the final case, we reconsidered the policy advice to focus in particular on reviving structural reform agendas as the most appropriate instruments to recover from the Great Recession. In itself, this approach makes sense as it would contribute in principle to rebuilding productivity and potential output. Our final example revealed that the presence of hysteresis raises the importance/possible benefits of structural reforms. However, there is also a risk that reform efforts are annihilated if overly restrictive monetary and fiscal policies are present in a hysteretic economy.

Another important result from our simulation study relates to the (regained) importance of macroeconomic stabilization policies. It was demonstrated that if fiscal stabilization is stronger, the hysteresis channel is less pronounced/can be mitigated; a similar conclusion would pertain to the use of monetary policy as a tool for output stabilization, even if in that case there are also considerations relating to inflation stabilization. In that sense, the recent debates about 'self-defeating' fiscal austerity and the use of non-standard monetary policy measures by the European Central Bank in the presence of a zero lower bound on interest rates can also be reinterpreted in the context of the hysteresis channel.

Our study did not provide any empirical evidence. Nevertheless, our take from the study is that in the case of the Euro Area the possibility of a hysteresis channel needs serious consideration: with monetary policy placed at the supra-national level and national fiscal policies restricted by a set of fiscal stringency requirements, there is a risk that hysteresis is particularly strong in countries that are hit by negative macroeconomic conditions.

Appendix

For analytical purposes it is convenient to write the macroeconomic model (5.1)–(5.5) in its state-phase form. To do this, (5.3) and (5.4) are substituted into (5.1).

Let

$$x_t' = [y_t, \pi_t, \overline{y}_{t-1}, r_{t-1}^n, i_{t-1}, g_{t-1}]'$$

and

$$v'_t = [v^y_{t-1}, v^\pi_{t-1}, v^i_{t-1}, v^g_{t-1}, v^{r^n}_{t-1}, v^{\bar y}_{t-1}]'$$

then the model's state-phase is given by

$$Ex_{t+1} = Ax_t + Bx_{t-1} + Cv_{t+1} \qquad (A5.1)$$

in which

$$A = \begin{bmatrix}
\dfrac{1+\sigma(1-\rho_i)-(1-\rho_g)\mu}{\omega} & -\dfrac{\rho_i}{\omega} & -\dfrac{\sigma(1-\rho_i)-(1-\rho_g)\mu}{\omega} & \dfrac{(1-n\rho_i)}{\omega} \\[2ex]
-n\dfrac{\kappa}{\beta} & \dfrac{1}{\beta} & \dfrac{\kappa}{\beta} & 0 \\[2ex]
\alpha & 0 & (1-n\alpha)\rho_{\bar y} & 0 \\[1ex]
0 & 0 & 0 & \rho_{r^n} \\[1ex]
\begin{matrix}(1-n\rho_i)\chi_x\\(1-\rho_g)\mu\end{matrix} & \begin{matrix}(1-\rho_i)\chi_\pi\\0\end{matrix} & \begin{matrix}-(1-\rho_i)\chi_x\\-n(1-n\rho_g)\mu\end{matrix} & \begin{matrix}1-\rho_i\\0\end{matrix} \\[2ex]
0 & 0 & 0 & 0 \\
0 & 0 & 0 & 0 \\
0 & 0 & 0 & 0 \\
0 & 0 & 0 & 0 \\
0 & 0 & 0 & 0 \\
0 & 0 & 0 & 0
\end{bmatrix}$$

$$\begin{bmatrix}
0 & 0 & -\dfrac{1}{\omega} & 0 & \dfrac{\sigma}{\omega} & -\dfrac{1}{\omega} & 0 & 0 \\[2ex]
0 & 0 & 0 & -\dfrac{1}{\beta} & 0 & 0 & 0 & 0 \\[2ex]
0 & 0 & 0 & 0 & 0 & 0 & 0 & 1 \\
0 & 0 & 0 & 0 & 0 & 0 & 1 & 0 \\
\rho_i & 0 & 0 & 0 & 1 & 0 & 0 & 0 \\
0 & \rho_g & 0 & 0 & 0 & 1 & 0 & 0 \\
0 & 0 & v_{\epsilon y} & 0 & 0 & 0 & 0 & 0 \\
0 & 0 & 0 & v_{\epsilon \pi} & 0 & 0 & 0 & 0 \\
0 & 0 & 0 & 0 & v_{\epsilon i} & 0 & 0 & 0 \\
0 & 0 & 0 & 0 & 0 & v_{\epsilon g} & 0 & 0 \\
0 & 0 & 0 & 0 & 0 & 0 & v_{\epsilon \bar y} & 0 \\
0 & 0 & 0 & 0 & 0 & 0 & 0 & v_{\epsilon r^n}
\end{bmatrix},$$

$$B = \begin{bmatrix} -\dfrac{1-\omega}{\omega} & 0 & 0 & 0 & \dfrac{\sigma\rho_i}{\omega} & \dfrac{\rho_g}{\omega} & 0 & 0 & 0 & 0 & 0 & 0 \\ 0 & -\dfrac{1-\beta}{\beta} & 0 & 0 & 0 & 0 & 0 & 0 & 0 & 0 & 0 & 0 \\ 0 & 0 & 0 & 0 & 0 & 0 & 0 & 0 & 0 & 0 & 0 & 0 \\ 0 & 0 & 0 & 0 & 0 & 0 & 0 & 0 & 0 & 0 & 0 & 0 \\ 0 & 0 & 0 & 0 & 0 & 0 & 0 & 0 & 0 & 0 & 0 & 0 \\ 0 & 0 & 0 & 0 & 0 & 0 & 0 & 0 & 0 & 0 & 0 & 0 \\ 0 & 0 & 0 & 0 & 0 & 0 & 0 & 0 & 0 & 0 & 0 & 0 \\ 0 & 0 & 0 & 0 & 0 & 0 & 0 & 0 & 0 & 0 & 0 & 0 \\ 0 & 0 & 0 & 0 & 0 & 0 & 0 & 0 & 0 & 0 & 0 & 0 \\ 0 & 0 & 0 & 0 & 0 & 0 & 0 & 0 & 0 & 0 & 0 & 0 \\ 0 & 0 & 0 & 0 & 0 & 0 & 0 & 0 & 0 & 0 & 0 & 0 \\ 0 & 0 & 0 & 0 & 0 & 0 & 0 & 0 & 0 & 0 & 0 & 0 \end{bmatrix},$$

$$C = \begin{bmatrix} 0 & 0 & 0 & 0 & 0 & 0 \\ 0 & 0 & 0 & 0 & 0 & 0 \\ 0 & 0 & 0 & 0 & 0 & 0 \\ 0 & 0 & 0 & 0 & 0 & 0 \\ 0 & 0 & 0 & 0 & 0 & 0 \\ 0 & 0 & 0 & 0 & 0 & 0 \\ 1 & 0 & 0 & 0 & 0 & 0 \\ 0 & 1 & 0 & 0 & 0 & 0 \\ 0 & 0 & 1 & 0 & 0 & 0 \\ 0 & 0 & 0 & 1 & 0 & 0 \\ 0 & 0 & 0 & 0 & 1 & 0 \\ 0 & 0 & 0 & 0 & 0 & 1 \end{bmatrix},$$

Equation (A5.1) describes a system of linear expectational difference equations. This system can be solved by uncoupling the unstable and stable components and then solving the unstable component forwards and the stable component backwards. There are a number of algorithms for working through this process as outlined by Klein (2000). Note that there are eight predetermined variables and two non-predetermined variables in the vector x_t and six predetermined variables in the vector v_t. Thus, if 12 of the generalized eigenvalues lie inside the unit circle and 2 of the generalized eigenvalues of the system lie outside the unit circle, the system has a unique solution. If more than two of the generalized eigenvalues lie outside the unit circle, then the system has no solution. If less than two of the

Table A5.1 Eigenvalues of the system dynamics in the case of the baseline parameter set

Modulus	Real	Imaginary
0	0	0
0	0	0
0	0	0
0	0	0
$9.819e-009$	$9.819e-009$	0
$9.819e-009$	$9.819e-009$	0
0.5	0.5	0
0.5	0.5	0
0.5	0.5	0
0.5	0.5	0
0.5866	0.5866	0
1.0	1.0	0
1.239	1.207	0.2796
1.239	1.207	-0.2796

generalized eigenvalues lie outside the unit circle, then the system has multiple solutions. See Blanchard and Kahn (1980) and Klein (2000) on this rank condition determining stability and nature of the system. In the baseline example of Table 5.1 that we use, the eigenvalues are as shown in Table A5.1.

There are two eigenvalue(s) larger than 1 in modulus for two forward-looking variable(s), so the rank condition is indeed verified.

Notes

1 See, e.g., Bruno and Sachs (1985), Blanchard and Summers (1986, 1987, 1988) and Lindbeck and Snower (1986) on the hysteresis experiences associated with the first and second oil crises of the 1970s and 1980s. The related empirical debate about unit roots in output also dates back to the same period (see Stock and Watson, 1986; Diebold and Rudebusch, 1987).
2 The standard New Keynesian models and their more worked out DSGE variants rely on exogenous business-cycle fluctuations in the sense that economic adjustments are the result of various types of shocks that hit the economy and transmit themselves through various transmission channels – exogenous transmission of shocks in other words – after which the economy returns to steady-state. In the case of endogenous fluctuations like hysteresis, shocks also imply that the transmission of shocks is endogenous since the steady-state itself is also affected by the temporary shock.
3 Strictly speaking, in the hysteresis case, these shocks need to be considered/implemented as deterministic processes, given that the mean and variance of the output and potential-output variables are not defined in the hysteresis case, as hysteresis implies that the various shocks can have permanent effects on the mean of potential and actual output, viz. potential and actual output are following random walks.
4 They denote cases with potential output persistence also as hysteresis. This seems somewhat confusing. As we will see, it is more useful to reserve hysteresis for the case $\alpha = 1$ and persistent potential output for the case where $0 < \alpha < 1$, since both cases are fundamentally different in the resulting adjustment dynamics.

5 Structural reforms in that sense are comparable to positive technology shocks. For an insightful analysis on the effects of technology shocks in the New Keynesian model, see Galí *et al.* (2003) and Ireland (2004).

References

Anderton, B., T. Aranki, A. Dieppe, C. Elding, S. Haroutunian, P. Jacquinot, V. Jarvis, V. Labhard, D. Rusinova and B. Szorfi (2014), 'Potential output from a Euro Area perspective', *European Central Bank Occasional Paper Series no. 156.*

Ball, L. (2014), 'Long-term damage from the Great Recession in OECD countries', *European Journal of Economics and Economic Policies: Intervention*, vol. 11, no. 2, pp. 149–160.

Blanchard, O. and C. Kahn (1980), 'The solution of linear difference models under rational expectations', *Econometrica*, vol. 48, pp. 1305–1311.

Blanchard, O. and L. Summers (1986), 'Hysteresis and the European unemployment problem', in S. Fischer (ed.), *NBER Macroeconomics Annual*, Vol. 1, Cambridge, MA: MIT Press, pp. 15–78.

Blanchard, O. and L. Summers (1987), 'Hysteresis in unemployment', *European Economic Review*, vol. 3, no. 1–2, pp. 288–295.

Blanchard, O. and L. Summers (1988), 'Beyond the natural rate hypothesis', *American Economic Review*, vol. 78, no. 2, pp. 182–187.

Bruno, M. and J. Sachs (1985), *Economics of Worldwide Stagflation*, Cambridge, MA: Harvard University Press.

Delong, B. and L. Summers (2012), 'Fiscal policy in a depressed economy', *Brookings Papers on Economic Activity*, Spring 2012, pp. 233–290.

Diebold, F. and G. Rudebusch (1987), 'Long memory and persistence in aggregate output', *Journal of Monetary Economics*, vol. 24, pp. 189–209.

Ehrmann, M. and F. Smets (2003), 'Uncertain potential output: Implications for monetary policy', *Journal of Economic Dynamics and Control*, vol. 27, pp. 1611–1638.

European Commission (2009), 'Impact of the current economic and financial crisis on potential output', *European Economy, Occasional Papers* no. 49.

Furceri, D. and A. Mourougane (2012), 'The effect of financial crises on potential output: New empirical evidence from OECD countries', *Journal of Macroeconomics*, vol. 34, pp. 822–832.

Galí, J. (2008), *An Introduction to the New Keynesian Framework and Its Applications*, Princeton, NJ: Princeton University Press.

Galí, J., D. Lopez-Salido and J. Valles (2003), 'Technology shocks and monetary policy: Assessing the Fed's performance', *Journal of Monetary Economics*, vol. 50, pp. 723–743.

Ireland, P. (2004), 'Technology shocks in the New Keynesian model', *Review of Economics and Statistics*, vol. 86, no. 4, pp. 923–936.

Klein, P. (2000), 'Using the generalized Schur form to solve a multivariate linear rational expectations model', *Journal of Economic Dynamics and Control*, vol. 24, pp. 1405–1423.

Kienzler, D. and K. Schmid (2014), 'Hysteresis in potential output and monetary policy', *Scottish Journal of Political Economy*, vol. 68, no. 4, pp. 371–396.

Lindbeck, A. and D. Snower (1986), 'Long-term unemployment and macroeconomic policy', *American Economic Review*, vol. 78, no. 2, pp. 38–43.

OECD (2009), 'Beyond the crisis: Medium-term challenges relating to potential output, unemployment and fiscal positions', *OECD Economic Outlook*, vol. 85, pp. 211–241.

Ollivaud, P. and D. Turner (2014), 'The effect of the global financial crisis on OECD potential output', *OECD Economics Department Working Papers*, no. 1166.

Stock, J. and M. Watson (1986), 'Does GNP have a unit root?', *Economics Letters*, vol. 22, pp. 147–151.

Summers, L. (2014), 'U.S. economic prospects: Secular stagnation, hysteresis, and the zero lower bound', *Business Economics*, vol. 49, no. 2, pp. 65–73.

Teulings, C. and R. Baldwin (eds) (2014), *Secular Stagnation: Facts, Causes and Cures*, A VoxEU.org Book, London: CEPR Press.

Woodford, M. (2003), 'Optimal interest-rate smoothing', *Review of Economic Studies*, vol. 70, pp. 861–886.

Part II

Policies

6 Public finance and the optimal inflation rate

Giovanni Di Bartolomeo and Patrizio Tirelli

Introduction

In the economic literature, there are three main alternative theories of inflation prescribing different optimal policies. Friedman (1977) calls for a negative steady-state inflation rate as long as the steady-state real interest rate is positive to equalize the social and private cost of producing money (Friedman rule). Optimal monetary policy analyses based on New Keynesian sticky price models identify the driving force in the adjustment cost of the price of goods for the optimal level of long-run (or trend) inflation, which has to be set to zero to eliminate the price dispersion effects or price adjustment costs (e.g., Khan *et al.*, 2003; Schmitt-Grohé and Uribe, 2004a). Finally, Phelps (1973) conjectured that to alleviate the burden of distortionary taxation, it might be optimal for governments to resort to monetary financing, driving a wedge between the private and the social cost of money, thereby setting a positive inflation rate.

Schmitt-Grohé and Uribe's (2004a) numerical simulations suggest that the optimal inflation rate is about zero or moderately negative, even accounting for the Phelps effect.[1] In their survey of the literature, Schmitt-Grohé and Uribe (2011) also argue that the optimality of zero inflation is robust to other frictions, such as nominal wage adjustment costs, downward wage rigidity, hedonic prices, incompleteness of the tax system, and the zero bound on the nominal interest rate. Their conclusion carries over to the optimality of near-zero volatility of inflation and near-random-walk behavior in government debt and tax rates in response to shocks. A consensus therefore seems to exist that monetary transactions costs are relatively small at zero inflation and that implementing low and stable inflation is the proper policy.

As noticed by the same Schmitt-Grohé and Uribe (2011), the above result is in sharp contrast to empirical evidence. A zero inflation rate is never observed either as a monetary policy target or as a policy outcome. The targets set by inflation targeting countries in fact somehow contradict the theories of the optimal inflation rate—being between 2 percent and 4 percent. Moreover, even in periods of relatively stable inflation, average inflation rates are not lower than 2 percent. For instance, between 1990 and 2008, a period of relative price stability, average inflation was about 2.8 percent in the United States, 2.2 percent in Germany, and 4 percent in OECD (Organization for Economic Co-operation and Development) countries. Between 1970 and 1999, both the United States and the Euro area experienced an average inflation rate close to 5 percent.

Recently, Di Bartolomeo *et al.* (2015) show that the inclusion of public transfers into New Keynesian models challenges the dogma of a zero (or below zero) optimal inflation rate. They suggest that a moderate inflation rate might indeed be optimal: specifically, in a standard framework which is only characterized by price stickiness, the optimal inflation rate monotonically increases from 2 percent to 12 percent as the transfers-to-gross domestic product (GDP) ratio goes from 10 percent to 20 percent, which is a realistic figure for OECD countries. The effect is due to the different incentives to finance public expenditures through taxes or seigniorage deriving from transfers and public consumption. To grasp the intuition behind this result, it is useful to refer to the different effects of public consumption and transfers on tax and inflation revenues. In fact, an increase in public consumption reduces private consumption and money holdings (thus eroding the inflation tax base), while raising labor supply (thus making an increase in the distortionary tax rate unnecessary) and the tax base. By contrast, transfers have no impact on consumption and labor supply and thus do not favor ordinary tax financing of public expenditure vis-à-vis the inflation tax.

By considering a richer framework this chapter studies the interplay between the above "transfer effect"and some relevant features of New Keynesian models. In other words, we investigate how commonly used features of New Keynesian models affect the incentive to use different instruments to finance public transfers, and, therefore, optimal inflation. Specifically, we consider the impact on inflation of different degrees of real distortions in goods and labor markets, sticky monopolistic wages, and price and wage indexation. We also extend Di Bartolomeo *et al.* (2015) by taking account of potentially non-unitary elasticity of demand for money with respect to consumption by introducing consumption scale effects in the monetary transactions technology. We find that some of these features (such as market distortions, indexation, and consumption scale effects) raise the level of the optimal inflation rate. Wage stickiness reduces it, but reductions are contained.

The rest of the chapter is structured as follows. The next section introduces the model. Then we define the competitive equilibrium and the Ramsey policy. The following section briefly illustrates the "transfer effect"derived in Di Bartolomeo *et al.* (2015). Then we consider the effects of real distortions in goods and labor markets, wage stickiness, and price and wage indexation. We then extend the model to consumption scale effects on the transaction costs. The final section presents the conclusions.

The model

We consider a simple infinite-horizon production economy populated by a continuum of households and firms whose total measures are normalized to one. Monopolistic competition and nominal rigidities characterize both product and labor markets. A demand for money is motivated by assuming that money facilitates transactions. The government finances an exogenous stream of expenditures by levying distortionary labor income taxes and by printing money. Optimal policy is set according to a Ramsey plan.

Right from the outset, it should be noted that the focus here is on the identification of the optimal financing mix for exogenous levels of public expenditures, including both consumption and transfers. Our model therefore cannot explain government size and its composition. In this regard, our approach is identical to Klein *et al.* (2005), who investigate the optimal combination of labor, capital, and corporate taxes for a given amount of total public expenditure.

Households

The representative household (i) maximizes the following utility function

$$U = E_{t=0} \sum_{t=0}^{\infty} \beta^t u\left(C_{t,i}, l_{t,i}\right); \quad u\left(C_{t,i}, l_{t,i}\right) = \ln C_{t,i} + \eta \ln\left(1 - l_{t,i}\right) \tag{6.1}$$

where $\beta \in (,1)$ is the intertemporal discount rate, $C_{t,i} = \left(\int_0^1 c_{t,i}(j)^\rho dj\right)^{\frac{1}{\rho}}$ is a consumption bundle, and $l_{t,i}$ is a differentiated labor type that is supplied to all firms. The consumption price index is $P_t = \left(\int_0^1 p_t(i)^{\frac{\rho}{\rho-1}} di\right)^{\frac{\rho-1}{\rho}}$.

The flow budget constraint in period t is given by

$$C_{t,i}\left(1 + S_{t,i}\right) + \frac{M_{t,i}}{P_t} + \frac{B_{t,i}}{P_t} = \frac{(1 - \tau_t)\, w_{t,i} l_{t,i}}{P_t} + \frac{M_{t-1,i}}{P_t} + \theta_t + T_t + \frac{R_{t-1} B_{t-1,i}}{P_t} \tag{6.2}$$

where $w_{t,i}$ is the nominal wage, τ_t is the labor income tax rate, T_t denotes real fiscal transfers, θ_t are firms profits, R_t is the gross nominal interest rate, and $B_{t,i}$ is a nominally riskless bond that pays one unit of currency in period $t + 1$. $M_{t,i}$ defines nominal money holdings to be used in period $t + 1$ in order to facilitate consumption purchases.

Consumption purchases are subject to a transaction cost

$$S_{t,i} = s(v_{t,i}), \quad s'(v_{t,i}) > 0 \tag{6.3}$$

where $v_{t,i} = \frac{P_{t,i} C_{t,i}}{M_{t,i}}$ is the household's consumption-based money velocity. The features of $s(v_{t,i})$ are such that a satiation level of money velocity ($v^* > 0$) exists where the transaction cost vanishes and, simultaneously, a finite demand for money is associated with a zero nominal interest rate. Following Schmitt-Grohé and Uribe (2004a) the transaction cost is parameterized as

$$s(v_{t,i}) = A v_{t,i} + \frac{B}{v_{t,i}} - 2\sqrt{AB}. \tag{6.4}$$

The first-order conditions of the household's maximization problem are[2]

$$c_t(j) = C_t \left(\frac{P_t(j)}{P_t} \right)^{\frac{1}{\rho-1}}$$
(6.5)

$$\lambda_t = \frac{u_c(C_t, l_t)}{1 + s(v_t) + v_t s'(v_t)}$$
(6.6)

$$\frac{\lambda_t}{\lambda_{t+1}} = \beta R_t \frac{P_t}{P_{t+1}}$$
(6.7)

$$\frac{R_t - 1}{R_t} = s'(v_t) v_t^2.$$
(6.8)

Equation (6.5) is the demand for the good j. As in Schmitt-Grohé and Uribe (2004a), equation (6.6) states that the transaction cost introduces a wedge between the marginal utility of consumption and the marginal utility of wealth that vanishes only if $v = v^*$. Equation (6.7) is a standard Euler condition. Equation (6.8) implicitly defines the household's money demand function.

Firms' pricing decisions

Each firm (j) produces a differentiated good using the production function

$$y_t(j) = z_t l_{t,j}$$
(6.9)

where z_t denotes a productivity shock[3] and $l_{t,j}$ is a standard labor bundle

$$l_{t,j} = \left[\int_0^1 l_{t,j}(i)^{\frac{\sigma-1}{\sigma}} di \right]^{\frac{\sigma}{\sigma-1}}.$$
(6.10)

Firm (j) demand for labor type (i) is

$$l_{t,j}(i) = \left(\frac{w_{t,i}}{W_t} \right)^{-\sigma} l_{t,j}$$
(6.11)

where $W_t = \left[\int_0^1 w_{t,i}^{1-\sigma} di \right]^{\frac{1}{1-\sigma}}$ is the wage index.

We assume a sticky price specification based on Rotemberg (1982)'s quadratic cost of nominal price adjustment:

$$\frac{\xi_p}{2} \left(\frac{P_t(j)/P_{t-1}(j)}{\pi_{t-1}^{\delta}} - 1 \right)^2$$
(6.12)

where $\xi_p > 0$ is a measure of price stickiness, $\pi_t = P_t/P_{t-1}$ denotes the gross inflation rate, and $\delta \in [0, 1]$ is the degree of price indexation to past inflation.

In a symmetrical equilibrium the price adjustment rule satisfies

$$\frac{z_t l_t (\rho - mc_t)}{1 - \rho} + \xi_p \frac{\pi_t}{\pi_{t-1}^{\delta_p}} \left(\frac{\pi_t}{\pi_{t-1}^{\delta_p}} - 1 \right) = E_t \beta \frac{\lambda_{t+1}}{\lambda_t} \xi_p \left[\frac{\pi_{t+1}}{\pi_t^{\delta_p}} \left(\frac{\pi_{t+1}}{\pi_t^{\delta_p}} - 1 \right) \right]$$

(6.13)

where

$$mc_t = \frac{1}{z_t} \frac{W_t}{P_t}.$$

From (6.5) it would be straightforward to show that the inverse of ρ is the price markup that obtains under flexible prices (μ^p).

Wage-setting decisions

The labor market is also characterized by monopolistic competition and rigid nominal wages. Under flexible wages

$$\frac{W_t}{P_t} = -\mu^w \frac{1 + s(v_t) + v_t s'(v_t)}{1 - \tau_t} \frac{u_l (C_t, l_t)}{u_c (C_t, l_t)}$$

(6.14)

where $\mu^w = \sigma (\sigma - 1)^{-1}$ denotes the gross wage markup.

We model nominal wage stickiness as in Rotemberg (1982). Each household maximizes the expected value of (6.1) subject to (6.2), (6.11) and to

$$\frac{\xi_w}{2} \left(\frac{W_t(i)/W_{t-1}(i)}{\pi_{t-1}^{\delta_w}} - 1 \right)^2$$

(6.15)

where $\xi_w > 0$ is a measure of wage stickiness and $\delta_w \in [0, 1]$ is the degree of wage indexation to past inflation.

As a result, in a symmetrical equilibrium, the wage adjustment rule satisfies

$$\left[(1 - \tau_t) \frac{W_t}{P_t} + \frac{\mu^w u_l (C_t, l_t) (1 + s(v_t) + v_t s'(v_t))}{u_c (C_t, l_t)} \right] \frac{l_t}{\mu^w - 1}$$
$$+ \xi_w \left[\frac{\omega_t}{\pi_{t-1}^{\delta_w}} \left(\frac{\omega_t}{\pi_{t-1}^{\delta_w}} - 1 \right) \right] = E_t \beta \frac{\lambda_{t+1}}{\lambda_t} \xi_w \left[\frac{\omega_{t+1}}{\pi_t^{\delta_w}} \left(\frac{\omega_{t+1}}{\pi_t^{\delta_w}} - 1 \right) \right]$$

(6.16)

where $\omega_t = W_t / W_{t-1}$.[4]

The government

The government supplies an exogenous, stochastic, and unproductive amount of public good G_t and implements exogenous transfers T_t. Government financing is obtained through a labor-income tax, money creation, and issuance of one-period, nominally risk-free bonds. The government's flow budget constraint is then given by[5]

$$R_{t-1} \frac{B_{t-1}}{P_t} + G_t + T_t = \tau_t \frac{W_t}{P_t} l_t + \frac{M_t - M_{t-1}}{P_t} + \frac{B_t}{P_t}. \tag{6.17}$$

It is worth noticing that the focus of the chapter is the identification of the optimal financing mix, where optimality is driven by efficiency considerations. Justifying the existence of government transfers as an optimal outcome would require some form of heterogeneity across households. This is beyond the scope of this chapter.

The competitive equilibrium

The competitive equilibrium is a set of plans $\{C_t, l_t, \lambda_t, mc_t, \pi_t, v_t\}_{t=0}^{+\infty}$ that, given the policies $\{R_t, \tau_t\}_{t=0}^{+\infty}$, the exogenous processes $\{z_t, g_t\}_{t=0}^{+\infty}$, and the initial conditions, satisfies (6.6), (6.7), (6.8), (6.13), (6.16), (6.17), and the aggregate resource constraint

$$Y_t = C_t (1 + S_t) + G_t + \frac{\xi_p}{2} \left(\frac{\pi_t}{\pi_{t-1}^{\delta_p}} - 1 \right)^2 + \frac{\xi_w}{2} \left(\frac{\omega_t}{\pi_{t-1}^{\delta_w}} - 1 \right)^2. \tag{6.18}$$

Ramsey policy

The Ramsey policy is a set of plans $\{R_t, \tau_t\}_{t=0}^{+\infty}$ that maximize the expected value of (6.1) subject to the competitive equilibrium conditions (6.6), (6.7), (6.8), (6.13), (6.16), (6.17), (6.18), and the exogenous stochastic process driving the fiscal and technology shocks. The solution requires numerical simulations.[6]

The role of public expenditure variables

The first step in our analysis is to illustrate the "transfer effect" derived in Di Bartolomeo *et al.* (2015). For the sake of comparison we calibrate the model as in Schmitt-Grohé and Uribe (2004a) with the addition that $0 < T/Y < 20$ percent. Therefore, in this section, the labor market is perfectly competitive, $\mu^w = 1$, the nominal wage is flexible, $\xi_w = 0$, and there is no indexation, $\delta_p = \delta_w = 0$. The time unit is meant to be a year; we set the subjective discount rate β to 0.96 to be consistent with a steady-state real rate of return of 4 percent per year; transaction cost parameters A and B are set at 0.011 and 0.075, respectively; we assume the debt-to-GDP ratio is 44 percent; in the goods market, monopolistic competition implies a gross markup of 1.2; and the annualized Rotemberg price adjustment cost is 4.375.[7] The preference parameter η is set so that in the flexible-price steady-state, households allocate 20 percent of their time to work.

In Figure 6.1 we describe the optimal inflation response to the transfer increase and to a corresponding variation in public consumption. Simulations show that

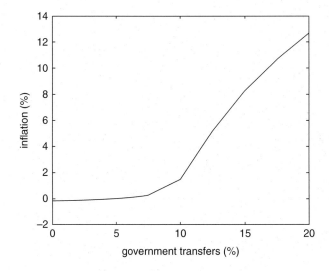

Figure 6.1 Public transfers and optimal inflation.

inflation rapidly increases when T/Y grows beyond the 8 percent threshold. For instance, the optimal inflation rate is close to 3 percent when T/Y is 10 percent, and exceeds 13 percent when the transfer ratio is 20 percent. Simulations also show that in the case where public expenditure is confined to public consumption, optimal inflation would exceed 5 percent only for ratio G/Y larger than 35 percent.

One key mechanism driving the choice of the optimal policy mix is related to the distortionary taxation necessary to finance the additional transfers, which adversely affects the labor supply and reduces the tax base. Thus an increase in public consumption is associated with a fall in private consumption and an increase in the labor supply. The reduction in private consumption, in turn, is associated with a fall in real money holdings, which implies a reduction in the inflation tax base. By contrast, revenues from labor income tax increase due to the labor supply expansion. In this case, the incentive to increase inflation is much reduced.

Real distortions, wage stickiness, and indexation

Recent studies suggest that firms adjust prices more frequently than previously thought. For instance Eichenbaum and Fisher (2007) infer that firms reoptimize prices once every 2.3–3 quarters, but cannot reject the hypothesis that firms reoptimize prices once every two quarters. In Figure 6.4 we consider the effects of different degrees of stickiness (measured as the average duration of price-setting decisions), assuming that $T/Y = 10$ percent. The optimal inflation rate depends on the firms' average adjustment to rest price and substantially increases when the average duration is between 2 and 3 quarters (see Figure 6.2).

Optimal inflation also depends on monopolistic distortions. For instance, when $\mu^p = 1.1$ optimal inflation remains very close to zero for $T/Y \leq 15$ percent. It increases with the price markup, as shown in Figure 6.3.

Introducing wage stickiness has two opposite effects on the optimal inflation rate. On the one hand, monopolistic distortions raise the incentive to substitute labor taxation with inflation tax. On the other, nominal wage adjustment costs strengthen the case for price stability. After setting[8] $\mu^w = 1.2$, we postulate that

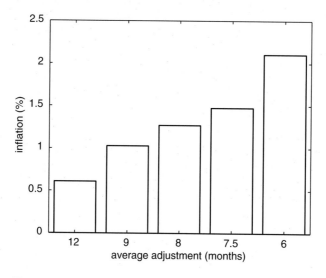

Figure 6.2 Price adjustment and trend inflation.

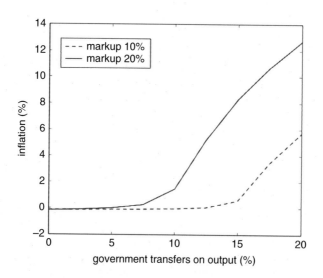

Figure 6.3 Public transfers, market distortions, and optimal inflation.

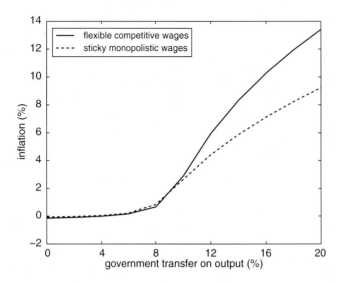

Figure 6.4 Optimal inflation: flexible vs. sticky wages.

price and wage adjustment costs are identical ($\xi_w = \xi_p = 4.37$). Simulations show that for $T/Y < 10$ percent the two effects offset each other (Figure 6.4). Beyond that threshold the wage adjustment cost dominates and the optimal inflation rate falls relative to the perfect competition case.

Inflation costs associated with nominal rigidities depend crucially on assumptions about the prices set by firms that cannot reoptimize. A commonly studied indexation scheme is one whereby non-reoptimized prices increase mechanically at a rate proportional to the economy-wide lagged rate of inflation (Christiano *et al.*, 2005). In many estimated DSGE models, it is assumed that the price and wage are indexed to a weighted average of past and trend inflation, in order to obtain a vertical long-run Phillips curve (see, for instance, Smets and Wouters, 2005, 2007). Recent contributions provide conflicting evidence on the extent of price indexation.[9] In Figure 6.5 we assume an identical degree of wage and price indexation ($\delta_p = \delta_w$) ranging between 0 and 40 percent.[10] When $T/Y > 10$ percent, even a moderate degree of indexation (20 percent) has a non-negligible impact on optimal inflation.

Monetary transactions technology: consumption scale effects

The transaction cost specification adopted in (6.3) constrains the consumption elasticity of money demand to one, in contrast to a large body of empirical literature.[11] Theoretical models accounting for consumption scale effects include Baumol (1952) and Khan *et al.* (2003). Attanasio *et al.* (2002) find substantial economies of scale in cash management using microdata. In a different model,

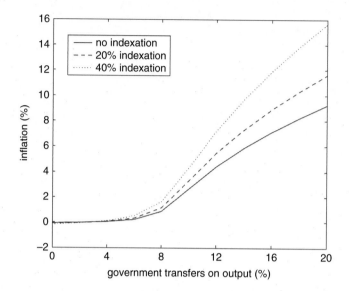

Figure 6.5 Public transfers, indexation, and optimal inflation.

Guidotti and Végh (1993) show that the constant elasticity of scale is an unduly restrictive assumption and that it is optimal to resort to the inflation tax if the transaction costs technology does not exhibit constant returns to scale. We therefore propose a definition of $S_{t,i}$ which accounts for such scale effects

$$S_{t,i} = s(v_{t,i})g(C_{t,i}); \qquad g(C_{t,i}) > 0, \quad g'(C_{t,i}) < 0 \tag{6.19}$$

where $S_{t,i}$ still vanishes at v^* and $g'(C_{t,i}) < 0$[12] allows us to obtain that unit transaction costs are decreasing in consumption. We assume the following specification for the monetary transaction cost[13]

$$g(C_{t,i}) = C_{t,i}^{-\theta} \quad \theta \ge 0. \tag{6.20}$$

Note that for $\theta = 0$, scale effects in consumption expenditure vanish and (6.19) converges to (6.4).

The resulting money demand function

$$\frac{M_t}{P_t} = \frac{C_t}{\sqrt{\frac{B}{A} + (R_t - 1)\frac{C_t^\theta}{A}}} \tag{6.21}$$

is characterized by a consumption elasticity (η_m)

$$\eta_m = \frac{\partial (M_t/P_t)}{\partial C} \frac{C}{M_t/P_t} = \left[1 - \frac{1}{2}\frac{\theta (R-1) C^\theta}{B + (R-1) C^\theta}\right] \le 1. \tag{6.22}$$

Table 6.1 Baseline calibration

$\beta = 0.96$	$\mu^p = 1.20$	$\mu^w = 1.00$
$A = 0.011$	$\xi_p = 4.37$	$\xi_w = 0.00$
$B = 0.075$	$\delta_p = 0.00$	$\delta_w = 0.00$

Table 6.2 Consumption scale effects

θ	Scenario 1		Scenario 2		Scenario 3	
	π	η_m	π	η_m	π	η_m
0.0	−0.15	1.000	4.43	1.000	7.87	1.000
0.4	0.00	0.959	4.63	0.962	8.26	0.962
0.8	0.12	0.956	4.80	0.963	8.55	0.963
1.2	0.19	0.967	4.92	0.974	8.95	0.974
1.6	0.23	0.978	4.98	0.984	9.13	0.984
2.0	0.25	0.987	5.00	0.991	9.22	0.991

This apparently innocuous modification can have substantial implications for our model. In fact, condition (6.6) now becomes

$$\lambda_t = \frac{u_c(C_t, l_t)}{1 + S_t + C_t \frac{\partial S_t}{\partial C_t}} = \frac{u_c(C_t, l_t)}{1 + \frac{s'(v_t)v_t + (1-\theta)s(v_t)}{c^\theta}}. \tag{6.23}$$

The transactions-induced wedge between the marginal utility of consumption and the marginal utility of wealth unambiguously falls in θ for any level of money velocity. Our conjecture is that this should support an increase in the optimal inflation rate. To consider this, observe that in (6.14) the policy wedge Ω_t now falls in θ (as $S_{t,i}$ accounts for scale effects of transaction costs technology). This, in turn, implies that the adverse effect of inflation on the desired real wage is reduced.

We compare three different scenarios. In scenario 1 we represent an economy calibrated as in Schmitt-Grohé and Uribe (2004a), where parameters are calibrated as in Table 6.1 with $G/Y = 0.2$, $T/Y = 0$. In scenario 2 we assume sticky wages (with $\mu^p = 1.2$ and $\xi_w = 4.37$), 20 percent indexation on both prices and wages, public consumption set at 20 percent, and a transfer equal to 11 percent of output. In scenario 3 we assume that prices are relatively flexible and the degree of price indexation to past inflation is modest, whereas wages are characterized by strong indexation, as found in Galí and Rabanal (2005), Rabanal and Rubio-Ramírez (2005), Fernandez-Villaverde and Rubio-Ramirez (2008), and Christiano *et al.* (2010). Relative to scenario 2, we set $\xi_p = 2.5$ (i.e., prices are reset about every six months on average), $\delta_p = 0.15$, and $\delta_w = 0.85$.[14]

Our simulations (Table 6.2) confirm that optimal trend inflation is increasing in θ. The strongest impact on inflation is obtained in scenario 3, when price and nominal wage adjustment costs are relatively milder. In steady-state equilibrium consumption scale effects have a limited, reversed hump-shaped effect on consumption elasticity of money demand, which reaches a minimum value for about $\theta = 0.6$.

Conclusions

Since the work of Phelps (1973), we know that a positive inflation rate might mitigate the distortions induced by the need to finance government budgets. In contrast to previous research, we show that this argument is relevant given the policy mix between government consumption and transfers that we observe in OECD countries. This result holds for plausible parameterization of price and nominal wage adjustment costs. In addition, the size of monopolistic distortions, the degree of price and wage indexation, and the consumption scale effect in monetary transaction costs unambiguously increase the optimal inflation rate. Unfortunately, empirical evidence on these latter variables is rather limited. In fact, estimated DSGE models typically impose markup parameters, assume a vertical long-run Phillips curve, and neglect monetary transaction costs.

Our calibrations show that the prediction of a positive inflation rate holds for countries similar to the United States, where the government size is relatively small. A fortiori, our reconsideration of the Phelps, conjecture appears even more appropriate when considering countries in the Euro area where the welfare state plays a more important role. In contrast with Schmitt-Grohé and Uribe (2011), who argue that central bank inflation targets are too high, our contribution shows that a 2 percent target might be too low, at least for countries where the burden of taxation is rather high, such as those of continental Europe. The explanation for this might be that commitment to a low inflation rate is used to discipline spending decisions, which we assume to be exogenous in our model. In fact, several political economy models point out that distorted policy makers' incentives inflate public expenditures.[15] As shown in Acemoglu *et al.* (2009), the Ramsey-optimal taxation is substantially affected when taxes and public good provision are decided by a self-interested politician who cannot commit to policies. In a similar vein, further research should investigate how these two frictions, i.e., politicians' self-interest and lack of commitment, might affect the choice of the optimal inflation target.

Notes

1 Similar results are found by Khan *et al.* (2003).
2 When solving its optimization problem, the household takes as given goods and bond prices. As usual, we also assume that the household is subject to a solvency constraint that prevents them from engaging in Ponzi schemes.
3 We assume that $\ln z_t$ follows an $AR(1)$ process.
4 For the sake of comparison with the standard New Keynesian framework, following Erceg *et al.* (2000), we neglect the effects of strategic interaction assuming the wage setters are atomistic. The effects of interactions are however introduced by, among others, Bratsiotis (2008), Gnocchi (2009), and Tirelli *et al.* (2013).
5 We assume that $\ln g_t$, $g_t = G_t / Y_t$ evolves exogenously following an independent $AR(1)$ process. By contrast, the level of the real transfer is not stochastic.

6 These are obtained implementing Schmitt-Grohé and Uribe (2004b) second-order approximation routines.
7 This implies that contracts are re-optimized on average every nine months (see Schmitt-Grohé and Uribe, 2004a).
8 Our choice of the wage markup follows Erceg *et al.* (2006) and is close to the value reported in Galí *et al.* (2007), but is lower than the calibration in Erceg *et al.* (2000). It should be noted, however, that Christiano *et al.* (2005, 2010) choose values much closer to one. We will consider a different calibration later.
9 Cogley and Sbordone (2008) estimate a New Keynesian Phillips Curve, finding that price indexation in the U.S. is zero once a time-varying inflation trend is accounted for. By contrast, Barnes *et al.* (2009) show that this result is not robust in the introduction of more flexible indexation schemes. Aruoba and Schorfheide (2009) find that 15 percent of firms optimize in each period, 60 percent of firms fully index their price to past inflation, and the remaining firms hold their price constant. Microdata analyses suggest that indexation parameters are lower for consumption prices than for nominal wages (Du Caju *et al.*, 2008; Maćkowiak and Smets, 2008). In line with this result, Fernandez-Villaverde and Rubio-Ramirez (2008) find that $\delta = 0.15$, $\delta_w = 0.85$.
10 Introducing asymmetries in the degrees of price and wage indexation would not affect our conclusions (simulations' results available upon request).
11 See Choi and Oh (2003), Dib (2004), Knell and Stix (2005), and references therein. Christiano *et al.* (2005) obtain an estimate of 0.1.
12 We also assume that $g(C)$ is twice continuously differentiable.
13 When $\theta = 0$, scale effects in consumption expenditure vanish and (6.19) converges to the transaction technology specified in Schmitt-Grohé and Uribe (2004a).
14 These indexation parameters are taken from Fernandez-Villaverde and Rubio-Ramirez (2008).
15 See Tornell and Lane (1999) and Persson and Tabellini (2003, 2004).

References

Acemoglu, D., M. Golosov and A. Tsyvinski (2009), "Political economy of Ramsey taxation," *NBER Working Papers* No 15302.
Attanasio, O. P., L. Guiso and T. Jappelli (2002), "The demand for money, financial innovation, and the welfare cost of inflation: An analysis with household data," *Journal of Political Economy*, 110: 317–351.
Aruoba, S. B. and F. Schorfheide (2009), "Sticky prices versus monetary frictions: An estimation of policy trade-offs," *NBER Working Paper* No 14870.
Barnes, M., F. Gumbau-Brisa, D. Lie and G. Olivei (2009), "Closed-form estimates of the New Keynesian Phillips curve with time-varying trend inflation," *Federal Reserve Bank of Boston Working Paper* No 09-15.
Baumol, W. J. (1952), "The transactions demand for cash: an inventory theoretic approach," *Quarterly Journal of Economics*, 66(4): 545–556.
Bratsiotis, G. J. (2008), "Influential price and wage setters, monetary policy and real effects," *European Journal of Political Economy*, 24: 503–517.
Choi, W. G. and S. Oh (2003), "A money demand function with output uncertainty, monetary uncertainty, and financial innovations," *Journal of Money, Credit and Banking*, 35: 685–709.
Christiano, L. J., M. Eichenbaum and C. L. Evans (2005), "Nominal rigidities and the dynamic effects of a shock to monetary policy," *Journal of Political Economy*, 113: 1–45.
Christiano, L. J., M. Trabandt and K. Walentin (2010), "DSGE models for monetary policy analysis," *NBER Working Paper* No 16074.

Cogley, T. and A. Sbordone (2008), "Trend inflation, indexation and inflation persistence in the New Keynesian Phillips curve," *American Economic Review*, 98: 2101–2126.

Di Bartolomeo, G., P. Tirelli and N. Acocella (2015), "The comeback of inflation as an optimal public finance tool," *International Journal of Central Banking*, 11: 43–70.

Dib, A. (2004), "Nominal rigidities and monetary policy in Canada," *Journal of Macroeconomics*, 28: 303–325.

Du Caju, P., E. Gautier, D. Momferatou and M. Ward-Warmedinger (2008), " Institutional features of wage bargaining in 22 EU countries, the US and Japan," *European Central Bank Working Paper* No 974.

Eichenbaum, M. S. and J. D. M. Fisher (2007), "Estimating the frequency of price re-optimization in Calvo-style models," *Journal of Monetary Economics*, 54(7): 2032–2047.

Erceg, C. J., D. W. Dale and A. T. Levin (2000), "Optimal monetary policy with staggered wage and price contracts," *Journal of Monetary Economics*, 46: 281–313.

Erceg, C. J., L. Guerrieri, and C. Gust (2006), "SIGMA: A new open economy model for policy analysis," *International Journal of Central Banking*, 2: 1–50.

Fernandez-Villaverde, J. and J. Rubio-Ramirez (2008), "How structural are structural parameters?," in Acemoglu, D., K. Rogoff and M. Woodford (eds), *NBER Macroeconomics Annual 2007*, Cambridge, MA, MIT Press: 83–137.

Friedman, M. (1977), "Nobel lecture: Inflation and unemployment," *Journal of Political Economy*, 85: 451–472.

Galí, J. and P. Rabanal (2005), "Technology shocks and aggregate fluctuations: How well does the real business cycle model fit postwar U.S. data?," in Gertler M. and Rogoff K. (eds), *NBER Macroeconomics Annual 2004*, Cambridge, MA, MIT Press: 225–318.

Galí, J., M. Gertler and J. D. López-Salido (2007), "Markups, gaps, and the welfare costs of business fluctuations," *The Review of Economics and Statistics*, 89: 44–59.

Gnocchi, S. (2009), "Non-atomistic wage setters and monetary policy in a New Keynesian framework," *Journal of Money, Credit and Banking*, 41: 1613–1630.

Guidotti, P. and C. Végh (1993), "The optimal inflation tax when money reduces transaction costs," *Journal of Monetary Economics*, 31: 189–205.

Khan, A., R. G. King and A. L. Wolman (2003), "Optimal monetary policy," *Review of Economic Studies*, 70: 825–860.

Klein, P., V. Quadrini and J. V. Rios-Rull (2005), "Optimal time-consistent taxation with international mobility of capital," *The B.E. Journal of Macroeconomics*, 5(1): doi 10.2202/1534-6013.1142.

Knell, M. and H. Stix (2005), "The income elasticity of money demand: A meta-analysis of empirical results," *Journal of Economic Surveys*, 19: 513–533.

Maćkowiak, B. and F. R. Smets (2008), "On implications of micro price data for macro models," *CEPR Discussion Papers* No 6961.

Persson, T. and G. Tabellini (2003), *The Economic Effects of Constitutions*, Cambridge, MA: MIT Press.

Persson, T. and G. Tabellini (2004), "Constitutional rules and fiscal policy outcomes," *American Economic Review*, 94: 25–45.

Phelps, E. S. (1973), "Inflation in the theory of public finance," *The Swedish Journal of Economics*, 75: 67–82.

Rabanal, P. and J. F. Rubio-Ramírez (2005), "Comparing New Keynesian models of the business cycle: A Bayesian approach," *Journal of Monetary Economics*, 52: 1151–1166.

Rotemberg, J. J. (1982), "Sticky prices in the United States," *Journal of Political Economy*, 90: 1187–1211.

Schmitt-Grohé, S. and M. Uribe (2004a), "Optimal fiscal and monetary policy under sticky prices," *Journal of Economic Theory*, 114: 198–230.

Schmitt-Grohé, S. and M. Uribe (2004b), "Solving dynamic general equilibrium models using a second-order approximation to the policy function," *Journal of Economic Dynamics and Control*, 28: 755–775.

Schmitt-Grohé, S. and M. Uribe (2011), "The optimal rate of inflation," in Friedman, B. M. and M. Woodford (eds), *Handbook of Monetary Economics*, Amsterdam, Elsevier: 723–828.

Smets, F. and R. Wouters (2005), "Comparing shocks and frictions in US and euro area business cycles: A Bayesian DSGE Approach," *Journal of Applied Econometrics*, 20: 161–183.

Smets, F. and R. Wouters (2007), "Shocks and frictions in US business cycles: A Bayesian DSGE approach," *American Economic Review*, 97: 586–606.

Tirelli P., N. Acocella and G. Di Bartolomeo (2013), "Trend inflation as a workers' discipline device," *Empirica*, 40: 215–235.

Tornell, A. and P. Lane (1999), "Voracity and growth," *American Economic Review*, 89: 139–145.

7 The long-term effects of government budget constraints on GDP growth

An empirical study on OECD countries (1980–2009)

Silvia Fedeli and Francesco Forte

Introduction

Our chapter aims to explore the potential effects on long-term gross domestic product (GDP) growth of budget rules that limit the level of deficit, looking at whether the levels of taxation (and expenditure) are relevant from this point of view. Specifically, we analyze the long-term relationship between real GDP growth rate and government budget constraints as captured by total deficit (i.e., net lending government ratio to GDP, NLG/GDP) and tax burden with a panel dataset of 20 OECD (Organization for Economic and Co-operative Development) countries from 1980 to 2009.

Our research differs from the researches by Reinhart and Rogoff (2010, 2012) that focus on the effects of different levels of government debt and external debt on GDP growth and inflation from a centuries-long perspective. Reinhart and Rogoff (2010) used data on 44 countries spanning about 200 years and with more than 3,700 annual observations, covering a wide range of different political systems, institutions, exchange-rate arrangements, and historic circumstances. They found that the threshold for public debt (negative) impact on growth is similar in advanced and emerging economies. The threshold is lower for external debt (public and private), usually denominated in a foreign currency. There is no apparent contemporaneous link between inflation and high levels of public debt for the advanced countries as a group.[1] Consistently, Reinhart *et al.* (2012) find that public debt overhang episodes are associated with lower growth. The long duration belies the view that the correlation is caused mainly by debt build-up in recessions. The long duration also implies that the cumulative shortfall in output from debt overhang is potentially massive.

At a theoretical level, the negative consequences of fiscal deficit and tax increases as instruments used to cope with the debt burden were already pointed out in the classic Ricardo Theorem which establishes an equivalence between a current extraordinary property tax and the issue of government bonds with infinite maturity and annual interest payments in all following years to be financed by future permanent taxes on property income. Rational taxpayers would find the two methods equivalent—because the estate's value shall be equally reduced either by the extraordinary property tax or by future taxes on estate's income—and will therefore reduce their consumption. However, in the case of the extraordinary tax on property, taxpayers must depart from a share of their property equivalent to the tax, while in the case of public debt they face a much smaller immediate tax burden on their income. Therefore, in the first case they will increase their present savings to restore their own property, while in the second they will not do so. Thus, the burden of future taxes shall fall to future investors.[2]

In Barro's (1979) theorization of Ricardian equivalence, the expectation of future taxes increases present savings so that a budget deficit does not affect present demand, while its short-term effect on growth via supply may be negative because of the reduction of the return on savings. Within the strand of literature that tries to relate the components of government budget constraint with economic growth,[3] we exploit recent results on cointegration analysis and show that there exists a long-term equilibrium relationship between GDP growth rate and government budget constraints. We show that a budget deficit's reduction via expenditure cuts is more effective, from a long-term perspective, than that obtained via tax increases.

We do not explore the details of the composition of expenditures and taxes and do not deny that this issue may be relevant. In this respect, Barro's (1990) endogenous growth model argues that all taxes that reduce the return on capital have a negative impact on growth, while governments can also reduce spending to cope with their debt overhang. On the basis of Barro's 1990 model, Peretto (2007) demonstrates that the tax structure and public-expenditure composition are important, unlike the level of the deficit/GDP or of debt/GDP (or size of the government). That is, distortionary and other taxes have more damaging effects on growth than deficits, so that simultaneously reducing the latter and raising these taxes is bad for growth in net terms. However, deficit-financed increases in productive public spending would appear to be modestly growth-enhancing.

Kneller *et al.* (1999), examining the data of 22 OECD countries from 1970 to 1995, found a difference in the effects on growth of "non-distortionary" taxes (with respect to investment) and non-distortionary taxes and expenditures that are "productive" or "unproductive" (where the former appear in private production functions). Gemmell *et al.* (2011) study budgetary deficit or surplus in connection with GDP in the presence of non-distortionary and distortionary taxes, and productive and other expenditures with similar results. Nevertheless, in a long-term empirical research it is hardly possible to distinguish between distortionary and non-distortionary taxes and between current productive and non-productive expenditure considering their classification in existing standard categories. At any rate, what matters is what governments really do, and not what, in an abstract world, well-intentioned rational politicians should do.

A partly different stream of the empirical research is concentrated on the short/medium-term effects of fiscal consolidation on GDP growth in situations of debt crisis.[4] The huge literature on this subject—which appeared in the early 1990s and included, among others, Giavazzi and Pagano (1990), Ardagna (2004), Giavazzi *et al.* (2000), McDermott and Wescott (1996), Von Hagen and Strauch (2001), Blanchard and Perotti (2002), Romer and Romer (2010), Mountford and Uhlig (2008), Ramey (2008), and Alesina and Ardagna (2009)[5]— generally agreed that cuts in public expenditure should be preferred to increases in taxes. By exploiting recent results on cointegration analysis, our results for some aspects complement such literature by explaining that the reason why some short/medium-term policies work better is that, ceteris paribus, the estimated "long-term" growth effects of budget deficit and high tax burden (and the related Government size)[6] are negative, mainly for European Union (EU) countries.

As a result, the suggestion that the EU rule of budget balance shall in and of itself foster a long-term growth in the countries that adopt it is not expected to work. Budgetary rules intending to balance the budget and be effective for long-term growth should be completed with limits on the tax burden. In addition, our analysis, carried out for two sub-samples of 13 OECD EU countries and 7 non-EU countries with more flexible markets, shows that, among others, labor market flexibility might matter for the long-term effect of budgetary policies on growth. If price increases via monetary expansion and the devaluation of the rate of exchange is prevented by monetary stability rules, rigid wages cannot be devalued. The pursuance of budgetary balance may thus imply lower growth and higher unemployment. Although further empirical research is needed to throw light on this crucial theme, this outcome implies a criticism of the EU rules of "sound" budgetary behavior, which do not require labor flexibility, while prescribing a balanced budget in the medium term and price stability.

The rest of the chapter is structured as follows. In the next section we present the model to be empirically tested. Then we report the results for the 20 OECD countries over the period 1980–2009. We then repeat the same empirical analysis, splitting the sample into the 13 OECD countries belonging to the EU and the 7 non-EU OECD countries. Conclusions follow in the final section.

The model

We consider the rate of growth of GDP, NLG/GDP, and Government receipts (GR) to GDP and verify cointegration among them by using a panel consisting of 20 OECD countries and spanning the years 1980 to 2009; the data have annual frequency and the variables are taken in levels. Data on GDP growth and on the two fiscal variables are obtained from OECD sources. The countries considered are Japan, the United States, Australia, Canada, Iceland, Norway, and Korea, plus 13 OECD countries belonging to the EU (i.e., Austria, Belgium, Denmark, Finland, France, Greece, Ireland, Italy, the Netherlands, Portugal, Spain, Sweden, and the UK). The summary statistics for the considered variables are in Table 7.1.

The government budget is composed of expenditures, revenues, and deficits–surpluses. It is substantially a "closed system" and any change in one element must be balanced by an equal and opposite change in another element. For long-run growth analysis, the government budget constraint is thus correctly represented by the included fiscal variables, i.e., NLG/GDP and GR/GDP.[7] Therefore, we

Table 7.1 Summary statistics of the considered variables

Variable	No. of observations	Mean	Standard deviation	Min	Max
GDP rate of growth	600	2.535207	2.556599	−7.76897	10.88061
NLG/GDP	600	−2.47993	4.782617	−16.0091	18.76811
GR/GDP	600	42.65967	9.273697	19.4662	63.47088
Year	600	1994.5	8.662663	1980	2009
Country	600	14.75	8.877999	1	20

postulate the following model

$$Y_{it} = \theta_{1i} X_{it} + \ldots + \mu_i + \varepsilon_{it} \tag{7.1}$$

where Y is the rate of growth of GDP in real terms, X is the set of fiscal policy variables entering the cointegrating relationship (i.e., NLG/GDP and GR/GDP), μ_i are intercept country effects, ε_{it} are white noise errors, $i = 1, 2, \ldots, N$ is an index identifying the nations, and $t = 1, 2, \ldots, T$ identifies the periods (years). If the variables are $I(1)$ and cointegrated, then the error term is $I(0)$. The long-run coefficients, θ_{1i}, are of particular interest. The correct interpretation of each estimated fiscal parameter is the effect of a unit change in the relevant included fiscal variable offset by a unit change in the fiscal element omitted from the regression.

The setting of Equation (7.1) can be modified to account for cross-section dependence in the data. This can be generated by unobserved factors, which, in this framework, can be regarded as common shocks affecting all countries, but to a different degree. Considering the vector X_i of the regressors included in (7.1), the model can be described as follows

$$Y_{it} = \theta_{1i} X_{it} + \gamma_i f_{it} + \mu_i + \varepsilon_{it} \quad \text{and} \tag{7.2}$$

$$X_{it} = \alpha_i + \phi_i f_{it} + \psi_i g_{it} + u_{it} \tag{7.3}$$

where f and g are unobserved factors affecting Y directly or indirectly (i.e., impacting on the set of variables X), and ϕ_i and ψ_i are the country-specific factor loads which cause a heterogeneous response to the common shocks. Failure to detect cross-section correlation and, thus, to take it into account when producing estimates, will give rise to the omitted-variables problems, thus causing bias in estimates and erroneous inference.

The result of the analysis is a cointegrating relationship that includes the rate of growth of GDP as dependent variable, and both the size of fiscal deficit and government revenues as a percentage of GDP as explanatory variables. That is, the long-run equilibrium for the rate of growth of GDP is affected by the government budget constraint. We will refer to "long-run" empirical growth effects of fiscal policies in the context of a stochastic autoregressive distributed lag (ARDL) where the "long run" describes the equilibrium (see Pesaran *et al.*, 1997). Given our annual dataset covering about 30 years per country, where equilibrium effects of fiscal policy are observed, they would appear to persist within the time span of our data. Whether they represent the "permanent" or "steady-state" effects envisaged by some theories is less clear.

The empirical analysis for the 20 OECD countries

The first step in our analysis is to test whether the variables are non-stationary. We employ the test of Im *et al.* (2003). The tests are normally distributed under the null hypothesis of non-stationary and permit the individual autoregressive roots to differ across the cross-sectional units. For the implementation of the test, all bandwidths and lag lengths are chosen according to $4(T/100)^{2/9}$. The number of lags chosen according to the Akaike criterion is 3. The results reported in Table 7.2 indicate that, once a linear time trend has been accommodated, we end up with a rejection of the null at the 1 percent level of significance for a number of lags going from 2 to 6 (in Table 7.2 we have marked in grey the statistics that accept the null). We therefore conclude that the variables appear to be non-stationary.

To provide evidence in favor of the cointegration hypothesis we apply the Westerlund (2007) tests on cointegration (see also Persyn and Westerlund, 2008). This tests lifts a restriction that is embedded in previous tests for cointegration requiring that the long-run parameters for the variables in their levels are equal to the short-run parameters for the variables in their differences; when the above restriction is not correct, it causes a significant loss of power and the failure to reject the null of no cointegration. Table 7.3 reports the outcome of four tests; in the first two the hypothesis alternative to the null is that the panel is cointegrated as a whole, while

Table 7.2 Im–Pesaran–Shin (2003) test on 22 OECD countries

Test statistic t-bar	Augmented by 1 lag	Augmented by 2 lags	Augmented by 3 lags	Augmented by 4 lags	Augmented by 5 lags	Augmented by 6 lags
GDP growth rate – deterministic chosen: constant and trend						
IPS	−2.637	−2.221	−2.115	−1.784	−1.502	−1.477
GDP growth rate – deterministic chosen: constant						
IPS	−2.541	−2.106	−1.960	−1.567	−1.288	−1.233
NLG/GDP – deterministic chosen: constant and trend						
IPS	−2.251	−2.001	−1.754	−1.345	−1.189	−1.278
NLG/GDP – deterministic chosen: constant						
IPS	−2.341	−2.198	−1.893	−1.522	−1.582	−1.470
GR/GDP – deterministic chosen: constant and trend						
IPS	−2.119	−2.038	−1.930	−1.756	−1.525	−1.534
GR/GDP – deterministic chosen: constant						
IPS	−1.771	−1.719	−1.598	−1.396	−1.387	−1.370

Notes: The unit-root tests take a unit root as the null hypothesis. IPS: Im–Pesaran–Shin test.

Table 7.3 Westerlund ECM panel cointegration tests: GDP growth on NLG/GDP, GR/GDP

Statistic	Value	Z-value	P-value
G_t	−3.340	−8.357	0.0000
G_a	−14.439	−7.045	0.0000
P_t	−15.133	−8.235	0.0000
P_a	−12.075	−8.738	0.0000

Notes: Average AIC selected lag length: 0.9; average AIC selected lead length: 0. Results for H_0: no cointegration.

Table 7.4 Long-run equation normalized on GDP growth rate

	Coefficient	Standard error	t
NLG/GDP	0.179691	0.017864	10.06
GR/GDP	−0.079990	0.009213	−8.68
Constant	6.572609	0.413493	15.9

Notes: Robust regression, number of observations $= 600$, $F(2, 597) = 72.67$, prob $> F = 0.0000$.

the other two test the alternative that at least one unit is cointegrated. The values of the statistics suggest that we can reject the null hypothesis of no cointegration at the 1 percent level in either case.

On the basis of the Westerlund panel cointegration test, in Table 7.4, we estimate the equation representing the long-term relations obtained for the 20 OECD countries.

The result shows a clear significant impact of both NLG/GDP and the tax burden on GDP growth rate as follows. In the long term, improving the budget balance (recall that NLG/GDP takes on a negative sign in the presence of a budget deficit) increases the GDP rate of growth and, at any given NLG/GDP, reducing the tax burden also increases the GDP rate of growth.

Before adding further comments, notice that the presence of cross-section dependence within the framework of our dataset is highly likely. Developed economies tend to be hit by globally common shocks even though they are affected in a heterogeneous manner, i.e., the impact varies according to their institutions and, in particular, to their fiscal framework. For a review of the panel time series literature, see Eberhardt and Teal (2011). Here we investigate this issue by implementing the most commonly used test for cross-section dependency (Pesaran, 2003, 2004).' The cross-section dependency (CD) test allows for the computation of the tests' statistics as reported in Table 7.5.

The above tests reject the null of lack of cross-section dependence. We thus proceed by repeating the same sequence of procedures—i.e., testing for unit root and for the presence of cointegration and finally estimating cointegrating relationships—but allowing for cross-section dependence.

We first run the t-test for unit roots in heterogeneous panels with cross-section dependence (Covariate Augmented Dickey–Fuller (CADF)), proposed by Pesaran

Table 7.5 Average correlation coefficients and Pesaran (2004) CD test

Variables series tested	CD test	P-value	Corr	abs(Corr)
GDP growth rate	36.17	0.000	0.479	0.483
NLG/GDP	31.13	0.000	0.412	0.465
GR/GDP	14.98	0.000	0.198	0.514

Notes: Group variable: country; number of groups: 20. Under the null hypothesis of cross-section independence CD $\sim N(0,1)$.

(2003), which is the homologous of Im, Pesaran and Shin's (IPS, 2003) test. This test is based on the mean of individual Dickey–Fuller (DF) (or Augmented Dickey–Fuller (ADF)) *t*-statistics of each unit in the panel and it assumes as the null hypothesis that all series are non-stationary.[8] We consider also a truncated version of CADF statistics which has finite first- and second-order moments. It allows the avoidance of size distortions, especially in the case of models with residual serial correlations and linear trends (Pesaran, 2003). As in this case, the size of T is fixed (and is not large enough to rely on asymptotic properties). The test is applied to the deviations of the variable from initial cross-section mean ensuring that the CADF statistics do not depend on the nuisance parameters. Lags of the dependent variable are introduced with the aim of controlling for serial correlation in the errors. All bandwidths and lag lengths are chosen according to $4(T/100)^{2/9}$. The number of lags chosen according to the Akaike criterion is 3. However, we investigated results for a number of lags spanning from 1 to 6, with the ensuing statistics $Z[t\text{-bar}]$ distributing standard normal under the null hypothesis of non-stationary. The vast majority of the statistics, reported in Table 7.6, confirm the non-stationary already found under the assumption of cross-section independence. Only statistics numbers highlighted in grey provide a different outcome.

This result prompts a further test to confirm that the variables are still cointegrated. Following Westerlund (2007) and Persyn and Westerlund (2008), we assume their same data-generating process for their error correction test and test for cross-sectional independence in its residuals by means of the Breusch–Pagan statistic. Notice that the test requires $T > N$. We tested for independence of the 20 cross-sectional units and assumed the same short-term dynamics for all series. In this case, based on 24 complete observations over panel units, the Breusch–Pagan Lagrange multiplier (LM) test of independence is $\chi^2(190) = 362.354$ ($Pr = 0.000$). As the result strongly indicates the presence of common factors affecting the cross-sectional units, we bootstrapped (1,500 replications) robust critical values for the test statistics related to the Westerlund error correction model (ECM) panel cointegration tests. Given that the Akaike optimal lag and lead search is time consuming when combined with bootstrapping, we kept the short-term dynamics fixed. The outcome in Table 7.7 shows that when we take into account cross-sectional dependencies, the tests still reject the null hypothesis of no cointegration.

Table 7.6 Panel unit-root tests Pesaran (2007)

Test statistic	$P=1$	$P=2$	$P=3$	$P=4$	$P=5$	$P=6$
Rate of growth of GDP constant and trend						
CIPS	−3.543	−2.754	−2.300	−2.083	−1.595	−1.766
CIPS*	−3.543	−2.754	−2.300	−2.083	−1.595	−1.766
Rate of growth of GDP constant constant						
CIPS	−3.258	−2.488	−1.984	−1.641	−1.131	−1.084
CIPS*	−3.258	−2.488	−1.984	−1.641	−1.131	−1.084
NLG/GDP constant and trend						
CIPS	−2.737	−2.186	−2.069	−1.832	−1.666	−1.416
CIPS*	−2.737	−2.186	−2.069	−1.832	−1.666	−1.416
NLG/GDP GDP constant						
CIPS	−2.320	−1.940	−1.738	−1.551	−1.478	−1.219
CIPS*	−2.320	−1.940	−1.738	−1.551	−1.478	−1.219
GR_GDP constant and trend						
CIPS	−2.126	−1.948	−1.868	−1.669	−1.435	−1.376
CIPS*	−2.126	−1.948	−1.868	−1.669	−1.435	−1.348
GR GDP constant						
CIPS	−1.722	−1.575	−1.595	−1.589	−1.433	−1.401
CIPS*	−1.722	−1.575	−1.595	−1.589	−1.433	−1.401

Notes: Rejection of the null hypothesis indicates stationary in at least one region. The considered critical values are at 1%. CIPS: cross-section augmented Im–Pesaran–Shin test; CIPS*: truncated cross-section augmented Im–Pesaran–Shin test.

Table 7.7 Westerlund ECM panel cointegration tests on rate of growth of GDP, NLG/GDP, GR/GDP. Bootstrapped critical values

Statistic	Value	Z-value	P-value	Robust P-value
G_t	−3.526	−9.152	0.000	0.000
G_a	−10.969	−4.208	0.000	0.000
P_t	−15.274	−8.341	0.000	0.007
P_a	−11.87	−8.551	0.000	0.003

Notes: Average Akaike Information Criterion (AIC) selected lag length: 0.9; average AIC selected lead length: 0.9. Results for H_0: no cointegration.

Given this outcome, we evaluated if, first of all, the presence of cross-section correlation changes the results when estimating the cointegration vector. The long-term coefficients estimated by means of the augmented mean group (AMG) estimator by Bond and Eberhardt (2009) and Eberhardt and Teal (2010) are reported in Table 7.8. As a robustness check, we also estimate the long-term coefficients by means of the augmented mean group estimator where a common dynamic process is imposed with unit coefficient (see Bond and Eberhardt, 2009; Eberhardt and Teal, 2010).[9] Details are available upon request.

Table 7.8 Augmented mean group estimator (Bond and Eberhardt, 2009; Eberhardt and Teal, 2010). Dependent variable GDP growth rate

	Coefficient	*Standard error*	z
NLG/GDP	0.293141	0.057893	5.06
GR/GDP	−0.259	0.068226	−3.8
Z	0.910156	0.090316	10.08
Constant	12.08296	2.551203	4.74

Notes: Number of observations = 600; group variable: country; number of groups = 20; observations per group: min = 30, avg = 30.0, max = 30; Wald $chi^2(2) = 31.91$; Prob > $chi^2 = 0.0000$. Root mean squared error (sigma): 1.5031.

Common dynamic process Z included as additional regressor. All coefficients represent averages across groups (country). Coefficient averages computed as unweighted means.

The standard errors reported in the averaged regression results are constructed following Pesaran and Smith (1995), thus testing the significant difference of the average coefficient from zero. In practice, the group-specific coefficients are regressed on an intercept, either without any weighting or attaching less weight to "outliers."

Results of the AMG estimator provide additional evidence in favor of our specification. They are visibly aligned with those presented in the absence of cross-section dependence; in particular they are very similar to the estimates produced in Table 7.4. The regressors are still significant and correctly signed, but, interestingly, their size is much bigger. In particular, the budget balance coefficient, NLG/GDP, is positive. The budget balance measures the difference between tax revenues and government expenditure. The result, showing that deficits reduce GDP growth rate in the long run, indicates that if GDP growth is a dominant policy objective, efforts and specific policy actions are needed to redress the situation. The estimated coefficient for GR/GDP is again significant and negative. This result confirms that a reduction in the tax burden, under an invariant NLG/GDP, stimulates GDP growth. Indeed, high taxes may weigh heavily on labor (directly, through the fiscal wedge, or indirectly, taxing mass consumptions), on capital, or on entrepreneurs, thus discouraging employment, savings, investments, productivity, and the development of enterprises.

Notice also that the estimated parameters are of similar absolute magnitudes and opposite signs. As for the magnitude of the estimated parameters of fiscal deficit and tax burden, we find that positive growth effects associated with budget surplus (0.29) are counteracted by tax burden changes with negative growth effects (−0.26). The estimated coefficients suggest that a reduction in the budget deficit has an effect on GDP growth which is bigger than that achieved by a reduction in the tax burden. Therefore a reduction in the budget deficit by means of a reduction in public expenditure is more effective than a reduction in the deficit obtained by an increased tax burden. Moreover, there is clear evidence that this effect on GDP growth is persistent over many years. The different effect in the growth rate between the two policies is 0.03. Anyway, clearly, the result thus reached may be positive from the point of view of the budgetary soundness, but not much from the point of view of its effects on the low growth of a developed country. The results change if the reduction of the deficit is undertaken entirely by reducing the expenditure. Indeed, a change of 0.3 points in the long-run rate of growth for any reduction of 1 point in the deficit implies that a country with a long-run deficit of 4 percent balancing its budget obtains an increase in the average growth rate of 1.16 percent. Only if they have operated a massive persistent tax cut without a corresponding increase in the deficit was the result significant for the GDP rate of growth.

Splitting the sample into two groups: 13 EU countries and 7 non-EU countries

A likely observation from previous analysis is that the countries considered are very different both in terms of their public economies and their economic markets' structures and institutions. For example, considerivng the 13 countries belonging to the EU as compared with the 7 non-EU countries, we see the following behavior of the critical variables (Figure 7.1: panels (1)–(4)). Notice that the EU group includes the UK, not included in the Euro area, but excludes Germany, because of statistical problems after the unification.

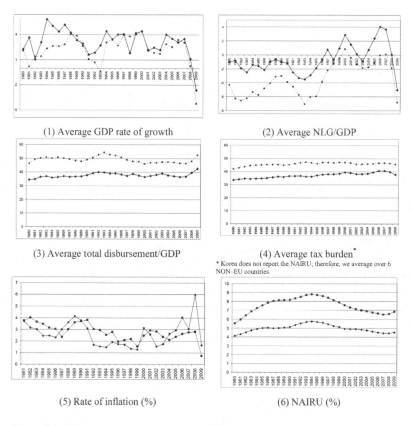

(1) Average GDP rate of growth   (2) Average NLG/GDP

(3) Average total disbursement/GDP   (4) Average tax burden[*]

* Korea does not report the NAIRU; therefore, we average over 6 NON–EU countries.

(5) Rate of inflation (%)   (6) NAIRU (%)

Figure 7.1 EU countries (squares) vs. non-EU countries (diamonds).

The average yearly GDP growth rates (Figure 7.1(1)) of the EU countries are lower than those of the non-EU developed countries and show smaller downward fluctuations and smaller peaks, so that the general picture is one of mature economies with a modest elasticity upward and downward in their growth path. On the other hand, the yearly average budgetary deficits (Figure 7.1(2)) of the EU countries are much greater than those of the non-EU countries. It is true that the trend of public deficits in EU countries was different before and after the Maastricht Treaty. However, the non-EU countries, without the constraint of this Treaty, have systematically shown a better performance. Moreover, the constraints of the Treaty, which reduced the level of the deficits in the EU countries, generated surpluses for only a few years between the end of the twentieth century and the beginning of the twenty-first century, with the non-EU countries having more years with higher surpluses. There were probably loopholes in the Maastricht Treaty constraints.

Clearly the average ratio of public expenditures to GDP (Figure 7.1(3)) is much greater in EU than in non-EU countries, ranging, respectively, around 50 percent against 40 percent. The ratio of public expenditures to GDP of EU countries, after the Maastricht Treaty, decreases below the 50 percent level, and the difference between the ratio of public spending to GDP of EU and non-EU OECD countries changes only a little.

The average ratio of GR to GDP (Figure 7.1(4)) of EU countries, with the exception of the early 1980s, is around 45 percent or above, while that of the non-EU developed countries is below 40 percent for almost the whole period. Moreover, in the two groups of countries, even the rate of inflation (Figure 7.1(5)) makes a difference.

From the 1990s up to 2004, paradoxically the inflation rate in EU countries is higher than in non-EU countries in spite of the monetary policy of the European Central Bank (ECB). Since the ECB has actually pursued a cautious monetary policy, the explanation of the differential in inflation rate has to be found in other factors such as the lower growth of productivity caused by a greater size of the public sector and rigidities of the structures of the market economy. Among them, there emerges the difference in the labor market structures, of which the level of the Natural Rate of Unemployment (NAIRU) may be a proxy (Figure 7.1(6)).

It is clear that the Natural Rate of Unemployment in EU countries is higher than that in non-EU countries. Its average level ranges from 5.5 at the beginning of the period to 7 at the end of the period, with a peak close to 9 in the mid-1990s. In non-Euro countries, it was about 4 percent, at the beginning of the period and increased to a level close to 6 percent during the 1990s, then diminished constantly to about 5 percent and less in the current century. It is also interesting to note that the difference between the two average NAIRUs tends to remain at about 2.5–3.0 percentage points, so that the EU average is about 50 percent higher than the non-EU average NAIRU. One may thus argue that in the EU countries there are greater structural rigidities in the labor supply.

On this basis, we further test the above relationship for the 13 OECD countries belonging to the EU and the 7 non-EU OECD countries. With this purpose, we repeat for the reduced samples the same set of tests carried out in the previous section. In particular, we repeat the same battery of tests in the absence or not of cross-section dependence. Details are available upon request.

In Table 7.9 and 7.10 we report the long-term relationship in the absence of cross-section dependence in the two samples.

It is interesting to note that with respect to the long-term relationships obtained for the 19 OECD countries (Table 7.4), considering the sample of 13 EU countries determines a slight worsening of the effect of public surplus on the rate of GDP

Table 7.9 Long-term equation, dependent variable: GDP growth rate

	Coefficient	*Standard error*	*t*
Panel A – 13 OECD/EU countries			
NLG/GDP	0.167902	0.024564	6.84
GR/GDP	−0.06576	0.013221	−4.97
Constant	5.998006	0.648646	9.25
Panel B – 7 OECD/ non-EU countries			
NLG/GDP	0.269691	0.033369	8.08
GR/GDP	−0.1443	0.018982	−7.6
Constant	8.775166	0.72998	12.02

Notes: Panel A: Number of observations $= 390$; $F(2,387) = 26.56$; Prob $> F = 0.0000$; robust regression.

Panel B: Number of observations $= 210$; $F(2,207) = 43.45$; Prob $> F = 0.0000$; robust regression.

Table 7.10 Bond and Eberhardt (2009) and Eberhardt and Teal (2010) augmented mean group estimator, dependent variable GDP growth rate

	Coefficient	*Standard error*	*Z*
Panel A – 13 OECD/EU countries			
NLG/GDP	0.164713	0.035115	4.69
Gov.Rec/GDP	−0.157520	0.059518	−2.65
R	0.983477	0.081729	12.03
Constant	9.413440	2.703746	3.48
Panel B – 7 OECD/ non-EU countries			
NLG/GDP	0.348224	0.095695	3.64
Gov.Rec/GDP	−0.352590	0.116982	−3.01
K	0.914402	0.110225	8.30
Constant	13.320550	3.921347	3.40

Notes: Panel A: Mean group type estimation; number of observations $= 390$; group variable: country; number of groups $= 13$; observations per group: min $= 30$, avg. $= 30.0$, max $= 30$; Wald $\text{chi}^2(2) = 29.17$; Prob $> \text{chi}^2 = 0.0000$. Root mean squared error (sigma): 1.2098.

Panel B: Mean group type estimation; number of observations $= 210$; group variable: country; number of groups $= 7$; observations per group: min $= 30$, avg $= 30.0$, max $= 30$; Wald $\text{chi}^2(2) = 15.01$; Prob $> \text{chi}^2 = 0.0006$. Root mean squared error (sigma): 1.7528.

Common dynamic process included as additional regressor K. All coefficients present represent averages across groups (country). Coefficient averages computed as unweighted means.

growth. The estimated coefficient in this relationship passes from about 0.18 to about 0.17. As for the effect of the tax burden on the GDP rate of growth, the estimated coefficient passes from about -0.8 to about -0.7.

As before, we again evaluate whether the presence of cross-section correlation changes the results when estimating the cointegration vectors for the 13 OECD EU countries and the 7 OECD non-EU countries.[10]

Results of the AMG estimator again provide additional evidence in favor of our specification in both cases. They are aligned with those obtained in the presence of "no cross-section dependence" and with those obtained for the 20 OECD countries. Now, however, the difference between EU and non-EU countries becomes clear. The effect of a reduction in the budget deficit on GDP growth is now much smaller for the EU countries than that observed for the non-EU countries: 0.165 points versus 0.348 for the sample of non-EU countries. Additionally, the negative effect of a tax increase on the rate of growth of GDP is smaller: 0.157 points against 0.352 points. In both cases, however, the result is that the increase in tax burden nearly compensates for the expansionary effect on the long-term GDP growth rate of the reduction in the deficit. However, for the non-EU countries, the negative effect of the tax increase is slightly greater than the positive effect of the reduction in the deficit, while the opposite occurs for the EU sample. Considering these differences, one can say that the result of the reduction of the deficit through tax increases has a smaller positive effect on the long-term rate of growth for the EU countries than the reduction of the deficit via expenditure cuts, whereas the opposite occurs for the non-EU countries, where the still minimal net effect of tax increase is more effective than the cut in expenditure. On the other hand, there is a much greater difference between the two groups of countries in the case of a fiscal policy of reduction in the deficits through a cut in public spending. For the non-EU countries, the effect is an increase of 0.348 in the long-term rate of growth, while for the EU countries the increase is 0.165. The explanation of the differences in the coefficient may be found in the different characteristics of the average GDP growth rate of the EU countries with respect to those of the non-EU countries. Indeed (see Figure 7.1(1)), the average long-term EU growth rate is smaller and less elastic upward and downward than the average long-term rate of the aggregate of all the non-EU countries. Therefore the stimulus provided by a given percentage of deficit reduction in the growth rate in the EU countries is smaller than that of the non-EU countries. For the same reason, the reduction of GDP growth rate caused by an increase in the tax burden is lower for the EU countries than for the non-EU countries.

To sum up, the developed countries that adopt tax policies to obtain a budget balance should not expect, on the basis of past experience, to obtain as a dividend an increase in the long-term growth rate. Jones's (1995) view that it would be an "astonishing coincidence" if two non-stationary variables that drive growth compensated for each other in such a way as to generate a stationary growth process, is not surprising here. The only way to get this dividend would be to cut the deficit by cutting expenditures in the EU (and by increasing taxes in the non-EU group). However, given the hysteresis of their growth path, the EU countries need to undertake important cuts in their high level of public spending to achieve a significant impact on their long-term rate of growth. Indeed, if they cut the spending by four points they may achieve a change in their long-term growth rate of about 0.64 percent. Similarly, a reduction in the tax burden, with an invariant budgetary deficit, may have smaller effects for the EU countries than for the non-EU, notwithstanding their EU higher tax burdens.

Conclusions

We have analyzed the effects of the government budget constraint on GDP growth, with a panel of 20 OECD countries, for the period from 1980 to 2009, considering the role of the main variables determining its dimension, i.e., revenues and expenditure on GDP. Subsequently, we have considered the panel of the 13 EU OECD countries as compared with the 7 non-EU members of the group, in order to analyze the likely different results in the light of the lower performance of EU GDP growth rates, of the higher ratios of average deficit to GDP, of the greater size of the public sector as measured by the ratio of public expenditure on GDP, of a higher tax burden, of higher rates of inflation and NAIRU—taken as a proxy of (more rigid) structures of the labor supply. We have found cointegration in both cases.

For the OECD countries as a whole, results show that persistent deficits significantly reduce long-term GDP growth rates, in comparison with a situation of budget balance. A reduction in tax burden tends to significantly improve the long-term rate of growth. On the other hand, a reduction in the deficit obtained through a tax increase has a lower effect than a reduction in the deficit from public-expenditure cuts. As for the EU countries, the net results are similar as far as fiscal policies aimed at reducing the deficits through tax increases are concerned, but the magnitude of the effect is smaller. In the case of the non-EU countries, the negative coefficient of a point of increase in the tax burden is in absolute value (slightly) greater than the coefficient of the deficit, implying that for non-EU countries the increase in tax burden might be more effective than a reduction in public expenditure. In other words, if the reduction of the deficit is achieved by reducing expenses, in the EU countries this causes an increase in the long-term rate of growth, whereas, in the non-EU countries the positive effect on growth occurs with an increased tax burden.

We have not explored the details of the composition of expenditures and taxes and do not deny that this issue may be relevant. However, in long-term empirical research it is hardly possible to distinguish between distortionary and non-distortionary taxes and between current productive and non-productive expenditure given their classification in the existing standard categories. Moreover, these seem to be further qualifications to be achieved within the framework of our research, which for some aspects complement the existing literature with the caveat that Keynesian or New Keynesian policies in the long term should be precluded. Indeed, our results validate long-term budget balance rules. However, they imply also a severe criticism of the EU rules because they overlook the negative effects on growth of achieving the budget balance by increased tax burden and because they allow for labor market rigidities while prescribing a rigid price stability as that for monetary policy.

Notes

1 Growth-reducing effects of high public debt are not necessarily transmitted via high real interest rates: in 11 episodes, interest rates are not substantially higher.
2 "In point of economy there is no real difference in either of the modes, for 20 millions in one payment, 1 million per annum forever, or £1,200,000 for forty-five years are precisely of the same value . . . But the people who paid the taxes never so estimate them, and therefore do not manage their private affairs accordingly . . . It would be difficult to convince a man possessed of £20,000, or any other sum, that a perpetual payment of £50 per annum was equally burdensome with a single tax of £1000" (Ricardo, 1888).
3 See, for instance, Devarajan *et al.* (1996)and Kneller *et al.* (1999).
4 Apart from a few exceptions (e.g., Bleaney *et al.*, 2001; Romero-Avila and Strauch, 2008; Gemmell *et al.*, 2011), regression tests for long-run fiscal-growth effects in OECD countries have typically relied on cross-section or panel data using five- or ten-year averages to smooth out short-run effects (see Lee and Gordon, 2005; Angelopoulos *et al.*, 2007; Bania *et al.*, 2007). For a single country, Romer and Romer (2010) provide an alternative "intermediate" approach between short-term structural vector autoregressive (SVAR) and long-term regression methods. However, for multiple countries with shorter time series, this method is not feasible.
5 A substantial body of literature has also investigated political and institutional effects on fiscal policy and, in particular, on the propensity of different parties in different institutional settings to prolong fiscal imbalances (see, among others, Alesina and Drazen, 1991; Alesina *et al.*, 1998; Persson and Tabellini, 2003; Milesi-Ferretti *et al.*, 2002).
6 A high tax burden combined with a high deficit implies a high ratio of public expenditure on GDP.
7 Even if our focus is on the relationship between GDP growth and both deficits/GDP and tax burden, we have also considered their inverse relationship in order to take into account their possible interaction. Therefore we have tested the direction of the relationship among the mentioned variables by means of the Granger causality (details are available upon request).
8 To eliminate the cross dependence, the standard DF (or ADF) regressions are augmented with the cross-section averages of lagged levels and first-differences of the individual series.
9 The Augmented Mean Group estimator (AMG) was developed in Eberhardt and Teal (2010) as an alternative to the Pesaran (2006) estimator in which the set of unobservable common factors is treated as a nuisance, something to be accounted for which is not of particular interest to the empirical analysis. See Eberhardt and Teal (2011) for a detailed discussion of the literature on growth empirics. The AMG procedure is implemented in a three-step procedure (for details, see Bond and Eberhardt, 2009).
10 We repeat the same battery of tests carried out in the previous section in the presence of cross-section independence. Details are available upon request.

References

Alesina, A. and A. Drazen (1991), "Why are stabilizations delayed?," *American Economic Review*, 81: 1170–1188.
Alesina, A. and S. Ardagna (2009), "Large changes in fiscal policy: Taxes versus spending," *NBER Working Paper* No. 15438.

Alesina, A., R. Perotti and J. Tavares (1998), "The political economy of fiscal adjustments," *Brooking Papers on Economic Activity*, 29.

Angelopoulos, K., G. Economides and P. Kammas (2007), "Tax-spending policies and economic growth: Theoretical predictions and evidence from the OECD," *European Journal of Political Economy*, 23: 885–902.

Ardagna, S. (2004), "Fiscal stabilizations: When do they work and why," *European Economic Review*, 48: 1047–1074.

Bania, N., J. A. Gray and J. A. Stone (2007), "Growth, taxes, and government expenditures: Growth hills for U.S. states," *National Tax Journal*, 60: 193–204.

Barro, R. (1979), "On the determination of the public debt," *Journal of Political Economy*, 87: 940–971.

Barro, R. (1990), "Government spending in a simple model of endogenous growth," *Journal of Political Economy*, 98: 103–117.

Blanchard, O. J. and R. Perotti (2002), "An empirical investigation of the dynamic effects of changes in government spending and revenues on output," *Quarterly Journal of Economics*, 117: 1329–1368.

Bleaney, M., N. Gemmell and R. Kneller (2001), "Testing the endogenous growth model: Public expenditure, taxation and growth over the long run," *Canadian Journal of Economics*, 34: 36–57.

Bond, S. and M. Eberhardt (2009), "Cross-section dependence in nonstationary panel models: A novel estimator," paper presented at the Nordic Econometrics Conference, Lund, Sweden, October 2009.

Devarajan, S., V. Swaroop and H. Zoo (1996), "The composition of public expenditure and economic growth," *Journal of Monetary Economics*, 37: 313–344.

Eberhardt, M. and F. Teal (2010), "Productivity analysis in global manufacturing production," *Economics Series Working Papers* 515, University of Oxford, Department of Economics.

Eberhardt, M. and F. Teal (2011), "Econometrics for grumblers: A new look at the literature on cross-country growth empirics," *Journal of Economic Surveys*, 25: 109–155.

Gemmell, N., R. Kneller and I. Sanz (2011), "The timing and persistence of fiscal policy impacts on growth: Evidence from OECD countries," *The Economic Journal*, 121(550): F33–F58.

Giavazzi, F. and M. Pagano (1990), "Can severe fiscal contractions be expansionary? Tales of two small European countries," *NBER Macroeconomic Annual*, MIT Press, Cambridge, MA: 95–122.

Giavazzi, F., T. Jappelli and M. Pagano (2000), "Searching for non-linear effects of fiscal policy: Evidence from industrial and developing countries," *European Economic Review*, 44: 1259–1289.

Im, K. S., M. Pesaran and Y. Shin (2003), "Testing for unit roots in heterogeneous panels," *Journal of Econometrics*, 115: 53–74.

Jones, C. I. (1995), "Time series tests of endogenous growth models," *Quarterly Journal of Economics*, 110: 495–525.

Kneller, R., M. Bleaney and N. Gemmell (1999), "Fiscal policy and growth: Evidence from OECD countries," *Journal of Public Economics*, 74: 171–190.

Lee, Y. and R. H. Gordon (2005), "Tax structure and economic growth," *Journal of Public Economics*, 89: 1027–1043.

McDermott, J. and R. Wescott (1996), "An empirical analysis of fiscal adjustments," *IMF Staff Papers*, 43: 723–753.

Milesi-Ferretti, G. M., R. Perotti and M. Rostagno (2002), "Electoral systems and public spending," *Quarterly Journal of Economics*, 117: 609–657.

Mountford, A. and H. Uhlig (2008), "What are the effects of fiscal policy shocks?," *NBER Working Paper* No. 14551.

Peretto, P. F. (2007), "Corporate taxes, growth and welfare in a Schumpeterian economy," *Journal of Economic Theory*, 137: 353–382.

Persson, T. and G. Tabellini (2003), *The Economic Effects of Constitutions*, Munich Lectures in Economics, Cambridge, MA, MIT Press.

Persyn, D. and J. Westerlund (2008), "Error-correction–based cointegration tests for panel data," *Strata Journal*, 8: 232–241.

Pesaran, M. H., Y. Shin and R. P. Smith (1997), "Estimating long-run relationships in dynamic heterogeneous panels," *DAE Working Papers Amalgamated Series* 9721.

Pesaran, M. H. (2003), "A simple panel unit root test in the presence of cross section dependence," *Cambridge Working Papers in Economics* 0346, Faculty of Economics (DAE), University of Cambridge.

Pesaran, M. H. (2004), "General diagnostic tests for cross section dependence in panels," *Cambridge Working Papers in Economics* 435, and *CESifo Working Paper Series* No. 1229.

Pesaran, M. H. (2006), "Estimation and inference in large heterogeneous panels with multifactor error structure," *Econometrica*, 74: 967–1012.

Pesaran, M. (2007), "A simple panel unit root test in the presence of cross-section dependence," *Journal of Applied Econometrics*, 22: 265–312.

Ramey, V. (2008), "Identifying government spending shocks: It's all in the timing," *NBER Working Paper* No. 15464.

Reinhart, C. M. and K. S. Rogoff (2010), "Growth in a time of debt," *American Economic Review*, 100: 573–578.

Reinhart, C. M., V. Reinhart and K. Rogoff (2012), "Public debt overhangs: Advanced-economy episodes since 1800," *Journal of Economic Perspectives*, 26: 69–86.

Ricardo, D. (1888), "Essay on the funding system," in *The Works of David Ricardo. With a Notice of the Life and Writings of the Author, McCulloch, J. R.*, London: John Murray.

Romer, C. D. and D. H. Romer (2010), "The macroeconomic effects of tax changes: Estimates based on a new measure of fiscal shocks," *American Economic Review*, 100: 763–801.

Romero-Avila, D. and R. Strauch (2008), "Public finances and long-term growth in Europe: Evidence from a panel data analysis," *European Journal of Political Economy*, 24: 172–191.

Von Hagen, J. and R. Strauch (2001), "Fiscal consolidations: Quality, economic conditions, and success," *Public Choice*, 109: 327–346.

Westerlund, J. (2007), "Testing for error correction in panel data," *Oxford Bulletin of Economics and Statistics*, 69: 709–748.

8 On productivity as an intermediate target for economic policy

Andrew Hughes Hallett

Introduction

Most developed economies now maintain a list of fairly standard targets to define the success of their economic policies and a well-articulated programme of strategies to achieve them. The standard targets would usually include a high but not excessive rate of growth in output, high rates of employment, of investment, plus low inflation, easily financed fiscal and external imbalances, and stable public finances.

However, alongside those targets, a number of intermediate or secondary targets often appear as components of the strategies by which the more fundamental targets are to be achieved. These additional targets are likely to include:

1   increasing productivity and competitiveness levels, to rank in the top quartile of the OECD (Organization for Economic Co-operation and Development) economies (say) and top among the main trading partners;[1]
2   increasing employment and participation rates, to match the OECD rates of growth in both of them and/or to stem the outflow of skills;
3   increasing the rate of investment, skills, and research and development (R&D) in the business sector, to match the principle trade partners in education/skills, and in innovation and business start ups.

The instruments/strategies most often suggested to achieve these goals are:

1   improving R&D spending or its effectiveness, and improving learning capacity and skills;
2   improving general productivity levels and the proportion of high productivity or high value added industries and jobs in the national economy;
3   improving the business environment: lower overhead costs and business taxes, better or more effective infrastructure and planning procedures, improving market flexibility and the functioning of the private sector.

Since these instruments are necessary, but not in themselves sufficient, we need to provide clear incentives for firms and policymakers to take advantage of the better conditions offered. First, those incentives should be based on achieving lower costs of production per unit produced. Lower relative costs across the board (a lower real exchange rate), not just in labour costs alone, are the only sure way to induce businesses to set up or expand their activities locally rather than elsewhere. Hence we need to consider:

1   new incentives for R&D and investment and to adopt technical and organizational measures that enhance productivity;
2   a competitive tax regime (lower business taxes, business rates and those taxes which can attract mobile factors of production);
3   incentives for regional governments to support business development and for agencies and firms to devolve employment policy and wage bargaining;
4   create incentives for particular sectors that have high productivity, or high value added potential, to set up or expand. This might involve improving or supporting infrastructure, skills and training, networks of specialized services, or to lower production costs directly.

This chapter explores the mechanisms by which an intermediate productivity target can lead to the basic targets of economic policy. In our analysis, productivity is defined as output per unit input used in the production process. We can therefore speak of labour productivity, capital productivity or productivity with respect to a particular factor such as information technology (IT). Total-factor productivity (TFP) is the increase in output that remains when the contributions of other inputs are taken out. The techniques and information required for measuring these different forms of productivity are discussed in detail in Harris *et al.* (2006).

The chapter then breaks into two parts. We first consider productivity of private-sector production with a special emphasis on the sector, factor or market-structure productivities that underlie the policy problem. Second, we look at the key role played by public-sector productivity – an aspect of the productivity which is often ignored in most policy discussions.

Economic growth in an era of low population growth

The most striking fact from the recent economic statistics for many OECD economies has been the lack of growth in the working population. For example, population growth in Scotland was just 0.4 per cent over the period 1997–2006 compared to around 3 per cent for the UK as a whole. And it is projected to shrink slightly (−0.1 per cent) over the period 2004–2031, while the population of the UK as a whole will rise by 12 per cent. More dramatically, the working population is scheduled to shrink in every age group to 59 per cent, while the numbers in the 60 and above group will expand. The working population can therefore be expected to shrink quite sharply over the next two decades. It is difficult to see how the rate of economic growth could be permanently increased, or how the target of matching the growth rates of other OECD countries can be achieved against the background of a shrinking work force.

Four possible remedies suggest themselves.

1   To increase the participation rates. However, the participation rate in Scotland is already high, and higher than that in the rest of the UK, so the scope for raising growth rates from that source must be limited (however welcome and desirable for other reasons).
2   To increase population growth rate through higher migration in or lower migration out. While desirable, this remedy will require the economic growth rate itself to increase in order to attract the extra people (given that we can do little to influence the birth rate) in the first place. So little can be expected from this source either.
3   To increase the productivity of the existing work force, either across the board or by changing the industrial mix to increase the weight of high productivity industries in total national output, so that the output produced per person (or per hour worked) increases.
4   However, with a labour force that already produces more per hour and works as many hours as comparable OECD economies (see the next section), the bulk of these productivity gains are going to have to come *either* from gains in the productivity of capital inputs (deploying higher technology production methods given the labour force) *or* from the gains in productivity that arise from a better organization of production, better work practices or a better use of IT, R&D, specialized services, innovations in management or a more effective use of education, skills and training (TFP).

To illustrate the problems caused by having no growth in the work force, we can use a standard model of economic growth:[2] Figure 8.1. Here national output is represented as total production (Y) from inputs of capital (K), labour (N), at a given level of technology or productivity (A), with diminishing marginal returns to increases in either input alone.[3] If the economy as a whole shows approximately constant returns to scale, then output per head, Y/N, will be given by the same output relationship in terms of the capital used per head, K/N. As a result, investment in any period would be made using the savings generated from that output, say sY or sY/N, where s represents the savings rate of the economy (savings are proportional to income). If government and trade accounts are held balanced to keep things simple, the capital stock will be last year's capital stock plus any new investment $(I = sY)$ less any depreciation or replacement investment which is proportional to the existing stock of capital $(\delta K$ say). Dividing everything through by N leads to Figure 8.1, all variables being displayed in per capita terms.

Similarly dividing through by AN, where AN shows the output of the work force increased by the current productivity level per employee, gives exactly the same diagram with everything measured in 'per effective worker' units, that is, corrected for increases in the productivity of the workers employed, as well as for any increases in the numbers actually employed. In this case, it is evident that any lack of growth in N could be made up by growth in A.

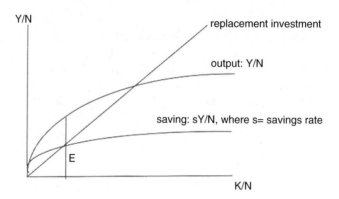

Figure 8.1 Output per head when the work force does not grow.

It is obvious that the economy's equilibrium is at point E, where the amount being saved and invested equals the amount of capital being retired, depreciated or replaced. To the left of E, savings are greater than depreciation, so the capital stock (per head) will be increasing each period. To the right, savings will be less than depreciation and the capital stock decreases each period. So we always end up back at E. But at that point, K/N is constant and the associated Y/N level is also constant. In other words, there is no long-term growth in either output *per head* or in capital *per head*. Hence, if the work force employed doesn't grow, then output cannot grow. That is the predicament of many advanced economies just now.

Of course, to allow for productivity, if we had divided through by AN instead of just N, exactly the same argument would lead us to end up at an equilibrium point where capital per productive worker, K/AN, is constant and the associated level of output per productive worker, Y/AN, is also constant. In that case, if neither the workforce nor productivity grows, then output cannot grow. But if either or both grow, then a constant value of Y/AN means output itself must be growing at the same rate to keep that ratio constant. The implication is that output can only grow in the longer run if the labour inputs grow, or if productivity grows. Similarly, to increase the rate of growth, you need to increase the growth rate of the work force employed, or increase the rate of growth of productivity among those employed or both. But if the local workforce is set to shrink, and if there is limited scope to increase the (already high) employment rate, then the economy's growth rate can only be increased by increasing the growth in productivity. As noted earlier, that can either be done by increasing the average productivity per person or other inputs employed, or by altering the industrial mix to increase the number and size of high productivity firms in total output.

It is worth noting that increasing savings, investment and hence the capital stock will not, on its own, increase the growth rate permanently. If we were to do this, *s* in Figure 8.1 would increase and hence move the sY/N curve up. That would establish a new equilibrium point to the right of the current one and hence at a higher *level* of capital per head or output per head. But as soon as we arrive there, those two ratios would be constant again. In the transition, there would be additional growth. But at the new equilibrium, that extra growth would vanish. Output would only continue to grow if the workforce grows, since the ratio Y/N is constant. Similarly, in the case where we allow for productivity, output would only continue to grow long term if either the workforce or productivity grows, since the ratio Y/AN will be constant – although there could be some growth in the transition to the new equilibrium.

One can see the same result in Figure 8.1 as it stands (in terms of output per employee) if A, the general level of productivity, or TFP, increases. That too will shift both the Y/AN and sY/AN curves up, creating a new equilibrium point to the right of the old one. There would be short-term growth in Y/AN as the economy adjusts to the new equilibrium. But things would stop there, as in the higher savings case, if productivity never increased again. The difference from the higher savings rate case is that increases in the savings rate are necessarily limited, since employees have to consume to survive and enjoy the fruits of their labour. However, there is no reason to suppose that productivity growth cannot continue indefinitely, faster or slower, and therefore be a source of increased growth into the future when increases in the workforce are difficult to engineer. In that case, both the Y/AN and sY/AN curves would continue to shift up the diagram.

Productivity policies as a secondary objective

The challenge for economic policy is then: (a) to find ways to translate the implications of an improvement in productivity into specific and concrete policy actions that can be implemented to achieve those improvements; (b) to separate those actions that can enable productivity gains (but which would not in themselves imply an incentive for firms to make the necessary changes in the absence of explicit policy interventions), from those that would provide a positive incentive for firms to do so; and (c) to examine the extent to which R&D activity is a sufficient indicator of innovation and the potential for raising productivity.

Solow's work on technical progress (Solow, 1957), and the Rostow–Porter analysis of stages of economic development (Rostow, 1962), show that R&D spending will reflect a significant part of the innovations process. But it is not sufficient. Recent empirical work[4] indicates that the ability to exploit innovations is as important as the ability to create them. Measures of entrepreneurial activity tend to identify risk aversion, cultural support, the ease of doing business, presence of technical expertise, internationalization, the availability of finance and, of course, (relative) costs or structural reform, as the factors that translate innovations into productivity gains. These are all elements in TFP (see the section on 'Total-factor productivity' below).

Productivity as a factor in growth

Impact on costs

It is a common perception that increased labour productivity is a key element in a successful growth strategy because it lowers unit labour costs to make the home economy more competitive than others with lower productivity or slower productivity gains. This was the thinking that led to the expectation that the East German economy would grow fast after reunification in 1990, and that economic convergence (integration) would be complete within five to ten years. At the time, East German wages were at about 60 per cent of their counterparts in the West, while the productivity level was about one-third of that in the West. As a result, unit production costs remained, even ten years after the event, around 10 per cent higher in the East. There was little or no convergence, and zero growth but rising unemployment in both German economies for 15 years after the initial shock until the structural reforms of 2003–2004, which reduced German relative prices, took effect in 2007–2009. Thus lower costs per se are not sufficient; productivity levels or rates of productivity growth must be higher by more than raw costs are lower than their counterparts in the competitor economies.

In another example, labour productivity in Scotland has been about 3 per cent lower than the UK average or comparable EU economies since 2000. Yet wages were 6 per cent lower, at least for the 2004–2006 period, on ONS (Office for National Statistics) data. This implies that unit labour costs were 3 per cent lower in Scotland. However, unit production costs as a whole were not lower in Scotland, since otherwise the Scottish economy would have been more competitive and would have grown faster. In the event, Scotland has grown slower by an average of 0.5–1 percentage points each year over the past 30 years. Again, lower unit labour costs (higher labour productivity) are not themselves sufficient for successful growth policies. Evidently, TFP (productivity of other factors of production, or of the way in which they are combined) has been lower in Scotland. This shortfall in one aspect of total productivity needs to be corrected if successful growth is to follow.

Different forms of productivity policy

The second example above can be extended. It is widely accepted that productivity gains can best be obtained through policies that encourage R&D activities and innovation: for example, R&D tax credits or subsidies, reductions in corporation tax, patent law to encourage R&D itself and the leasing of patents for facilitating the diffusion of the results, and a coherent science and technology policy. However, in practice, it would pay to take a more nuanced approach. The data for the second example show that the Scots work harder than their counterparts in the rest of the UK, but to less effect (Table 8.1), which suggests they are working in lower productivity industries as well as in a lower productivity environment. In short, that labour is being substituted for capital as well as technology in the absence of innovation and improvements to the production process. A more detailed analysis

Table 8.1 Components of growth, Scotland vs. the UK, percentage change per year, 1997–2007

Components of change in GDP	Scotland	UK	Differential (Scotland – UK)
Productivity (GDP/hrs worked)	1.9	2.3	−0.4
Employment rate	0.6	0.3	0.3
Average hours worked	−0.7	−0.4	−0.3
Working age population	0.4	0.7	−0.3
GDP	2.3	2.9	−0.6

Source: Scottish Government.

shows that Scotland has 'specialized' in low productivity industries relative to the UK, with more industries being less productive than the UK average, but fewer being more productive (Scottish Economic Statistics 2009). But where productivity has improved, it has done so through changes in the industry mix. That suggests a two-level approach is more useful: a general approach of trying to increase TFP with improved technology, capital deepening, better production processes, work practices and upgraded skills across the board; plus sectorial policies designed to shift the industry mix towards the high productivity sectors and those with specialized services, skills and external economies of scale. These two options are not exclusive; they can both be followed to good effect at the same time.

R&D spending and innovation

Indicators of R&D expenditure show that the location of R&D spending and innovation matters. Continuing with the Scottish example, Scotland ranks very highly on R&D and innovation in the public sector – principally in the higher-education sector – but does less well in the business and industry sector. In fact business R&D spending and innovation runs at half the UK rate (Table 8.2) and less than the European average. At the same time, employment in the medium-to-high-tech firms is below the UK and EU averages with knowledge diffusion rated no more than average.

These are the dominant facts in the innovations data. Three possible explanations suggest themselves. There could be:

a   a lack of capacity (in smaller firms) to create or absorb the new techniques, products and new ways of doing things;
b   insufficient capacity to do so because they are not where the business or production decisions, or technical/process design decisions, are being made;
c   a lack of skills or understanding in the work force.

Of these three, in smaller economies, the first two are very likely to be true; and, with easy emigration of those with skills, often the third one is too.

In that context, it is interesting, as an illustration, that business sector R&D and innovation in Scotland is largely done by US-, Scottish- and EU-owned firms,

Table 8.2 Gross spending on R&D in 2007 – Scotland vs. the UK

	Scotland	UK	Scotland (UK = 100)
R&D spending as percentage of GDP	1.52	1.79	84.9
... and per head of population	£332	£417	79.6
Public R&D as percentage of GDP (incl. higher education)	1.07	0.62	173.2
Business R&D as percentage of GDP	0.46	1.13	40.3
... and per employee	£311	£665	46.8
... and per employee in services	£42	£195	21.6

	R&D in business	R&D in government	R&D in Higher Ed
Scotland, £m	513	327	870
Scotland as percentage of UK	3.2	14.6	13.3

and very little by UK-based firms. In figures, 53 per cent is done by US firms, 25 per cent by Scottish-owned firms, 16 per cent by EU firms and 3 per cent by UK-owned firms.[5] In terms of value added, 8 per cent of firms in Scotland are US owned, 31 per cent are non-UK and 61 per cent are UK owned. Taken together, this means that the UK-based firms undertake just 5 per cent of the R&D or innovation spending per unit value added, that non-UK firms do.

Given that most high-value-added and high-productivity activities take place at or near head office, these disparities must account for a large part of the differences in productivity and hence GDP growth rates between Scotland and the UK. If, other things being equal, productivity is to be the key to achieving growth and other objectives of policy, the simplest policy strategy is to find measures that will bring high-productivity, high-tech activities to the local economy – if not the head offices themselves – by offering lower operating costs, lower personal or business taxes, lifestyle advantages, proximity or collaboration with universities/research centres, or support (or information) to clusters of similar firms to share specialized services, and so on.

A programme of this type gives direction and focus to the general structural reform policies so often demanded as part of the austerity and restructuring efforts in the advanced economies in recent years. It is interesting that, in the Scottish case, just a few sectors account for the lion's share of R&D and innovation: pharmaceutical firms (41 per cent), precision instruments (20 per cent), services (12 per cent) and IT (4 per cent). At first sight, this shows how much might be gained by exploiting the use of IT in reorganizing production processes (process innovation or TFP) – especially when used in combination with other activities such as medical diagnostics, measurement, digital technologies, communications or energy. These are prime cases where IT and networking can increase competitiveness and market competition by increasing the size and efficiency of firm organization, and by making ownership and tradable output more contestable. A deeper response is to recognize that this suggests policies should be designed to raise productivity in specific sectors, as well as across the board, in the sectors mentioned above, for example, and also in financial services, environmental services, precision measurement, health care, etc. As such, they fit right into the two-level strategy highlighted in the previous subsection.

The role of productivity in convergence or economic integration

One implication of the model behind Figure 8.1 is that productivity is the key factor needed to achieve economic convergence as measured by levels of income per head. Convergence in this sense requires convergence in productivity levels (Hughes Hallett and Ma, 1993, 1994). That is the condition we need to achieve full integration in a single economic area such as the Eurozone. The reasoning is as follows. Output per effective worker, Y/AN, as demonstrated in Figure 8.1, can stay equal in steady state in different economies only if the movements in productivity (A) and those in capital per productive worker, K/AN, exactly match and balance each other. But diminishing marginal returns in output, with linear replacement of capital depreciation, implies a long-run equilibrium value for K/AN; and that in turn means Y/AN can remain equal in different places only if productivity growth equalizes across the common economic zone.

A different argument for focusing on productivity growth

The traditional argument for the gains from trade is that, given the ability to trade freely, those gains derive from the capacity of an economy to specialize either in the industries where it has comparative advantage, or in those industries where it has established economies of scale in production (or could establish such economies). These economies of scale might be internal, where efficient production (low per unit costs) means very large plants and production runs and hence a small number of large firms in the industry. Or they might be external economies, where efficient (low-cost) production arises from many firms in a cluster providing specialist services or sharing inputs with particular characteristics (a kind of economies of scale in providing certain high-value inputs, as happens in the creative, information or financial services industries). That suggests a large number of smaller specialist firms in an industry. Scotland could, and probably does, benefit from both types of gains from trade, but may have been more successful with the external economies of scale type in recent years.

However, a new argument has been made by Marc Melitz (2003), that an important part of the gains from trade come from the fact that, being exposed to competition from a wider range of firms with comparative advantage or economies of scale on the world markets (and hence to competition from levels of comparative advantage or scale economies that are close to or surpass the best available at home), the extra competition from abroad will either drive the lower productivity firms out of business or force them to update their technology and production methods to the best available in order to survive. In other words, the gains from trade will come (in part) as the extra competition forces domestic firms to increase their productivity or quit, and as high productivity firms take over or enter the domestic market. This may be an explanation for why productivity is often found to be higher in multi-nationals. More importantly, it suggests a strategy that would raise productivity levels directly, rather than indirectly via transfers of productivity, technologies or work practices from subsidiaries of firms located elsewhere that are not exposed to international competition to the same degree.

Similar arguments can be made that the pressures of financial liberalization will force increased productivity through the mobility of capital; or that the pressures of trade competition will force structural or market reforms that increase efficiency and hence raise productivity indirectly.

Total-factor productivity

The discussion in the second section above makes it clear that we should really be concerned with TFP, rather than just labour productivity. It is an important point, as the empirical studies by Jorgenson *et al.* (2008) and van Ark *et al.* (2008) emphasize, that for the United States and Europe much of the recent growth in productivity has come from employing more productive capital and making better use of that capital (organizational and the tasks to which it can be put), as well as from 'higher quality' labour or from better work practices. Moreover, concentrating on labour productivity alone might not produce any benefits if capital productivity turns out to be lower in say Scotland than in the UK or elsewhere. And this must be the case. Although we have no direct numbers for capital productivity in Scotland, we do know that labour productivity is 3 per cent lower than in the rest of the UK (and falling) while wages are 6 per cent lower.[6] That means unit labour costs are 3 per cent lower than in the rest of the UK. Hence, if all else were equal, output should be growing faster in Scotland. But it is not growing faster: national output growth has in fact been between 0.5 and 1 percentage points slower on average since 1976. So all other things are not equal; and the most plausible culprit is that capital or TFP is significantly lower in Scotland (if we take capital and TFP to include the contributions of transport, infrastructure, R&D and organizational methods). That in turn means that, unless we can come up with some dramatic increases in labour productivity, there is no real reason why firms would want to start or expand their operations in Scotland. Hence higher productivity in general is needed in order to overcome the constraints on growth, and to provide the cost incentives for firms to expand in the domestic economy rather than elsewhere.

At this point it might be useful to review what we can infer about capital productivity from the data that we do have. For installed capital, we know that investment in R&D in the business sector is much lower in Scotland than in the rest of the UK (in 2004 business R&D expenditures were running at just less than half the UK rate), even if it is above the UK average in the higher-education sector. Similarly, patents filed per inhabitant were at 68 per cent of the UK level. Likewise the shortfall in value-added tax (VAT) registrations is greater than the shortfall in VAT deregistrations. But the registrations per inhabitant were just 80 per cent of the UK average, so business formation lags behind the rest of the UK even if the survival rate is less bad than the formation rate.[7] Both sets of figures imply capital productivity, widely defined, must be lower in Scotland – and will probably fall further behind if the new or surviving firms are more likely to be the high productivity ones.

More pertinent evidence comes from direct comparisons of labour productivity. Relative to UK averages, all the available measures of labour productivity are a bit lower. The lowest, relatively, is output per job, then comes output per head and, finally, output per hour worked. Since the outputs produced are the same in each case, and since the employment rate is actually higher in Scotland, the first difference – output per job less than output per head – is obviously true. But the 'output per job less than output per hour' ranking shows that the Scots are working harder per hour. If the number of hours worked is not different in both places, and they are not, then this second difference could be because more capital or more technology is being used per worker. But that would have to mean a higher rate of output, since the employment rate is higher in Scotland. However, output is not higher; it is lower. Alternatively, it could be that the workforce is substituting a greater labour input for less-productive capital. Given the relative output figures, this has to be the explanation. In other words, what is holding Scotland back is low capital productivity – or, since so many firms operating in Scotland are headquartered elsewhere, a 'branch office' problem in which the high-productivity/high-value production work is done at headquarters and the lower-productivity work in Scotland.

Productivity in public services, infrastructure, education and training

A model of public-sector productivity

The model used here is based on Yakita's (2008) overlapping generations model with population ageing and public capital accumulation the driving force behind economic growth.[8] Specifically, we suppose an overlapping generations economy populated by homogenous individuals, with symmetric firms and a government. Individuals are assumed to have a life span divided into a working and a retirement period. In each period, the generation working forms the young cohort. Their working lifetime is of fixed length, whereas their retirement is of uncertain length. We assume that each individual is alive at the beginning of their second period with probability $(1 - \lambda) \in (0, 1)$. This probability is the same for every agent. Individuals who survive into the second period of life are retired. Denoting the population of young agents as N_t, total population in period t is $N_t + (1 - \lambda)N_{t-1}$.

Public investment and productivity

Suppose we assume a large number of symmetric firms which produce a homogenous product by combining the services of private capital and labour. The production technology available to firm j is described by a constant returns to scale production function with labour augmenting productivity

$$Y_{j,t} = A K_{j,t}^{\alpha} (h_t L_{j,t})^{1-\alpha} \tag{8.1}$$

where $Y_{j,t}$, $K_{j,t}$, $L_{j,t}$ denote respectively: the output level, private capital stock and labour inputs in firm j for period t; and where $A > 1$ and h_t are constants representing scale effects (TFP) and labour productivity which is not firm specific, and $0 < \alpha < 1$. Assuming perfect competition in both the goods and private factor markets, and denoting r_t and w_t as the rental rate of private capital and wage rate, the first-order conditions of firm j's profit maximization are

$$r_t = A\alpha \left(\frac{K_{j,t}}{L_{j,t}}\right)^{\alpha-1} (h_t)^{1-\alpha} \quad \text{and} \quad w_t = A(1-\alpha)\left(\frac{K_{j,t}}{L_{j,t}}\right)^{\alpha} (h_t)^{1-\alpha}. \quad (8.2)$$

According to these two conditions, the marginal product of each factor of production, labour and private capital is equal to its price.

In line with other papers, such as Kalaitzidakis and Kalyvitis (2004) and Yakita (2008), we assume that labour productivity is composed of private and public elements

$$h_t = \frac{K_t^{\beta} G_t^{1-\beta}}{L_t} \quad (8.3)$$

where $0 < \beta < 1$; and where, being not firm specific $K_t = \sum_j K_{j,t}$ stands for the aggregate stock of private capital, G_t is the stock of public capital and $L_t = \sum_j L_{j,t}$ the aggregate labour input. This specification of labour productivity implies the existence of positive externalities from aggregate public and private capital, G_t and K_t, onto production, with the result that the per-capita labour input itself (i.e. stripped of productivity increases) is unity. This is the standard specification.[9]

The first-order conditions in (8.2) imply that the private capital to labour ratio is the same in all firms. Therefore, in equilibrium, we have that $\frac{K_{j,t}}{L_{j,t}} = \frac{K_t}{L_t}$ – which then allows us to rewrite (8.3) in aggregate terms

$$Y_t = A K_t^{\alpha} (h_t L_t)^{1-\alpha} = A K_t^{\alpha+\beta(1-\alpha)} G_t^{(1-\beta)(1-\alpha)} \quad (8.4)$$

where $Y_t = \sum_j Y_{jt}$. Defining $\omega = \alpha + \beta(1-\alpha)$, we rewrite the *aggregate* production function as

$$Y_t = A K_t^{\omega} G_t^{1-\omega} \quad (8.5)$$

and the corresponding first-order conditions for aggregate private capital and labour inputs

$$r_t = A\alpha \left(\frac{K_t}{G_t}\right)^{\omega-1} \quad \text{and} \quad w_t = A(1-\alpha)\left(\frac{K_t}{G_t}\right)^{\omega}\left(\frac{G_t}{L_t}\right).$$

More conventionally, these first-order conditions imply capital income shares as follows: $\alpha = r_t K_t / Y_t$ from (8.4) and $\beta = r_t K_t / h_t$ from (8.3).

The first represents the usual capital income share of output; but the second is the private capital income share derived from the level of labour productivity. To simplify expressions that follow, we assume that neither private nor public capital depreciate over time. We write the public-to-private capital ratio as $X_t = G_t / K_t$.

Public investment and optimal public debt

The rest of the model can now be presented in abbreviated form. In this economy, there are two generations of consumers and workers. The young agents consume, work and have children. If they survive into old age, they retire and enjoy the savings made while young. The typical agent of generation t has preferences represented by a lifetime utility function

$$\ln c_t + (1 - \lambda)\rho \ln d_{t+1} + \varepsilon \ln n_t \tag{8.6}$$

where c_t and d_{t+1} denote consumption in periods t and $t + 1$, n_t denotes the number of children, ε denotes the priority for having a certain number of children in the utility function, λ is the probability that the individual will die before the next generation and $\rho \in (0, 1)$ is a time discount factor.

Each young agent is endowed with one unit of time for their working period (a unit labour input). Young agents earn income w_t to be allocated between consumption, savings and tax payments determined by a tax rate of θ_t. They receive a subsidy for child-rearing time on which taxes are paid: a constant fraction, ρ_w, of w_t. The budget constraint of the young generation is

$$(1 - \theta_t)[w_t(1 - zn_t) + \rho_w w_t zn_t] = c_t + s_t \tag{8.7}$$

where $z > 0$ denotes the rearing time per child, θ_t is the tax rate on labour, subsidy and capital incomes, and s_t denotes savings. Older individuals, if alive, will then receive an actuarially fair payment from their assets equal to $\frac{1+r_{t+1}}{(1-\lambda)} s_t$. Given that taxes have to be paid on those earnings, we can write the second generation's budget constraint as

$$\frac{1 + (1 - \theta_{t+1})r_{t+1}}{(1 - \lambda)} s_t = d_{t+1}. \tag{8.8}$$

The problem of the young agent is then to choose consumption while working, their purchases of annuity assets/savings and the number of children, all to maximize lifetime utility subject to the budget constraints (8.7) and (8.8).

At the same time, the government is subject to a budget constraint. In each period, it levies taxes at rate θ_t on wages w_t, subsidies and savings s_{t-1}. It also issues public debt b_t and invests the proceeds in public capital G_t. The government's budget constraint is therefore

$$\begin{aligned} b_{t+1} = (1 + r_t)\, b_t + (G_{t+1} - G_t) + \rho_w w_t zn_t N_t \\ - \theta_t(w_t L_t + \rho_w w_t zn_t N_t + r_t s_{t-1} N_{t-1}). \end{aligned} \tag{8.9}$$

If interest payments and public consumption are financed via taxes on wages, subsidies and savings income, and public debt is issued to finance public capital accumulation (the golden rule of public finance), then the following two conditions will hold

$$r_t b_t + \rho_w w_t z n_t N_t = \theta_t (w_t L_t + \rho_w w_t z n_t N_t + r_t s_{t-1} N_{t-1}) \tag{8.10}$$

and $b_t = G_t$.

Putting all this together allows us to solve for the growth-maximizing level of debt. First, there is a balanced growth path in which all variables grow at a constant rate defined by

$$\frac{G_{t+1}}{G_t} = \frac{K_{t+1}}{K_t} = \frac{Y_{t+1}}{Y_t} = \gamma n \equiv \gamma^A \tag{8.11}$$

where n is the population growth rate across a generation. The ratio of public to private capital is therefore constant in steady state, which implies that the tax rate θ_t and interest rate r_t will also be constant. Given (8.5), the optimal debt to GDP ratio is now $d^* = \frac{1}{A} X^{*\omega}$ implying a certain stock of public capital, and associated productivity, to match private capital and private-sector productivity. It then follows that, if the subsidy rate $\rho_w \to 0$, the optimal level of debt will be independent of demographic parameters. But otherwise, since $\omega < 1$, the optimal debt burden $d*$ increases with ρ_w.

Public-sector productivity in action

To give specific illustrations of the role of public-sector productivity in the policy problem, we have simulated this model with plausible but stylized parameter values. It turns out that the only parameter values that matter for the state of the economy in this context are income inequality (α) and the public-to-private-sector participation rate in creating advances in productivity (β). Figure 8.2 shows how. The parameter values used are set out in Table 8.3. They are calibrated to a typical small OECD economy, such as Denmark.

They show very little discounting between generations: equal utility between lifetime consumption and children for the average two-child family; a generous labour share of income, but private capital getting the larger share of any productivity increases; a small scale effect (outside of labour enhancing productivity); a low probability of dying before retirement (scaled to the proportion of people over 65 in the population); and generous child-rearing subsidies with time spent on doing so to match. The result is a steady-state debt ratio of 43 per cent, a public-to-private capital ratio of 31 per cent and annual growth of just over 3 per cent.

More detailed numerical results are provided in Figure 8.2. The horizontal axis shows increasing inequality (a larger share of national income going to capital), and the vertical axis an increasing private-sector share in creating productivity (a larger share of any productivity gains going to private capital). The hatched lines meanwhile show the different parameter combinations that yield 20 per cent growth over a ten-year period for example, or a 60 per cent public debt ratio, and so on.

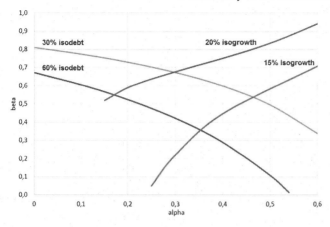

Figure 8.2 Public debt, growth, and income inequalities with public investment.

Table 8.3 Parameter calibration

ρ	discounting	0.99
ε	importance of children in utility	0.5
α	income inequality	0.25
β	private share of productivity gains	0.6
A	scale effect	1.03
λ	hazard rate	0.1
z	rearing time per child	0.4
ρ_w	child rearing subsidy	0.5
Number of years in two generations $= 45$		
Outcomes:		
d^*	optimal debt to GDP ratio	0.4351
X	public private capital ratio	0.3177
γ^A	growth rate of output per year	3.1973

Narrative

If we go northeast up the diagram we get lower debt and some extra but increasingly elusive additional growth (and maybe none at all if there is too much movement east), together with increasing income or wealth inequality in a conventional sense. By contrast, moving up the diagram northwest brings higher growth more rapidly, together with greater income and wealth equality in the conventional sense and lower debt ratios – although these debt reductions will likewise become increasingly elusive and may not materialize at all if there is too much movement west. In both cases, the income gains from higher productivity gains would increasingly go to the owners of capital – and necessarily so because to get any reductions in debt ratios we have to persuade the private sector to invest in productivity improvements, since public investment, in this model, is funded by public debt.

The clear implication of this example is that, although usually overlooked in most analyses, public-sector productivity matters a great deal. But more than that, it matters how it is deployed. Second, there are a series of unwelcome trade-offs to be navigated (or resolved). Greater income inequality inhibits growth, but having to promote productivity and growth through public-sector involvement increases debt. Thus an appropriate productivity policy could allow higher growth, and possibly lower debt, with or without greater inequality of incomes. But whichever route is chosen, it will require a greater share of the (income) gains made possible by higher productivity to go to the owners of private capital if higher debt ratios are to be avoided, or if the burden of public debt is to be reduced at the same time.

Similarly, higher productivity can be used to lower public-debt ratios, with or without increasing income inequalities; but at the cost of weaker, or even falling growth if income inequalities increase too sharply. And again, a greater share of the gains from this higher level of productivity will go to the owners of capital if growth rates are to be maintained or increased at the same time. Similarly, reversing this argument, policies designed to increase the public participation in raising productivity will typically reduce growth but increase debt, whereas those designed to reduce income inequalities directly will usually increase both growth and debt.

Conclusion

Productivity policies may function as an intermediate target for the usual targets of economic policy. But, as such, they are medium- to long-term policies and, of necessity, involve a degree of structural reform. Nevertheless, they are a good deal more subtle and nuanced than the structural-reform policies discussed in the literature or advocated in the austerity policies of recent years. They imply distinct roles for public-sector productivity and TFP and have clear and measurable consequence for income inequality in general, and for the distribution of gains from advances in productivity between capital and labour.

Notes

1 Krugman (1991) argues that increasing productivity is the only sustainable way to improve living standards.
2 This kind of model can be found in any undergraduate text; see Blanchard (2006) for example.
3 Formally $Y = Af(K, N)$, where the first derivative is positive, and the second negative, with respect to K and N.
4 See Jorgenson *et al.* (2008), and also Bloom, Sadun and van Reenen (2007).
5 Roberts (2005).
6 As above, data from Scottish Government (2007); also *Economic Pocket Databank*, Scottish Government (2007).
7 The data in this paragraph are taken from Scottish Government (2007).

8 This adaptation of Yakita's model is taken from Bokan *et al.* (2015), but has its origin in Arrow (1962) and Aiyagari and McGrattan (1998).
9 Arrow (1962), Aiyagari and McGrattan (1998) and Aschauer (2000) all use the same formulation.

References

Aiyagari, S. R. and E. R. McGrattan (1998), 'The optimum quantity of debt', *Journal of Monetary Economics*, 42, 447–469.
Arrow, K. J. (1962), 'The economic implications of learning by doing', *Review of Economic Studies*, 29, 155–173.
Aschauer, D. A. (2000), 'Do states optimise? Public capital and economic growth', *Annals of Regional Science*, 34, 343–363.
Blanchard, O. (2006), *Macroeconomics*, 4th edition, Prentice-Hall, Saddle River, NJ.
Bloom, N., R. Sadun, and J. Van Reenen (2007), 'Americans do I.T. better: US multinationals and the productivity miracle', *NBER Working Paper* No. 13085.
Bokan, N., A. Hughes Hallett and S. E. H. Jensen (2015), 'Growth maximising debt under changing demographics', *Macroeconomic Dynamics*, 12 pages. DOI: http://dx.doi.org/10.1017/S1365100514000947. Published online 17 August 2015.
Harris, R., M. O'Mahony and C. Robinson (2006), *Research on Scottish Productivity*, Chief Economic Advisors Office, Scottish Government, St Andrews House, Edinburgh.
Hughes Hallett, A. and Y. Ma (1993), 'East Germany, West Germany and their mezzogiorno problem', *Economic Journal*, 103, 416–428.
Hughes Hallett, A. and Y. Ma (1994), 'Adjustment mechanisms in a monetary union between asymmetric and incompletely converged economies', *European Economic Review*, 38, 1731–1761.
Jorgenson, D., M. S. Ho and K. J. Stiroh (2008), 'A retrospective look at the US productivity resurgence', *Journal of Economic Perspectives*, 22, 3–24.
Kalaitzidakis, P. and S. Kalyvitis (2004), 'On the macroeconomic implications of maintenance in public capital', *Journal of Public Economics*, 88, 695–712.
Krugman, P. (1991), *Geography and Trade*, MIT Press, Cambridge, MA.
Melitz, M. (2003), 'The impact of trade on intra-industry reallocations and aggregate industrial productivity', *Econometrica*, 71, 1695–1725.
Roberts, F. (2005), 'Ownership of firms in Scotland', *Scottish Economic Statistics*, Scottish Government, St Andrews House, Edinburgh.
Rostow, W. (1962), *The Stages of Economic Growth*, Cambridge University Press, Cambridge, UK.
Scottish Government (2007), *The Government Economic Strategy*, The Scottish Government, St Andrews House, Edinburgh.
Solow, R. M. (1957), 'Technical change and the aggregate production function', *Review of Economics and Statistics*, 39, 312–320.
Van Ark, B., M. O'Mahony and M. P. Timmer (2008), 'The productivity gap between Europe and the United States: Trends and causes', *Journal of Economic Perspectives*, 22, 25–44.
Yakita, A. (2008), 'Aging and public capital accumulation', *International Tax and Public Finance*, 15, 582–598.

9 Unifying framework for the evaluation of the composition of foreign exchange reserves for emerging economies

The case of South Africa

Lebogang Mateane and Willi Semmler

Introduction

The currency composition of foreign debt is a key reason for the currency composition of foreign exchange (FX) reserves (see Eichengreen and Mathieson, 2000; Papaioannou *et al.*, 2006). For example, euro debt obligations which are due soon for a government (or even any major domestic institution or firm) facing liquidity problems, can be financed using euro-denominated FX reserves. Empirical evidence by Dooley *et al.* (1989) shows that an increase in the weight of foreign-currency debt of developing countries results in a higher reserve weight in the same currency. Soesmanto *et al.* (2015) also find that foreign-currency debt influences the composition of FX reserves of Australia.

Against this background, much of the literature outlines that the currency composition of foreign debt is a motivating factor for the currency composition of FX reserves (composition of FX reserves henceforth). However, the literature does not emphasize the devastating effects of currency depreciations on foreign-currency debt and the resulting negative balance sheet effects which may result in investment and output contraction, especially in the context of emerging markets. These devastating effects are well documented in the currency crises literature and emerging economy literature (see Kamin, 1999; Jeanne, 2000; Aghion *et al.*, 2001, 2004; Mishkin and Savastano, 2001; Galindo *et al.*, 2003; Mishkin, 2004; Cook, 2004; Flaschel *et al.*, 2005; Kato *et al.*, 2011).

Claessens and Kreuser (2004) point out that research on financial crises directly shows that the balance sheet of a country needs to be accounted for and used as one of the motivating factors in the management of a country's FX reserves. Furthermore, risks that are faced by sovereigns are much broader as compared with those of firms and/or financial institutions. Thus, they note that this makes it more necessary for sovereigns to have an asset-liability management framework.

Following this set up, we propose that one portion of the total portfolio of FX reserves of South Africa is for liquidity and that another portion is motivated and consistent with the currency composition of foreign liabilities, where risk–return considerations are also accounted for. Thus, we propose a unifying framework which accounts for the two main motives proposed in the FX composition literature in a consistent manner using central-bank unique constraints. This procedure provides one possible mechanism under which the South African central bank may be able to safeguard the domestic economy, because of the well-documented effects of adverse exchange-rate movements on foreign-currency debt, especially in the context of emerging markets. We emphasize that our proposed framework is not a mechanism that we consider as one that can completely prevent or offset a fully fledged currency crisis. Instead, we propose one possible procedure that allows the central bank to safeguard the domestic economy in the event of foreign debt obligations that cannot be settled by domestic institutions whether or not the country is experiencing adverse exchange-rate movements and/or a currency crisis.

We also view this as one possible procedure to increase credibility among foreign-currency creditors because there is some financial backing associated with their assets. The main contribution of this chapter to the literature is to formalize through an existing quantitative framework and exploit the properties of the framework in such a way that the portfolio of FX reserves should exhibit a currency composition of FX reserves that is motivated and is consistent with the currency composition of foreign liabilities.

Although major reserve currencies are highly liquid, their respective exchange rates do not trade at a one-to-one rate. Hence, transactions costs can increase rapidly the larger and more rapid an attempt to convert between major currencies. Thus, our proposal is one that prevents the central bank from having to rapidly adjust its composition of FX reserves to match the composition of foreign liabilities of the country. This is a plausible, positive and direct proposal because, as is pointed out by Claessens and Kreuser (2004), emerging markets are typically faced with constraints in rapidly adjusting their assets and liabilities. Thus, they note that these constraints are in the form of high transaction costs and difficult market accessibility, especially during difficult market conditions. Furthermore, these factors can be exacerbated by negative investor sentiment which also depends on the prevailing conditions of international financial markets.

The rest of the chapter is structured as follows. The next section presents a literature review on the composition of FX reserves and presents an analysis of the composition of FX reserves using a transaction approach. Then we present a mean–variance model and our proposed unifying framework. We then describe the statistical properties of actual FX reserve data. The penultimate section presents estimation results of a mean–variance model and our unifying framework and the final section presents the conclusions.

Literature review

In this section we present a literature review on more factors that motivate the composition of FX reserves. In addition, we explain how these factors are explicitly connected with our analysis. There are two main approaches associated with the management of the composition of FX reserves. The first approach, noted by Dooley *et al.* (1989) and Borio *et al.* (2008), uses a mean–variance analysis to examine and determine an optimal composition of FX reserves. The mean–variance approach uses the risk, return and covariances of FX reserves to select an optimal composition of FX reserves. Alternative objective functions are used in the mean–variance approach and these are typically in the form of minimizing variance or maximizing expected return or using an objective function which is a linear combination of expected return and variance (see Ben-Bassat, 1980; Dellas and Yoo, 1991; Papaioannou *et al.*, 2006; and refer to Ramaswamy, 1999 and Gintschel and Scherer, 2004 for other representations).

The second approach that motivates the composition of FX reserves is the transaction approach and this generally uses a country's trade flows, composition of foreign liabilities and intervention in the FX market to examine and determine the optimality of a composition of FX reserves. Within this approach, Galati and Wooldridge (2009) outline that a reserve currency may be accumulated to serve as a medium of international exchange, a unit of account and a store of value and can be used for intervention in FX markets. Leahy (1996) notes that exchange-rate arrangements, such as unilateral currency pegs, may influence the composition of FX reserves. For developing countries, Eichengreen and Mathieson (2000) find that one of the main determinants of the currency composition of reserves is a country's trade flows. Recent literature argues and finds that transaction motives influence the composition of FX reserves (Soesmanto *et al.*, 2015, for Australia). Similarly, Ito *et al.* (2015) find that trade invoicing and currency movements influence the composition of FX reserves for five central and eastern European countries.

A relevant concept in the context of FX reserves is that ofnetwork externalities and is explained by Eichengreen (2005). The concept is based on an outcome that there are incentives associated with using currencies that are dominant in the market place. For example, when conducting international trade and settling international payments, it is cheaper and more sensible to use a currency used by other market participants. However, the concept of network externalities does not necessarily follow for the currency denomination of reserves.

Eichengreen (2005) emphasizes that although there are benefits of holding reserves associated with highly liquid markets, market liquidity is not the only relevant factor of relevance, and instead there may be gains for a central bank from greater diversification in exchange for less liquidity. Furthermore, without evidence of strong network externalities, then it should not be the case that a central bank is incapable of adjusting the composition of its FX reserves following relevant information about expected capital gains and losses.

Truman and Wong (2006) note that FX investment decisions by authorities are configured towards ensuring liquidity, preserving value and maximizing return subject to outlined constraints inclusive of exchange-rate movement. However, they note that reserve management practices are prudent and are highly influenced by inertia.[1]

Bernadell *et al.* (2004) and Cardon and Coche (2004) note that one possible investment philosophy of a central bank's FX reserve management is an asset and liability approach. Furthermore, Cardon and Coche (2004) note that the objective of this approach may be to incorporate reserve management with either a central bank's ability to handle financial risk or the respective country's external debt. In addition, they give an example where they document that in such a context, the objective of reserve management may be to find an optimal risk–return tradeoff and evaluate risk relative to the allocation of external public sector debt.

According to Putnam (2004), FX reserves should be divided into liquidity and capital preservation components because during periods of financial difficulty, central banks may have to intervene to safeguard the domestic economy and in turn they may have special needs to perform particular national duties.[2] Truman and Wong (2006) outline that reserve diversification and the role of active reserve management is relevant when a country's ratio of FX reserves relative to the size of the economy is significant. They also note that the composition of FX reserves may depend on the currency composition of debt, especially for a country concerned about settling its debt over a medium-term horizon.

Our proposed unifying framework is for South Africa, and the South African economy is a small open economy which exhibits a volatile currency, experiences volatile portfolio flows, went through financial-market liberalization and is susceptible to adverse exchange-rate shocks. These factors make South Africa vulnerable to liability dollarization, a currency crisis which in turn can result in investment and output contraction, among other things. This is evident insofar as the ratio of foreign-currency debt to gross domestic product (GDP) is rising (refer to Table 9A.1 in the appendix). Similarly, South Africa's ratio of FX reserves to GDP is rising (refer to Table 9A.1 in the appendix) and its FX reserves are comparable to other emerging markets that were in the top 30 of FX reserve holders (as of 2001, refer and compare with Table 1 in Truman and Wong, 2006). Furthermore, the percentage increase in South Africa's FX reserves has exceeded 200 per cent over the period 2001–2005, which is much higher than some of the emerging markets that were in the top 30 of FX reserve holders (Table 9.1 in Truman and Wong, 2006).

Aghion *et al.* (2001) emphasize that one of the two well-known facts surrounding the discourse on currency crises, is that countries with a high likelihood of experiencing a crisis are those in which firms hold a large amount of foreign-currency debt. This is evident in their findings under which all the countries that they evaluate that had a ratio of liabilities to claims with respect to foreign banks in excess of 1.5, went through a serious crisis in the 1990s. South Africa is one of the countries in these findings, and it has a ratio in excess of 2. Thus, based on these empirics and outlined devastating effect of currency depreciations, optimal management of the composition of FX reserves such as our proposed unifying framework may yield positive benefits for the domestic economy. This may also provide a positive signaling effect to international markets because of the sovereign assuming some accountability for foreign-currency debt.[3]

Data show that from the year 2000 onwards, the ratio of FX reserves as a percentage of GDP and the ratio of foreign-currency debt as a percentage of GDP for South Africa have evolved in a similar manner (refer to Table 9A.1 in the appendix). Moreover, the ratio of foreign-currency debt as a percentage of

GDP has partially exceeded the ratio of FX reserves as a percentage of GDP. We also examine whether the empirical composition of FX reserves of South Africa are optimal using the transaction approach and examine optimality using the mean–variance approach. We then proceed to our proposed unifying framework.

Transaction approach

Data outline

We first highlight the data we use and some of the problems associated with using and trying to obtain data associated with the composition of FX reserves. Empirically, central banks have always been reluctant to issue data on both the country and currency composition of FX reserves due to the sensitivity of the data because of fears surrounding speculative attacks, among other factors. Thus there has always been difficulty at the country level to obtain data on the country and currency composition of FX reserves and also on the country and currency composition of foreign-currency liabilities.

First, to highlight data problems in our context, we had to manually input the FX reserves data and foreign-liability data from various issues of the South African central banks' quarterly bulletins. We also had to compute the respective weights. This is unlike other data series which are readily available online and easy to download. The South African central bank is formally known as the South African Reserve Bank (SARB henceforth).

Second, ideally we should be working with net FX reserves, but gross FX reserves are reported and typically the literature evaluates gross reserves because this is what is usually reported or available. Third, we should ideally be evaluating foreign-currency composition of short-term liabilities because that poses a clearer and more immediate threat towards an emerging market. Furthermore, we should be evaluating the foreign-currency composition of unhedged liabilities. However, data on the foreign-currency composition of unhedged liabilities is not available. In addition, the composition of total liabilities is the only data series that is consistent, because data extracted from the SARB's quarterly bulletins do not distinguish whether some debt instruments are short term or long term. Such problems surrounding data are also documented by Honig (2005).

He notes that, because of a lack of data, he cannot determine the degree to which foreign-currency-denominated liabilities are hedged with forward contracts. However, he argues that total foreign-currency liabilities seem to be a reliable proxy for total unhedged foreign-currency liabilities, because not all forward contracts eliminate FX risk. Furthermore, he points out that the dominance of foreign lenders associated with major reserve currencies, results in these lenders usually being unwilling to sell foreign currencies in exchange for domestic currency, which in turn restricts hedging opportunities.[4]

Another problem is that data on actual FX reserves, actual trade flows and foreign liabilities of South Africa are denoted by the country of origin and not by currency denomination. For the purposes of our analysis, we consider, and from now on use, the country composition of FX reserves, trade flows and foreign liabilities as proxies for the currency-composition counterparties. We consider our proxies as reasonable, because the country composition of FX reserves, trade flows and foreign liabilities of South Africa all correspond to major reserve-currency countries such as the United States, the Euro area, Britain and Japan. Furthermore, the United States, the Euro area, Britain and Japan have empirically constituted a large combined weight in the total country composition of FX reserves, trade flows and foreign liabilities.[5] Wooldridge (2006) explains that one of the ways to determine the composition of reserves is by using counterparty data where for the holder of reserve assets, there is a corresponding liability for the issuer. As a result, he notes that counterparty data are a close proxy for reserve assets.

Transaction approach analysis

We now examine whether empirically the SARB has optimally managed its composition of FX reserves using variants of the transaction approach. More specifically, we examine whether empirically the actual weights of FX reserves are associated with trade flows in the form of trade weights, import weights and export weights. In addition, we examine whether empirically the actual weights of FX reserves are associated with the composition of foreign liabilities.

Table 9.1 reports data on average actual trade, import and export weights of South Africa by its trade partners. The trade flows and foreign liabilities that we examine are with respect to major reserve-currency countries which also happen to be South Africa's main trade partners and also comprise a large weight in the composition of South Africa's foreign liabilities. Trade flows and foreign liabilities are variables which are readily available and have explicit measures.

Other studies run regressions of FX reserve shares on variables such as trade shares, foreign-currency-debt shares and other variants of the transaction approach (see Dooley *et al.*, 1989; Eichengreen, 1998; Eichengreen and Mathieson, 2000; Ito *et al.*, 2015; and Soesmanto *et al.*, 2015). We use yearly international trade data to calculate the trade, import and export weights of South Africa.[6] Trade flows data are derived from Quantec's international trade database and spans from 1997–2012. For brevity, we report the average actual weights in Table 9.1 which cover three periods, namely 1997–2004, 2005–2012 and 1997–2012. For 2012, South Africa's two main continental trade partners are Asia in first place and Europe in second place. However, on a recognized and defined region/union the European Union is South Africa's main trade partner for the year 2012. Similarly for 2012, South Africa's four main country trade partners are China, the United States, Germany and Japan in rank order, the UK having been a main trade partner in previous years. Our data set for the composition of FX reserves and foreign liabilities is reported on an annual basis and is available over the period 1997–2012. Thus the data set is limited, which in turn makes us only conduct correlation analysis for the variants of the transaction approach.

Table 9.2 reports the average actual currency denomination of FX reserves and foreign-liability weights of South Africa. The yearly actual FX reserves and foreign-liabilities data of South Africa are only available over the period

Table 9.1 Average actual trade, import and export weights of South Africa (per cent)

Years	UK			Germany			US		
	TS	IM	EX	TS	IM	EX	TS	IM	EX
97–04	9.16	9.06	9.26	10.56	14.42	6.79	10.68	11.63	9.76
05–12	5.18	4.34	6.14	9.29	11.65	6.66	8.49	7.64	9.47
97–12	7.17	6.70	7.70	9.93	13.04	6.72	9.59	9.64	9.61
2012[1]	3.66	3.47	3.88	7.95	10.08	5.42	7.99	7.36	8.74

Years	Japan			China			Europe[2]		
	TS	IM	EX	TS	IM	EX	TS	IM	EX
97–04	7.18	7.32	7.06	3.02	4.50	1.56	19.39	21.23	17.63
05–12	7.13	5.61	8.84	9.95	12.01	7.53	17.96	18.44	17.46
97–12	7.16	6.46	7.95	6.49	8.30	4.55	18.68	19.83	17.54
2012[3]	5.36	4.56	6.31	13.09	14.36	11.58	15.54	16.62	14.26

Years	Americas[4]			Asia[5]			Africa		
	TS	IM	EX	TS	IM	EX	TS	IM	EX
97–04	3.30	3.97	2.63	17.19	21.39	13.10	8.82	3.54	13.97
05–12	3.79	5.00	2.43	20.09	25.20	14.36	11.18	7.74	15.00
97-12	3.54	4.49	2.53	18.64	23.29	13.73	10.00	5.64	14.48
2012[6]	3.78	4.58	2.82	22.71	27.30	17.26	13.38	9.88	17.53

Years	Oceania			Other[7]		
	TS	IM	EX	TS	IM	EX
97–04	2.34	2.73	1.95	8.36	0.23	16.28
05–12	1.98	2.05	1.91	4.95	0.22	10.21
97–12	2.16	2.39	1.93	6.66	0.22	13.25
2012[8]	1.44	1.63	1.22	5.10	0.16	10.98

Sources: Quantec – International trade database and author's computations.

Notes: Abbreviations: (UK) United Kingdom, (US) United States, (TS) Trade weight, (IM) Import weight, (EX) Export weight.
1, 3, 6, 8 – These are the actual trade, import and export weights for 2012.
2 – Europe excluding Germany and the UK. 4 – Americas excluding the US.
5 – Asia excluding Japan and China. 7 – Other refers to unidentified countries.

1997–2012. The average actual weights cover three periods, namely 1997–2004, 2005–2012 and over the total holding period 1997–2012. Table 9.2 excludes reserves from North and South America (except for the United States), Asia and Oceania because of their low weights over the holding period. For example, Japan is one of South Africa's main trade partners, but Japanese yen FX reserves have only featured twice in the actual portfolio of FX reserves, in 2001 with a 0.001 per cent weight and in 2012 with a 0.0003 per cent weight.

For 2012, 93.47 per cent of the total composition of FX reserves of the SARB consists of US dollar, British pound and euro-denominated reserves. This is in line

Table 9.2 Average actual FX reserve and liability weights of South Africa (per cent)

Years	British pound		Euro[1]		US dollar		Swiss franc		Other[2]	
	R	L	R	L	R	L	R	L	R	L
97–04	1.33	42.62	9.56	20.25	84.38	20.49	0.19	3.76	4.54	2.91
05–12	8.50	41.94	21.05	21.22	66.12	22.48	0.012	2.97	4.32	1.41
97–12	4.91	42.28	15.30	20.73	75.25	21.48	0.01	3.36	4.43	2.16
2012[3]	10.81	37.61	17.99	26.60	64.67	20.89	0.06	2.37	6.45	1.76

Source: Various issues of the *SARB Quarterly Bulletin* and author's computations.

Notes: Abbreviations: (R) FX Reserve weight, (L) Liability weight.
1 – We use Continental Europe excluding Switzerland as a proxy for the Euro.
2 – international organizations and unidentified countries.
3 – These are the actual FX reserve and liability weights for the year 2010. In Table 9.2, liability and FX reserve weights may not add up to 100 per cent because the table reports the weights which are significant and which are used in the analysis.

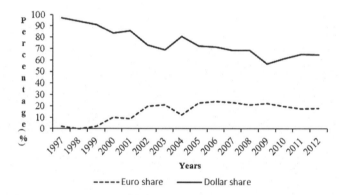

Figure 9.1 SARB dollar vs. euro share in reserves over 1997–2012.

with Eichengreen (1998), in which the US dollar, British pound, Deutsche marks, and Japanese yen constitute the largest weight for most of his sample period for industrial and developing countries.[7] Wooldridge (2006) identifies that over the late 1980s to the mid 2000s, fluctuations in the US dollar's weight of reserves have been mirrored by fluctuations in the euro's weight (inclusive of euro legacy currencies). This is exactly exhibited in the US dollar and euro weight of the SARB over the holding period 1997–2012, as shown in Figure 9.1.

Over the holding period 1997–2012, FX reserves of US dollar, British pound and euro denomination have constituted almost 96 per cent of the average total composition of FX reserves. Similarly, US dollar, British pound and euro-denominated foreign liabilities have also constituted a large weight, which is about 85 per cent of the average total composition of foreign-liability weights of South Africa over the period 1997–2012. We also include the Swiss franc because data are available. Some of the main trade partners, for example China, have never

Table 9.3 Correlation between reserve weights and other variables

Years	British pound			Euro			US dollar		
	TS	IM	EX	TS	IM	EX	TS	IM	EX
97–12	−0.93	−0.87	−0.90	−0.23	−0.48	0.03	0.85	0.87	0.27

Years	Swiss franc			British pound			Euro		
	TS	IM	EX	L			L		
97–12	−0.52	0.03	−0.54	−0.38			−0.04		

Years	US dollar			Swiss franc					
	L			L					
97–12	−0.55			−0.40					

Notes: Abbreviations: (TS) Trade weight, (IM) Import weight, (EX) Export weight, (L) Liability weight.

featured in the actual composition of FX reserves of South Africa over the period 1997–2012. Transaction costs may be a possible reason for not accumulating Chinese FX reserves. Unlike other FX assets, Chinese FX assets may not be traded regularly in FX markets.[8]

Table 9.3 reports the correlation between trade weights and FX reserves weights, the correlation between import weights the and FX reserves, the correlation between export weights and FX reserves and the correlation between foreign-liability weights and FX reserve weights. Over the holding period 1997–2012, it is only the correlation coefficients between trade, import and export weights with US dollar FX reserves that are always positive. Moreover, these are the only correlation coefficients which are high and positive, and this strongly suggests that US dollar FX reserves are accumulated for trade considerations. Moreover, this result possibly shows the international dominance of US assets as a medium of exchange and as a unit of account.

Most of the other correlation coefficients in Table 9.3 are either negative or are low and positive. Second to the US dollar, it is only the correlation between the export weights and euro FX reserves that are positive. This suggests that euro and US dollar reserves are possibly accumulated for exchange-rate intervention purposes, which is a point made by Dellas (1989). The intervention may be motivated by the desire to increase the competitiveness of South African exports.[9] This result is also supported by the fact that continental Europe and the United States have predominantly been the main export destinations for South Africa.

The correlation coefficient between British pound FX reserve weights and liability weights is −0.38 over the holding period 1997–2012. This value is low, negative, and raises concern. British pound liabilities have constituted the largest weight in the foreign-liability weights of South Africa over the holding period 1997–2012 with a 42.28 per cent average liability weight. Similar patterns are exhibited in the correlation coefficients between the FX reserve weights and the foreign-liability weights with respect to the US dollar, euro and Swiss franc, which are -0.55, -0.04 and -0.40 respectively over the holding period 1997–2012.

Based on correlation analysis, the empirical composition of FX reserve weights seems to reflect only a liquidity consideration and network externality effect because of the large allocation towards the US dollar. Thus, we propose that one portion is for liquidity and that another portion is managed and configured towards the composition of foreign liabilities. Thus, we propose a unifying framework which accounts for the composition of foreign liabilities and risk–return considerations, in a consistent manner.

Mean–variance and unifying framework

We now present the constrained mean–variance portfolio model that we use to examine whether the empirical composition of FX reserves of the SARB is optimal. We also present our proposed unifying framework. We first outline variants of the mean–variance portfolio model used in the literature on the composition of FX reserves. This allows us to distinguish our unifying framework from others.

Ben-Bassat (1980) uses a mean–variance model to select an optimal FX reserves portfolio using the consumption currency as a key factor. For the central bank of Korea, Dellas and Yoo (1991) compare the actual composition relative to portfolios generated by a mean–variance model with a no-short-selling constraint. Furthermore, using realized returns on FX reserves and actual currency denomination of imports as a proxy for consumption, they also evaluate whether portfolio decisions are associated with a welfare maximization criterion.

Ramaswamy (1999) proposes a framework that deviates from the dominant view by outlining a central bank's objective as minimizing the worst possible return outcome in different currency *numeraires*. Following this set up, the currency allocation problem is solved using a multi-objective optimization problem within the context of fuzzy decision theory.[10]

Gintschel and Scherer (2004) model the central-bank problem as a multiple benchmark optimization problem, with different weights attached to each problem and alternative risk regimes. In some representations of their constrained quadratic programming problem, they use an objective function which is synonymous with a mean–variance approximation of expected quadratic utility. Papaioannou *et al.* (2006) use a dynamic mean–variance optimization framework with portfolio rebalancing costs to estimate optimal-portfolio weights comprising major reserve currencies, with an objective function of maximizing expected portfolio return.[11]

Using compact vector and matrix notation, our central-bank portfolio selection problem in an n FX reserve asset framework, is characterized as follows[12]

$$\min \omega' \Omega \omega \tag{9.1}$$

subject to

$$\boldsymbol{\omega}'\mathbf{R} = r \tag{9.2}$$

$$\boldsymbol{\omega}'\mathbf{e} = 1 \tag{9.3}$$

$$\omega_i \geq 0, i = 1, 2, \ldots, n \tag{9.4}$$

where $\boldsymbol{\omega}$ is a weight vector of the FX reserves and each weight component ω_i is constrained to be greater than or equal to zero. This is shown in (9.4) and is our imposed no-short-selling constraint on each of the FX reserves. The covariance matrix of the expected real returns of the n FX reserves is given by $\boldsymbol{\Omega}$. The vector of expected returns is $\overline{\mathbf{R}}$, the unit vector is given by $\mathbf{e}$ and r is a given expected portfolio real return.[13] Equation (9.3) is a constraint that the sum of the weights of all the FX reserves is equal to one. Our no-short-selling constraint on each of the risky assets is the benchmark for constrained optimization throughout our analysis.[14] Thus, we use our constrained mean–variance portfolio model as shown in (9.1)–(9.4) to examine whether the empirical composition of FX reserves is optimal. In addition, we estimate optimal portfolios using our constrained mean–variance model consistent with (9.1)–(9.4).

More constraints can be imposed that are consistent with a no-short-selling constraint and these constraints can assume multiple forms, such as lower- and upper-bound constraints that are central-bank unique constraints. Thus, for our proposed unifying framework, the lower-bound constraints are arbitrary insofar as that given the associated empirical average foreign-liability weights exceed (0.2 or 20 per cent), they are allocated no less than 10 per cent. The upper-bound constraints are the associated individual empirical average foreign-liability weights (refer to Table 9.2).[15] Following this set up, the constraints guided by the empirical average foreign-liability weights are expressed as follows

$$0.10 \leq \omega_1 \leq 0.2073, \ 0.04 \leq \omega_2 \leq 0.08, 0.04 \leq \omega_3 \leq 0.08, \tag{9.5}$$

$$0.10 \leq \omega_4 \leq 0.4228, \ 0.10 \leq \omega_5 \leq 0.2148$$

The constraints in (9.5) can be incorporated along with those in (9.2), (9.3) and (9.4) and thus constitute our unifying framework in an n FX reserves framework.[16] The central-bank problem captured in (9.1), (9.2), (9.3), (9.4) and (9.5) is a quadratic programming problem and requires Kuhn–Tucker conditions in order to determine the optimal weights (see Bertsekas, 1999; Brandimarte, 2006).[17]

Our proposed unifying framework improves on frameworks that only use lower bound constraints by incorporating both lower- and upper-bound constraints. This allows our framework to preclude over-allocating weights beyond the associated actual foreign-liability weights and allows our framework to match the actual composition of foreign liabilities as best as possible.

The main contribution of this chapter to the literature is to exploit the properties of a mean–variance model in such a way that the currency composition of FX reserves is consistent with the currency composition of foreign liabilities, whether or not the country is experiencing adverse exchange-rate movements and/or a currency crisis. Thus, we propose a unifying framework for the evaluation of the composition of FX reserves which accounts for the two main motives proposed in the literature in a consistent manner using central-bank unique constraints.

Description of statistical properties of actual reserve data

Computing expected real returns on FX reserves

For robustness, we compute monthly expected real returns (which are annualized) using two different methods over the period 1997:01–2012:12. First, we compute expected real returns on FX reserves as follows[18]

$$R^e_{i,t+1} = r_{i,t} - \Delta P^{e*}_{t+1} + \Delta s^e_{i,t+1} \qquad (9.6)$$

where $R^e_{i,t+1}$ is the expected real return on FX reserve i at time $t+1$ (with the expectation formed at time t) and $r_{i,t}$ is the short-term nominal interest rate on FX reserve i. The log of nominal exchange rate is denominated as the domestic currency unit per foreign-currency unit, which is given by $s_{i,t}$ (i.e. South African rand per foreign currency) and $\Delta s^e_{i,t+1}$ is the expected percentage change in the exchange rate (the first difference of the log with the expectation formed at time t). The log of the foreign price index is denoted as P^*_t and ΔP^{e*}_{t+1} is expected foreign price inflation at time $t+1$ (the first difference of the log with the expectation formed at time t).

Our expected real returns incorporate expected exchange-rate changes, and forecasting exchange rates has proven to be difficult over the years. This difficulty is well known and has been well established through the seminal work of Meese and Rogoff (1982) who find that their candidate structural models do not perform any better than the random-walk model.[19] We assume the exchange rate follows a random walk in our first method of computing expected real returns and refer to this as the random-walk model. However, we also assume the disturbance term of the exchange rate is serially uncorrelated but is heteroscedastic, such as that characterized by Lo and MacKinlay (1989). We assume a heteroscedastic random-walk model because this theoretical construct allows us to capture the possibility of a time varying conditional variance of the exchange rate.[20] The first method includes a forecasted foreign price index.[21]

In the second method of computing expected real returns, we follow Papaioannou *et al.* (2006) and assume the central bank has perfect foresight of exchange-rate movements. We also assume the central bank has perfect foresight of exchange-rate movements purely because we want to capture the impact of realized actual exchange-rate changes in the real returns and their impact on portfolio selection. We also maintain our expected (forecasted) foreign inflation in the second method of computing real returns and denote the second method as the perfect-foresight model.[22]

Returns on FX reserves are computed for five major international currencies, namely the US dollar, the euro, British pound, Japanese yen and Swiss franc, and all our returns are annualized. We use the monthly producer price index of imported commodities as our foreign price index because this is the only reliable foreign price index we can use. The expected real returns we compute are South African rand denominated expected real returns. We incorporate returns for the Japanese yen and Swiss franc because these two currencies are internationally recognized and have featured at least once in the actual portfolio of FX reserves between 1997 and 2012. Moreover, data are available for returns on Japanese yen and Swiss franc denominated FX reserves.

The nominal interest rate for FX reserves denominated in the British pound, US dollar, Japanese yen and Swiss franc is the respective monthly treasury bill rate. For FX reserves denominated in euros, the nominal interest rate is the monthly money market rate because no treasury bill rate data are available.[23] Interest-rate data are derived from the International Monetary Fund's (IMF's) International Financial Statistics (IFS). Exchange rate and foreign price data are derived from the SARB. For all computations for the euro prior to 1999 (in our case for two years 1997–1998), we use the official European Currency Unit (ECU) for exchange-rate purposes. The South African rand/ECU rate we use is as defined by the SARB and from 1999 onwards we use the euro in our computations.

Variance–covariance and correlation matrices and volatility of real returns

We now report the empirical variance–covariance (covariance henceforth) matrix associated with both our computed expected real returns (real returns henceforth). Tables 9.4 and 9.5 report the sample covariance matrices over the monthly period 1997:01–2012:12.[24] We also evaluate the eigenvalue and eigenvector properties of the empirical covariance and correlation matrices.

Table 9.4 Variance–covariance matrix of annualized real returns using random walk

1997:01–2012:12	Euro	Yen	Swiss franc	British pound	US dollar
Mean return (%)	0.84	−1.63	−0.82	2.03	0.81
Standard deviation (%)	2.52	2.17	2.15	2.92	2.76
Variance–covariance (correlation coefficient)					
Euro	0.0006 (1.00)				
Yen	0.00045 (0.83)	0.0005 (1.00)			
Swiss franc	0.0005 (0.95)	0.00042 (0.90)	0.0005 (1.00)		
British pound	0.00069 (0.94)	0.00044 (0.69)	0.00053 (0.85)	0.0009 (1.00)	
US dollar	0.00062 (0.89)	0.00041 (0.69)	0.00051 (0.87)	0.00074 (0.93)	0.0008 (1.00)

Table 9.5 Variance–covariance matrix of annualized real returns using perfect foresight

1997:01–2012:12	Euro	Yen	Swiss franc	British pound	US dollar
Mean return (%)	2.15	0.027	1.07	3.11	1.96
Standard deviation (%)	13.32	15.52	13.85	13.42	14.08
Variance–covariance (correlation coefficient)					
Euro	0.018				
	(1.00)				
Yen	0.015	0.024			
	(0.75)	(1.00)			
Swiss franc	0.017	0.0167	0.019		
	(0.95)	(0.78)	(1.00)		
British pound	0.016	0.015	0.0158	0.018	
	(0.89)	(0.73)	(0.86)	(1.00)	
US dollar	0.0148	0.0175	0.015	0.016	0.0197
	(0.79)	(0.81)	(0.78)	(0.85)	(1.00)

We use empirical FX reserves returns and covariance matrices to evaluate the optimality of the empirical composition of FX reserves. We also use the empirical returns and covariances to determine alternative optimal compositions of FX reserves that are consistent with the composition of foreign liabilities. Thus we determine whether our empirical covariance matrices are invertible by computing their eigenvalues, the accuracy associated with their inverses by computing their condition numbers and determining whether these matrices exhibit information rather than noise as outlined in the random-matrix theory.

The condition number of a matrix is defined as follows

$$\gamma = \left[\frac{\lambda_{max}}{\lambda_{min}} \right]^{\frac{1}{2}} \tag{9.7}$$

where λ_{max} is the largest eigenvalue and λ_{min} is the smallest eigenvalue of the matrix. Greene (2011) points out that matrices with large condition numbers are difficult to invert accurately and a condition number greater than 20 is considered as problematic and its inverse does not exhibit a high degree of accuracy. Table 9.6 shows that our empirical covariance matrices are invertible because all their eigenvalues are positive and hence we can determine optimal weight vectors. Moreover, the condition numbers of our empirical covariance matrices are less than 20. They show a reliable degree of accuracy and in turn imply that the optimal FX reserves weight vectors also exhibit a reliable degree of accuracy.

Plerou *et al.* (1999, 2000) give a brief outline of the random-matrix theory that was developed in nuclear physics to allow for the interpretation of the spectra of complex nuclei and to be able to deal with the statistics of energy levels of complex quantum systems. This is of relevance in financial time-series data, more

Table 9.6 Eigenvalues of empirical covariance matrix 1997:01–2012:12

Actual eigenvalues: random walk

$\lambda_1 = 0.0028$ $\qquad$ $\lambda_2 = 0.00024$ $\qquad$ $\lambda_3 = 0.000068$ $\qquad$ $\lambda_4 = 0.000033$ $\qquad$ $\lambda_5 = 0.0000078$

Condition number $\qquad\qquad\qquad$ $\gamma = \left[\frac{\lambda_{\max}}{\lambda_{\min}} \right]^{\frac{1}{2}} = 18.95$

Actual eigenvalues: perfect foresight

$\lambda_1 = 0.084$ $\qquad$ $\lambda_2 = 0.0073$ $\qquad$ $\lambda_3 = 0.0047$ $\qquad$ $\lambda_4 = 0.0018$ $\qquad$ $\lambda_5 = 0.00085$

Condition number $\qquad\qquad\qquad$ $\gamma = \left[\frac{\lambda_{\max}}{\lambda_{\min}} \right]^{\frac{1}{2}} = 9.94$

---

specifically in large-dimensional systems which exhibit systematic associations between many variables such as those captured in covariance (correlation) matrices.

Laloux *et al.* (1999, 2000) highlight that the smallest eigenvalues of the correlation matrix are the ones that are most sensitive to noise, and it is the eigenvectors corresponding to the smallest eigenvalues that determine the set of least-risky portfolios. This shows that it is important to determine whether eigenvalues and eigenvectors of a given correlation matrix contain information. Portfolio-management recommendations are usually provided based on estimations that depend on empirical covariance (correlation) matrices. Our recommendations need to be based on empirical covariance (correlation) matrices that exhibit information (signal) rather than noise (see Pafka and Kondor, 2004; Frahm and Jaekel, 2008; Bouchaud and Potters, 2009). We conduct a three-stage test procedure using the predictions of the random-matrix theory so that we can determine whether both our empirical correlation matrices exhibit information or are random.

Our first-stage test procedure is to examine the ratio of the number of assets (N) in our portfolio relative to the length of the time series in our analysis. We define this ratio as $q = \frac{N}{T}$ and analyse this ratio first, because Pafka and Kondor (2003) argue that the effect of noise in variance–covariance (correlation) matrices depends on the ratio q. In a related manner, Bouchaud and Potters (2009) make an observation in the context of noisy matrices. They note that typical values of the inverse of the ratio of number of assets (N) relative to the number (length) of time-series data points or observations T, typically lie in the range $1 \to 10$. In the context of our analysis, the value of the ratio $\frac{T}{N} = 38.4$ provides us with our first indication that our empirical correlation matrices may not be random, but rather exhibit information (signal).

In our second-stage test procedure we examine whether the eigenvalues of our empirical correlation matrices fall in the region consistent with the theoretical prediction of the maximum and minimum values that the eigenvalues can assume, as proposed by the random-matrix theory. In line with Sharifi *et al.* (2004) and Daly *et al.* (2010), we construct a matrix **G** which is of dimension $N \times T$, where the components of **G** are g_i, where each g_i is constructed as follows

$$g_i(t) = \frac{R^e_{i,t+1} - \hat{R}^e_{i,t+1}}{\sigma_i} \qquad\qquad (9.8)$$

where $R_{i,t+1}^e$ is the expected real return on each FX reserve i at time $t+1$ (with the expectation formed at time t), $\hat{R}_{i,t+1}^e$ is the sample mean for each FX reserve i, and σ_i is the standard deviation of $R_{i,t+1}^e$ for each FX reserve i.

Let $\mathbf{C}$ denote the empirical correlation matrix and using matrix notation it can be written as follows

$$\mathbf{C} = \frac{1}{T}\mathbf{GG}^T. \tag{9.9}$$

Under the null hypothesis that the components of $\mathbf{G}$, namely g_i, are independent and identically distributed random variables, then the empirical correlation matrix is random. In addition, the density of the eigenvalues of the random matrix $\mathbf{C}$ is defined as follows

$$\rho_C(\lambda) = \frac{1}{N}\frac{dn(\lambda)}{d\lambda} \tag{9.10}$$

where $n(\lambda)$ is the number of eigenvalues of $\mathbf{C}$ less than λ. Furthermore if $\mathbf{G}$ is a random matrix, then $\rho_C(\lambda)$ is self-averaging and exactly known in the limit $N \to \infty$, $T \to \infty$ and $Q = \frac{T}{N} \geq 1$ fixed, then the density of the eigenvalues can be expressed as follows

$$\rho_C(\lambda) = \frac{Q}{2\pi\sigma^2}\frac{\sqrt{(\lambda_{max}-\lambda)(\lambda-\lambda_{min})}}{\lambda} \tag{9.11}$$

with $\lambda \in [\lambda_{min}, \lambda_{max}]$ and σ^2 is equal to the variance of the elements of $\mathbf{G}$ (see Sharifi *et al.*, 2004; Daly *et al.*, 2008, 2010). The symbol λ_{min}^{max} denotes the theoretical prediction of the maximum and minimum eigenvalues assumed that correspond to a random correlation matrix, and these are expressed as follows

$$\lambda_{min}^{max} = \sigma^2\left(1 + \frac{1}{Q} \pm 2\sqrt{\frac{1}{Q}}\right). \tag{9.12}$$

The results in Table 9.7 shows that using the empirical correlation matrices for both methods of computing real returns, all of the eigenvalues fall outside the

Table 9.7 Theoretical and actual eigenvalues for empirical correlation matrices

Empirical correlation matrix using random walk model				
$\lambda_{max} = 1.34$			$\lambda_{min} = 0.699$	
Actual eigenvalues				
$\lambda_1 = 4.43$	$\lambda_2 = 0.41$	$\lambda_3 = 0.013$	$\lambda_4 = 0.091$	$\lambda_5 = 0.0597$
Empirical correlation matrix using perfect foresight model				
$\lambda_{max} = 1.343$			$\lambda_{min} = 0.70$	
Actual eigenvalues				
$\lambda_1 = 4.28$	$\lambda_2 = 0.34$	$\lambda_3 = 0.24$	$\lambda_4 = 0.096$	$\lambda_5 = 0.046$

random (theoretical) bound. Based on our second-stage test procedure, we find that our empirical correlation matrices exhibit information and are not random.

For our third-stage test procedure, we plot and examine the distribution of the eigenvector components (corresponding to all the eigenvectors) of both our empirical correlation matrices. Plerou *et al.* (1999, 2001) note that the theory of random matrices predicts that the components of normalized eigenvectors of a Gaussian orthogonal ensemble follow a Gaussian distribution with a zero first moment and second moment equal to one. Similarly, Sharifi *et al.* (2004) examine the distribution of the eigenvector components corresponding to their empirical correlation matrix.

Figures 9.2 and 9.3 report the distribution of the eigenvector components of the empirical correlation matrices using the random-walk model and the perfect-foresight model. The eigenvector components are not clustered around the mean and the distribution is not consistent with a Gaussian distribution.

Our third-stage test procedure shows that our empirical correlation matrices are not random, but rather exhibit information (signal). Based on all three of our test procedures and using both our empirical correlation matrices, we do not find good agreement between our empirical correlation matrices and the predictions of the random-matrix theory. Thus, we conclude our empirical correlation matrices exhibit information (signal) rather than noise, as would be predicted by the random-matrix theory.

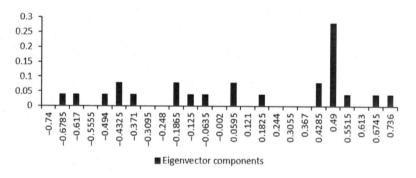

Figure 9.2 Distribution of eigenvector components (using random-walk model).

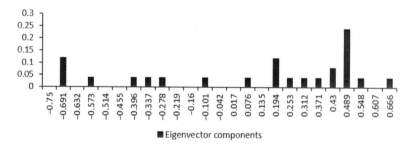

Figure 9.3 Distribution of eigenvector components (using perfect-foresight model).

Estimation results

No-short-selling constraint only

We first report optimal portfolios estimated only with a baseline no-short-selling constraint using both methods of computing real returns and compare them with the actual 2012 and average actual (over the total sample period 1997–2012) composition of FX reserves. In the next subsection we report optimal portfolios estimated with our unifying framework. We also report and compare the relevant means and standard deviations of the actual portfolios as shown in Tables 9.8 and 9.9.[25] We only report six optimal portfolios rather than all the optimal portfolios that lie on the efficient frontier (our reported optimal portfolios include the minimum-variance and maximum-return portfolio). We plot the efficient frontier and include the actual 2012 portfolio and average actual portfolio (over 1997–2012) positions for comparison purposes, as shown in Figures 9.4 and 9.5. The optimal portfolios represent a movement to the right along the efficient frontier, where this movement represents alternative risk–return trade-offs. Figures 9.4 and 9.5 show that the actual 2012 and average actual portfolios (over 1997–2012) are inefficient using both methods of computing returns. Although the British pound has the second-highest standard deviation (risk), the higher weight achieved in some of

Table 9.8 Actual and optimal foreign-reserve weights (random-walk model)

	2012 Act. port.		Av. act. port.		Min. var.
Port. mean (%)	0.909		0.847		−1.18
Port. std (%)	2.646		2.66		2.11
	Act. weights		Av. act. weights		Weights
Euro (%)	19.28		16.18		0.00
Yen (%)	1.29		0.88		44.30
Swiss franc (%)	1.35		0.979		55.70
British pound (%)	12.10		5.79		0.00
US dollar (%)	65.96		76.13		0.00
	Port. 1	Port. 2	Port. 3	Max. ret.	
Port. mean (%)	0.90	1.03	1.29	2.03	
Port. std (%)	2.51	2.55	2.63	2.92	
	Weights	Weights	Weights	Weights	
Euro (%)	41.68	48.46	54.90	0.00	
Yen (%)	12.03	11.16	2.44	0.00	
Swiss franc (%)	6.87	0.60	0.00	0.00	
British pound (%)	39.42	39.78	42.66	100	
US dollar (%)	0.00	0.00	0.00	0.00	

Notes: Abbreviations: (2012 Act. port.) 2012 actual portfolio, (Av. act. port.) average actual portfolio 1997–2012, (Min. var.) minimum variance, (Max. ret.) maximum return, (Port. mean) portfolio mean, (Port. std) portfolio standard deviation, (Port. 1,2,3) arbitrary optimal portfolios.

Table 9.9 Actual and optimal foreign-reserve weights (perfect-foresight model)

	2012 Act. port.		Av. act. port.		Min. var.
Port. mean (%)	2.099		2.03		2.22
Port. std (%)	13.23		13.42		12.84
	Act. weights		*Av. act. weights*		*Weights*
Euro (%)	19.28		16.18		44.85
Yen (%)	1.29		0.88		7.08
Swiss franc (%)	1.35		0.979		0.00
British pound (%)	12.10		5.79		26.63
US dollar (%)	65.96		76.13		21.43
	Port. 1	*Port. 2*	*Port. 3*	*Max. Ret.*	
Port. mean (%)	2.38	2.55	2.71	3.11	
Port. std (%)	12.85	12.89	12.98	13.42	
	Weights	*Weights*	*Weights*	*Weights*	
Euro (%)	42.94	37.47	29.09	0.00	
Yen (%)	2.43	0.00	0.00	0.00	
Swiss franc (%)	0.00	0.00	0.00	0.00	
British pound (%)	33.28	45.03	60.56	100	
US dollar (%)	21.35	17.50	10.34	0.00	

Notes: Abbreviations: (2012 Act. port.) 2012 actual portfolio, (Av. act. port.) average actual portfolio 1997–2012, (Min. var.) minimum variance, (Max. ret.) maximum return, (Port. mean) portfolio mean, (Port. std) portfolio standard deviation, (Port. 1,2,3) arbitrary optimal portfolios.

the optimal portfolios in Table 9.8 is anchored by the British pound having the highest mean return over the period 1997–2012. These findings are also augmented by the British pound's positive correlation with the other reserves, being fairly equal to the positive correlation between the US dollar and the other reserves.

Thus, the British pound is a better alternative for the risk–return trade-off on the basis of it having the highest mean return. Similarly, the euro has the second-highest mean return, and lower risk as compared with the US dollar, which in turn anchors it to having the highest weight in some optimal portfolios with higher returns. In Table 9.8 and in the context of optimal portfolios with the lowest risk, the Japanese yen and Swiss franc are allocated the highest weights. These weights are purely anchored by the Japanese yen having the second-lowest risk and the Swiss franc having the lowest risk. Moreover, these reserves exhibit the lowest positive correlation with all the other reserves. Thus, this works well for portfolio risk minimization and hence yields the substantial weights which gradually decline, however, as the optimal-portfolio mean return increases, because these reserves have negative mean returns and they are the two lowest mean returns over the period 1997–2012.

The low risk and negative mean returns of the Japanese yen and Swiss franc result in zero weights allocated in the optimal portfolios in Table 9.8, which have

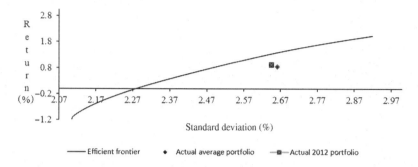

Figure 9.4 Efficient frontier vs. actual portfolios (using random-walk model).

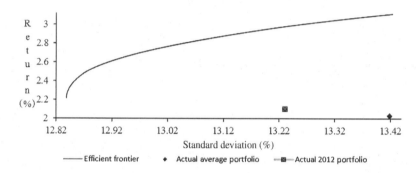

Figure 9.5 Efficient frontier vs. actual portfolios (using perfect-foresight model).

higher returns. This is more evident for the Swiss franc because it has higher positive correlation with the other reserves as compared with the positive correlation that the Japanese yen has with the other reserves. The US dollar achieves a zero allocation in all the optimal portfolios. The US dollar has a moderate return, the second-highest risk and has high positive correlation with the other reserves. Thus, these factors allocate a zero weight for the US dollar in all the optimal portfolios.

Table 9.9 reports the actual 2012 and actual average weights of FX reserves over the 1997–2012 period and reports their respective portfolio mean returns and standard deviations using the perfect-foresight model. Table 9.9 also reports the weights of six selected optimal portfolios which lie on the efficient frontier (including the minimum-variance and maximum-return portfolio) and their respective portfolio mean returns and standard deviations.

Table 9.9 shows that incorporating exchange-rate effects results in substantially different portfolio outcomes. The euro and the British pound are allocated the majority of the weight in the optimal portfolios. The higher weights are anchored by the British pound and the euro having the highest and second-highest mean return, respectively. The euro also has the lowest risk whereas the British pound has the second-lowest risk and these factors work well for alternative risk–return tradeoffs.

The Japanese yen is allocated some weight in the optimal portfolios with lower risk, which gradually declines, however, as the optimal-portfolio mean return increases, because the Japanese yen has the lowest mean return. Although the Japanese yen has the highest risk, it has the lowest positive correlation with the other reserves as compared with how the remaining reserves correlate among themselves. The low positive correlation works well for portfolio risk minimization and anchors its weight in the optimal portfolios that have lower risk.

Unlike in the random-walk model, the US dollar is allocated a substantial weight in the optimal portfolios that have lower risk using the perfect-foresight model. However, this weight gradually declines as the mean return of the optimal portfolios increases. The higher US dollar weight in the optimal portfolios that have lower risk is anchored by it having lower positive correlation with the other reserves as compared with the Swiss franc. In addition, the US dollar exhibits a similar correlation structure to the correlation structure of the British pound and euro. The Swiss franc achieves a zero allocation in all the optimal portfolios. The Swiss franc has the second-lowest return, moderate risk and high positive correlation with the other reserves. These factors make the Swiss franc a bad alternative for the optimal portfolios when balancing alternative risk–return trade-offs under the perfect-foresight model.

Unifying framework: foreign-liability weights constraint

We now report optimal portfolios using our unifying framework and all the relevant results are presented in Tables 9.10 and 9.11.

Tables 9.10 and 9.11 report the optimal weights of FX reserves using lower-bound and upper-bound constraints that are the consistent with the composition of the foreign liabilities of South Africa. Tables 9.10 and 9.11 also report the respective portfolio mean returns and standard deviations using the random-walk model and perfect-foresight model, respectively. Tables 9.10 and 9.11 show that the optimal weight of FX reserves using lower and upper bound constraints actually reflect the composition of foreign liabilities in the best possible manner. The risk and return of all the optimal portfolios using foreign-liability constraints and using both methods of computing real returns, perform better than the actual 2012 portfolio and the average actual (1997–2012) portfolio. Thus, using foreign-liability constraints, generates diversified and balanced optimal portfolios and exhibits better risk–return alternatives.

Next, using our unifying framework, we compare the optimal portfolios with the optimal portfolios generated only with a no-short-selling constraint. In this context, the optimal portfolios using our unifying framework perform better than some of the optimal portfolios generated only with a no-short-selling constraint. For example, using the random-walk model, the optimal minimum variance portfolio using our unifying framework has positive return, whereas the optimal minimum variance portfolio using only a no-short-selling constraint, has a negative return. Both these portfolios have similar risk, but the portfolios consistent with our unifying framework are more diversified and balanced. Incorporating

Table 9.10 Foreign-reserve weights using liability weights as constraints (random-walk model)

	2012 Act. port.		Av. act. port.	Constraints	
Port. mean (%)	0.909		0.847		
Port. std (%)	2.646		2.66		
	Weights		*Weights*	*Lower bound*	*Upper bound*
Euro (%)	19.28		16.18	10.00	20.73
Yen (%)	1.29		0.88	4.00	8.00
Swiss franc (%)	1.35		0.979	4.00	8.00
British pound (%)	12.10		5.79	10.00	42.28
US dollar (%)	65.96		76.13	10.00	21.48
	Min. var.	*Port. 1*	*Port. 2*	*Port. 3*	*Max. ret.*
Port. mean (%)	1.00	1.008	1.01	1.016	1.02
Port. std (%)	2.569	2.571	2.572	2.574	2.58
	Weights	*Weights*	*Weights*	*Weights*	*Weights*
Euro (%)	20.73	20.73	20.73	20.73	20.73
Yen (%)	8.00	7.98	7.89	7.64	7.51
Swiss franc (%)	8.00	8.00	8.00	8.00	8.00
British pound (%)	41.79	42.28	42.28	42.28	42.28
US dollar (%)	21.48	21.00	21.10	21.35	21.48

exchange rates exhibits similar patterns. The optimal minimum variance portfolio consistent with our unifying framework has a higher return than the optimal minimum variance using only a no-short-selling constraint, but has a marginally higher risk.

Based on the estimation results, our unifying framework exhibits multiple gains. First, the lower- and upper-bound constraints result in a more diversified and balanced portfolio as compared with portfolio weights constructed using only a no-short-selling constraint. Second, the optimal-portfolio risk–return characteristics using our unifying framework are comparable to the optimal portfolios using only a no-short-selling constraint and actual portfolios. In addition, in some instances they actually perform better. Third, the additional constraints allow the portfolio to be configured towards foreign-liability weights and actually reflect the composition of foreign liabilities in the best possible manner, while accounting for risk–return considerations.[26]

Our proposed unifying framework improves on models that only use lower-bound constraints by incorporating both lower- and upper-bound constraints. Only using lower-bound constraints may over-allocate some FX reserves beyond the associated foreign-currency-debt share (see Papaioannou *et al.* (2006), Tables 9.10 and A.2, comparing these tables for such an outcome). Thus our unifying framework precludes over allocating weights beyond the associated

Table 9.11 Foreign-reserve weights using liability weights as constraints (perfect-foresight model)

	2012 Act. port.		Av. act. port.	Constraints	
Port. mean (%)	2.099		2.03		
Port. std (%)	13.23		13.42		
	Act. weights		*Av. act. weights*	*Lower bound*	*Upper bound*
Euro (%)	19.28		16.18	10.00	20.73
Yen (%)	1.29		0.88	4.00	8.00
Swiss franc (%)	1.35		0.979	4.00	8.00
British pound (%)	12.10		5.79	10.00	42.28
US dollar (%)	65.96		76.13	10.00	21.48
	Min. var.	*Port. 1*	*Port. 2*	*Port. 3*	*Max. ret.*
Port. mean (%)	2.255	2.261	2.263	2.27	2.271
Port. std (%)	12.885	12.885	12.886	12.8863	12.89
	Weights	*Weights*	*Weights*	*Weights*	*Weights*
Euro (%)	20.73	20.73	20.73	20.73	20.73
Yen (%)	8.00	7.82	7.76	7.59	7.51
Swiss franc (%)	8.00	8.00	8.00	8.00	8.00
British pound (%)	41.79	41.97	42.03	42.20	42.28
US dollar (%)	21.48	21.48	21.48	21.48	21.48

actual foreign-liability weights. It also allows our framework to match the actual composition of foreign liabilities as best as possible.[27]

In the context of our unifying framework, the lower- and upper-bound constraints result in multiple gains. First, the lower- and upper-bound constraints result in a more diversified portfolio as compared with portfolio weights constructed using only a no-short-selling constraint. Second, the additional constraints allow the portfolio to be consistent with foreign-liability weights and thus account for central-bank unique constraints. This is one possible clear and direct procedure to safeguard the domestic economy because of the well-documented devastating effects of currency depreciations through liability dollarization effects and thus investment and output contraction. Furthermore, another possible procedure to increase credibility among external creditors (and domestic creditors that provide foreign-currency debt) is for there to be some financial backing associated with their assets, because the sovereign is taking responsibility for a proportion of the nation's foreign-currency debt. We consider this a plausible proposal, especially given that empirically foreign reserve weights of South Africa have been inconsistent with foreign liability weights.

We argue that the portfolio can be rebalanced period-by-period by taking into account whether factors such as the mean–variance and covariance structure between FX reserves exhibit changes and also accounting for changes in the central-bank unique constraints. In the context of using foreign-liability weights as constraints and changes in these constraints, we consider using average foreign-liability weights as constraints rather than the period-by-period composition of foreign liabilities as constraints. We consider this a better strategy because the average will most likely exhibit smaller changes as compared with the period-by-period change in the composition of foreign liabilities. Thus, it is highly likely that the rebalancing will not be as substantial as compared with a rebalancing strategy on the basis of a period-by-period change in the composition of foreign liabilities.[28]

Although major reserve currencies are highly liquid, their respective exchange rates do not trade at a one-to-one rate. Hence, transaction costs can increase rapidly the larger and more quickly an attempt to convert between major currencies. Thus, our proposal is one that prevents the central bank from having to rapidly adjust its composition of FX reserves to match the composition of foreign liabilities of the country. Claessens and Kreuser (2004) argue that emerging markets are typically faced with constraints in rapidly adjusting their assets and liabilities, where these constraints are in the form of high transaction costs and difficult market accessibility, especially during difficult market conditions. These factors can in turn be exacerbated by negative investor sentiment which also depends on the prevailing conditions of international financial markets.

Our proposed unifying framework is consistent with the views of Claessens and Kreuser (2004) who point out that research on financial crises directly shows that the balance sheet of a country needs to be accounted for and used as one of the motivating factors in the management of a country's FX reserves. Furthermore, risks that are faced by sovereigns are much broader compared with those of firms and/or financial institutions.

Conclusion

We propose that a proportion of the total portfolio of FX reserves should be consistent with the currency composition of foreign liabilities, whether or not South Africa is experiencing adverse exchange-rate movements and/or a currency crisis. Furthermore, risk–return considerations are taken into account. Thus, we propose a unifying framework for the evaluation of the composition of FX reserves for South Africa which accounts for the two main motives proposed in the literature in a consistent manner using central-bank unique constraints.

We estimate optimal portfolios using our proposed unifying framework and find optimal portfolios that are more diversified and balanced as compared with optimal portfolios constructed using only a no-short-selling constraint. In addition, the optimal-portfolio risk–return characteristics using our unifying framework are comparable with the optimal portfolios using only a no-short-selling constraint and perform better in some instances. Moreover, the optimal portfolios using our unifying framework always have better risk–return characteristics compared with the actual portfolios.

By imposing lower-bound and upper-bound constraints, our unifying framework precludes over-allocating weights beyond the associated central-bank unique constraints. As a result, this allows the actual composition of FX reserves to be consistent with the actual composition of foreign liabilities as best as possible. This is a plausible, positive and direct proposal.

Appendix: data on foreign-currency reserves and foreign-currency debt and ratios

We only report data on the level of FX reserves, foreign-currency debt, the ratio of FX reserves to GDP and the ratio of foreign-currency debt to GDP over the period 2002–2013 rather than over our sample holding period 1997–2012. Thus, we use a data series that can allow us to compare with Truman and Wong's (2006) analysis, because the data source we use is the same as theirs for extracting the level of FX reserves of South Africa and also the global FX reserves.[29] In addition, the currency denomination is the same, thus allowing the variables to be compared. Data on FX reserves are derived from the International Reserves Template of the IMF, and South African GDP data are derived from the World Economic Outlook of the IMF. Data on the level of foreign-currency debt are derived from the SARB's statistical and economic information site and it is also denominated in US dollars.

Table A9.1 shows that the level of FX reserves has been rising and so too has the ratio of FX reserves to GDP (as percentage). In addition, the ratio of foreign-currency debt to GDP (as a percentage) has been rising as well. Comparing with table 1 in Truman and Wong (2006), it is evident that for the year 2005, South Africa marginally falls out of the world's top 30 foreign reserve holders. South Africa has a very similar ratio of FX reserves to GDP (as percentage) to those in the top 30 and in some instances higher than that for some emerging market countries (we don't compare with advanced countries). Another interesting fact is that South Africa's FX reserves have exhibited a 216 per cent change over the period

Table A9.1 FX reserves and foreign currency denominated debt data and ratios

Years	FXR to GDP (%)	FCD to GDP (%)	FXR (USD billions)
2000	4.36	18.70	5.79
2001	4.86	20.28	5.77
2002	5.03	22.49	5.60
2003	3.66	16.26	6.16
2004	5.84	12.71	12.81
2005	7.40	11.43	18.28
2006	8.71	13.99	22.75
2007	10.24	16.30	29.27
2008	11.07	16.73	30.27
2009	11.38	15.97	32.47
2010	9.70	13.86	35.43
2011	9.86	13.58	39.85
2012	10.80	15.82	41.28
2013	11.96	17.45	41.94

Notes: (FXR) foreign exchange reserves, (FCD) foreign currency debt, (USD) US dollars.

2001–2005, which is a higher percentage change compared with some of the top 30 holders over the period 2001–2005 in Truman and Wong's (2006) analysis. Furthermore, South Africa's weight in world (global) weight of foreign-currency reserves has increased over the period 2001–2005 with a 0.28 per cent weight of world total in the year 2001 and a 0.44 per cent weight of world total in 2005, which is a positive percentage point increase.

Table A9.1 shows that from the year 2000, the ratio of FX reserves as a percentage of GDP and the ratio of foreign-currency debt as a percentage of GDP for South Africa have evolved in a similar manner. Moreover, the ratio of foreign-currency debt as a percentage of GDP has partially exceeded the ratio of FX reserves as a percentage of GDP. These are some of the factors that motivate our proposal that a proportion of the total portfolio of FX reserves is managed so that it is consistent with the currency composition of foreign liabilities. This is a procedure that allows the central bank to safeguard the domestic economy in the event of foreign debt obligations that cannot be settled by domestic institutions whether or not the country is experiencing adverse exchange rate movements and/or a currency crisis.

Notes

1 Fisher and Lie (2004), Ho (2004) and Putnam (2004) outline that the traditional objectives of reserve management are capital preservation, liquidity and investment return. Thus, simple objectives of maximizing portfolio returns are inconsistent with central banks' investment objectives and, instead, central banks have unique investment objectives and mandates.

2 Truman and Wong (2006) point out that countries may also allocate a proportion of their reserves for other reasons, such as recapitalizing government-owned banks.

3 There is always a possibility of moral hazard on the part of domestic firms and institutions. However, there is always a high possibility that stringent measures can be put into place by the sovereign, which also has legal jurisdiction over domestic institutions. Jeanne (2000) also discusses some aspects surrounding foreign-currency debt and the possibilities of moral hazard.

4 There are documented costs and benefits associated with foreign-currency-denominated debt. For example and from a borrower's perspective, one of the benefits of borrowing in foreign currency is because of the risk premium associated with borrowing externally in domestic-currency terms. This is a point made by Calvo (2002), who notes that foreign borrowing in domestic currency may have an interest-rate premium that may be over and above what is already captured by exchange-rate risk. On the other hand and with reference to earlier literature, Honig (2005) points out that foreign lenders force emerging markets to borrow externally using major foreign currencies because the diversification benefits of emerging market countries' currencies are low relative to their associated transaction costs.

5 Similarly, Dooley *et al.* (1989) argue that the trade flow patterns of a country can be used as an approximation of the currency composition of a country's trade flows. Papaioannou *et al.* (2006) do not have access to data on trade invoicing (currency composition of trade); instead they have data on the direction of trade and instead use these for evaluating the composition of reserves.

6 Trade shares are defined as the sum of export and import value of South Africa, with each respective country/region divided by the sum of export value and import value of South Africa with the world.

7 The similarity in the composition of FX reserves of the SARB, probably reflects Eichen-green's (1998, 2005) point on the herding behavior (network externality) aspect of having a composition similar to other international investors (and not restricted to central banks only).

8 We would also like to thank an anonymous referee for highlighting that over the sample period of this chapter, the Chinese currency was pegged (more or less closely) to the US dollar. Thus, having a large weight in US dollars and a low or zero weight on the renminbi in official reserves is not inconsistent with the transaction motive.

9 Although South Africa follows a floating-exchange-rate policy, just like some other central banks, we consider the exchange-rate policy to be a managed-float policy.

10 Matching currency composition of reserves to currency composition of imports is motivated by a desire to hedge against exchange-rate risk associated with purchasing imports. Ramaswamy (1999) argues that this is not necessarily suitable for many central banks, because reserve holdings may not necessarily be motivated by a need to finance imports.

11 They simulate optimal currency weights for four large emerging market countries and incorporate constraints such that the composition of FX reserves is consistent with currencies of a country's peg, foreign debt and international trade. In their model, they note that Russia had about 65 per cent of its external debt in US dollars and 29 per cent in Deutsche marks. Thus, they impose a constraint that the Russian central bank would desire to hold at least 32.5 per cent of its reserves in US dollars and 14.5 per cent of its reserves in Deutsche marks, where they note that the 50 per cent thresholds are arbitrary.

12 Markowitz's (1952) mean–variance portfolio framework and Tobin's (1958) mutual fund theorem, are two well-known frameworks that defined and elevated technical frameworks that can be used for portfolio selection. The constrained mean–variance quadratic programming model does not use an explicit utility function and hence does not explicitly characterize an investor's risk preferences. However, as pointed out by Markowitz (2014), a careful choice of an optimal mean–variance portfolio by an investor, even though an explicit utility function is not used, results in a portfolio with maximum or almost maximum expected utility, because it is an implicit expected utility maximization process.

13 Jorion (1994) notes that the optimization problem faced by an investor in a mean–variance framework involves maximizing an objective function that is positively related to a portfolio mean and negatively related to a portfolio variance. This is consistent with a mean–variance approximation of expected quadratic utility. Using a mean–variance approximation of expected quadratic utility allows us to characterize a central bank's preferences through a parameter of risk aversion. However, utility functions have associated problems and corresponding implications for the relevant parameters of absolute and relative risk aversion. Moreover, depending on a specific utility function, there are distributional assumptions associated with asset returns (see Campbell and Viceira, 2002; Danthine and Donaldson, 2005).

14 From a central-banking perspective, Dellas and Yoo (1991) avoid using a mean–variance framework which consists of a risk-free asset and a portfolio of risky assets. They avoid using this framework to characterize central-bank behaviour for the following reasons: (i) they avoid the ambiguity involved with choosing a risk-free asset because they argue that they do not know if such an asset exists in the context of FX reserves; and (ii) they avoid the problem of guessing values of the parameter of relative risk aversion or using information that may not be relevant. Dellas (1989) avoids using a risk aversion parameter because central banks do not have the same risk profile as private investors and there is no consensus view on particular risk aversion parameters.

We rule out using a mean–variance approximation of expected quadratic utility because it results in short selling some FX reserves so that the model can maximize the Sharpe ratio when the covariance matrix exhibits positive correlation among many of the FX reserves. A short-selling procedure seems to be inconsistent with central-bank conduct. However, we do have estimation results using a mean–variance approximation to expected quadratic utility under the perfect-foresight model. The weights exhibit substantial short selling in the Japanese yen (-40.20 per cent) and Swiss franc (-40.24 per cent) in the overall portfolio. Using the random-walk model results in infeasible portfolios because the model cannot obtain a tangency portfolio that maximizes the Sharpe ratio and it seems like the model requires excessive short selling. It may be possible to maximize the same objective function constraining the risky asset vector, using an approach such as a Hamilton–Jacobi–Bellman method. However, we do not explore such an approach and have not encountered it yet (to our knowledge) in the existing literature.

15 The Japanese yen and Swiss franc have associated empirical average foreign-liability weights that are less than 4 per cent. Thus to obtain feasible portfolios out of the five assets, these are the only two assets where both the lower- and upper-bound constraints have to be arbitrary. In the context of these two assets, the constraints are such that they are individually allocated no less than 4 per cent and no more than 8 per cent in all the optimal portfolios which use foreign-liability weights as constraints.

16 Using five specific FX reserves consistent with our analysis, ω_1 refers to the euro, ω_2 refers to the Japanese yen, ω_3 refers to the Swiss franc, ω_4 refers to the British pound and ω_5 refers to the US dollar.

17 Without the no-short-selling constraint, an optimal weight vector can be determined directly from the first-order conditions corresponding to a Lagrangian, in a manner outlined by Horii (1986). Furthermore, Best and Grauer (1991) evaluate the analytics of a portfolio problem formulated as a parametric quadratic programming problem.

18 As of September 2014, the most up-to-date available data on the composition of FX reserves of the SARB cover the period 1997–2012.

19 Dellas and Yoo (1991) and Baz *et al.* (2001) assume that the exchange rate follows a random-walk model in their portfolio frameworks.

20 We also don't examine whether each exchange rate follows a random walk or if they fit other types of models which may be useful for forecasting purposes. For comprehensive analyses on exchange-rate models and their forecasting ability, refer to the seminal work of Meese and Rogoff (1983), Clarida *et al.* (2003), Yilmaz (2003), Kim *et al.* (2004), Cheung *et al.* (2005), Kolari *et al.* (2008) and Proaño (2011, 2013) among others.

21 Our findings suggest that foreign price inflation is best estimated with an ARMA model, and details are available upon request.

22 In line with other research, we have assumed that the exchange rate follows a random walk in one instance and perfect foresight in another. This is without problems. Assuming random walk of the exchange rate results in an optimal composition geared towards reserve currencies with the highest yield. This is emphasized by Papaioannou *et al.* (2006), where they also note that this is an unlikely strategy for a central bank because it would imply continuous rebalancing. Papaioannou *et al.* (2006) also point out that assuming perfect foresight exhibits outcomes under which it is illogical to allocate substantial weight to reserves with negative returns unless a central bank needs to be invested in a reserve asset with its associated risk. Thus, our unifying framework addresses such problems because the central bank is not allocating reserves on the basis of the highest yield, and even if some reserves may exhibit negative returns such as the Japanese yen, the central bank is invested in such a reserve asset on the basis of constraints unique to a central bank's requirement, i.e. composition of foreign liabilities. This in turn shows that, our unifying framework is robust to the shortcomings associated with assuming that an exchange rate follows a random walk and a perfect-foresight model and addresses the problem of continuous rebalancing.

23 We use the money market rate instead of a monthly euro-area government bond rate because the money market rate has similar magnitude and exhibits similar variation with

that of the treasury bill rates of the other foreign exchange reserves. Thus, it is a better comparable short-term interest-rate measure. In addition, using the monthly government bond rate would bias results more to the euro because in general over the sample, the government bond rate has higher magnitude and less variation as compared with the other treasury bill rates.

24 We have also estimated the volatility of real returns. It is well known that financial time-series data exhibits a time varying conditional variance. Thus using both methods of computing real returns, we find that the foreign exchange reserves exhibit a time varying conditional variance. Estimation results for the time varying conditional variances, the corresponding implied unconditional variances, implied unconditional kurtosis and their sample counterparts, are available upon request.

25 Although we compare the actual 2012 portfolio and average actual (1997–2012) portfolio to the optimal portfolios, the weights of the actual 2012 portfolio consisting of the euro, Japanese yen, Swiss franc, British pound and US dollar only sum to approximately 93.53 per cent because the remaining 6.47 per cent is allocated to international organizations, other countries and unidentified countries. Similarly, the weights of the average actual (1997–2012) portfolio consisting of the same major reserve currencies, only sum to approximately 95.56 per cent because the remaining 4.44 per cent is allocated to international organizations, other countries and unidentified countries. In both instances, for the actual 2012 portfolio and average actual (1997–2012) portfolio, the majority of the residual is due to international organizations and unidentified countries. Thus, to be able to compare the actual portfolios with the estimated, which sum to 100 per cent, we equally allocate the residual to the relevant reserves in our analysis so that the actual portfolios sum to 100 per cent.

26 There are limitations to our unifying framework because it emphasizes risk benefits through diversification on the basis of the mean and variance of the distribution of returns. However, this model does not consider other higher moments and factors such as downside risk, which can matter and can result in different portfolio outcomes even when a portfolio is diversified and balanced. As emphasized by Ang (2012), a greater negative skewness results in greater downside risk of a portfolio relative to the downside risk of each individual asset. Furthermore, we only use portfolio standard deviation as a measure of portfolio risk, when in fact, there are other measures of risk such as Value-at-Risk (VaR). As noted by Kolm *et al.* (2014), in recent times, Conditional Value-at-Risk (CVaR) is a popular portfolio risk measure because it is logical and consistent and progresses from VaR, which possesses some undesirable mathematical properties such as non-subadditivity and non-convexity (see Fabozzi *et al.*, 2007). In the context of a central-banking environment, Ho (2004) outlines the benefits and shortfalls of VaR as a risk measure. Putnam (2004) evaluates and outlines aspects of VaR in a central-banking environment. Claessens and Kreuser (2004) outline CVaR in a central-banking environment and explain its relation with VaR and the corresponding advantages and disadvantages of each approach.

27 Holding reserves is costly and thus can also justify using lower- and upper-bound constraints to avoid over-allocating beyond the associated actual foreign-liability weights. For example, Feldstein (1999) and Rodrik (2006) note that the interest earned on the purchase of reserves is generally lower than the interest paid on domestic bonds which are used for financing the purchase of reserves. Furthermore, there is the foregone rate of return that could be realized from investment in the domestic economy.

28 It is a procedure that prevents the central bank from having to rapidly adjust its composition of FX reserves to match the composition of foreign liabilities of the country.

29 Data are available on the level of FX reserves from earlier times, but it is denominated in South African rands.

References

Aghion, P., Bacchetta, P. and Banerjee, A., 2001. Currency crises and monetary policy in an economy with credit constraints. *European Economic Review* 45, 1121–1150.

Aghion, P., Bacchetta, P. and Banerjee, A., 2004. A corporate balance-sheet approach to currency crises. *Journal of Economic Theory* 119, 6–30.

Ang, A., 2012. Mean-variance investing. Columbia Business School Research Paper No. 12/49. Columbia Business School – Finance and Economics, New York.

Baz, J., Breedon, F., Naik, V. and Peress, J., 2001. Optimal portfolios of foreign currencies: Trading on the forward bias. *The Journal of Portfolio Management* 28.1, 102–111.

Ben-Bassat, A., 1980. The optimal composition of FX reserves. *Journal of International Economics* 10, 285–295.

Bernadell, C., Cardon, P., Coche, J., Diebold, F. X. and Manganelli, S., 2004. *Risk Management for Central Bank FX*. European Central Bank, Frankfurt, Germany.

Bertsekas, D. P., 1999. *Nonlinear Programming*, second edition. Athena Scientific, Belmont, MA.

Best, M. J. and Grauer, R. R., 1991. On the sensitivity of mean-variance-efficient portfolios to changes in asset means: Some analytical and computational results. *The Review of Financial Studies* 4, 315–342.

Borio, C., Ebbesen, J., Galati, G. and Heath, A., 2008. FX reserve management: Elements of a framework. Monetary and Economic Department, BIS Papers No. 38, March 2008.

Bouchaud, J-P. and Potters, M., 2009. Financial applications of random matrix theory: A short review. Preprint, arXiv: 0910.1205v1 [q-fin.ST].

Brandimarte, P., 2006. *Numerical Methods in Finance and Economics: A MATLAB-Based Introduction*, second edition. John Wiley & Sons, Hoboken, NJ.

Calvo, G. A., 2002. On dollarization. *Economics of Transition* 10, 393–403.

Campbell, J. Y. and Viceira, L. M., 2002. *Strategic Asset Allocation: Portfolio Choice for Long-Term Investors*, Clarendon Lectures in Economics. Oxford University Press, Oxford.

Cardon, P. and Coche, J., 2004. Strategic asset allocation for FX reserves. In: Bernadell, C., Cardon, P., Coche, J., Diebold, F. X. and Manganelli, S., 2004. *Risk Management for Central Bank FX*. European Central Bank, Frankfurt, Germany.

Cheung, Y-W., Chinn, M. D. and Pascual, A. G., 2005. Empirical exchange rate models of the nineties: Are any fit to survive? *Journal of International Money and Finance* 24, 1150–1175.

Claessens, S. and Kreuser, J., 2004. In: Bernadell, C., Cardon, P., Coche, J., Diebold, F. X. and Manganelli, S., 2004. *Risk Management for Central Bank FX*. European Central Bank, Frankfurt, Germany.

Clarida R. H., Sarno, L., Taylor, M. P. and Valente, G., 2003. The out-of-sample success of term structure models as exchange rate predictors: A step beyond. *Journal of International Economics* 60, 61–83.

Cook, D., 2004. Monetary policy in emerging markets: Can liability dollarization explain contractionary devaluations? *Journal of Monetary Economics* 51, 1155–1181.

Daly, J., Crane, M. and Ruskin H. J., 2008. Random matrix theory filters in portfolio optimisation: A stability and risk assessment. *Physica* A 387, 4248–4260.

Daly, J., Crane, M. and Ruskin H. J., 2010. Random matrix theory filters and currency portfolio optimisation. *Journal of Physics: Conference Series* 221, 012003.

Danthine, J.-P. and Donaldson J. B., 2005. *Intermediate Financial Theory*, second edition, Academic Press Advanced Finance Series. Elsevier, Amsterdam.

Dellas, H., 1989. International reserve currencies. IMF Working Paper WP/89/15.

Dellas, H. and Yoo, C. B., 1991. Reserve currency preferences of central banks: The case of Korea. *Journal of International Money and Finance* 10, 406–419.

Dooley, M. P., Lizondo J. S. and Mathieson D. J., 1989. The currency composition of FX reserves. Staff Papers – International Monetary Fund 36, 385–434.

Eichengreen, B., 1998. The euro as a reserve currency. *Journal of the Japanese and International Economies* 12, 483–506.

Eichengreen, B., 2005. Sterling's past, dollar's future: Historical perspective on reserve currency competition. NBER Working Paper No. 11336, May 2005, JEL No. F0.

Eichengreen, B. and Mathieson, D., 2000. The currency composition of FX reserves: Retrospect and prospect. IMF Working Paper WP/00/131.

Fabozzi, F. J., Kolm, P. N., Pachamanova, D. and Focardi, S. M., 2007. *Robust Portfolio Optimization and Management*. John Wiley & Sons, Hoboken, NJ.

Feldstein, M., 1999. A self-help guide for emerging markets. *Foreign Affairs* 78, 93–109.

Fisher, S. J. and Lie, M. C., 2004. Asset allocation for central banks: optimally combining liquidity, duration, currency and non-government risk. In: Bernadell, C., Cardon, P., Coche, J., Diebold, F. X. and Manganelli, S., 2004. *Risk Management for Central Bank FX*. European Central Bank, Frankfurt, Germany.

Flaschel, P., Proano, C. R. and Semmler, W., 2005. Currency and financial crises in emerging market economies in the medium run. *The Journal of Economic Asymmetries* 2, 105–130.

Frahm, G. and Jaekel, U., 2008. Random matrix theory and robust covariance matrix estimation for financial data. Preprint, arXiv: physics/0503007v1 [physics.soc.ph]

Galati, G. and Wooldridge, P., 2009. The euro as a reserve currency: A challenge to the pre-eminence of the US dollar? *International Journal of Financial Economics* 14, 1–23.

Galindo, A. Panizza, U. and Schiantarelli, F., 2003. Debt composition and balance sheet effects of currency depreciation: A summary of the micro evidence. *Emerging Markets Review* 4, 330–339.

Gintschel, A. and Scherer, B., 2004. Currency reserve management by dual benchmark optimisation. In: Bernadell, C., Cardon, P., Coche, J., Diebold, F. X. and Manganelli, S., 2004. *Risk Management for Central Bank FX*. European Central Bank, Frankfurt, Germany.

Greene, W. H., 2011. *Econometric Analysis*, seventh edition. Prentice Hall, Upper Saddle River, NJ.

Ho, C., 2004. FX risk management in Hong Kong. In: Bernadell, C., Cardon, P., Coche, J., Diebold, F. X. and Manganelli, S., 2004. *Risk Management for Central Bank FX*. European Central Bank, Frankfurt, Germany.

Honig, A., 2005. Fear of floating and domestic liability dollarization. *Emerging Markets Review* 6, 289–307.

Horii, A., 1986. The evolution of reserve currency diversification. BIS Economic Papers No. 18, December 1986.

Ito, H., McCauley, R. N. and Chan, T., 2015. Currency composition of reserves, trade invoicing and currency movements. *Emerging Markets Review* 25, 16–29.

Jeanne, O., 2000. Foreign currency debt and the global financial architecture. *European Economic Review* 44, 719–727.

Jorion, P., 1994. Mean/variance analysis of currency overlays. *Financial Analysts Journal*, 50, 48–56.

Kamin, S. B., 1999. The current international financial crisis: How much is new? *Journal of International Money and Finance* 18, 501–514.

Kato, M., Proano, C, R. and Semmler, W., 2011. Currency runs, international reserves management and optimal monetary policy rules. *Review of World Economics* manuscript, 4 June 2011.

Kim, T.-H., Lee, Y.-S. and Newbold, P., 2004. Revisiting the martingale hypothesis for exchange rates. Discussion Papers in Economics No. 04/13, University of Nottingham, July 2004.

Kolari, J. W., Su, X. and Yang, J., 2008. Do Euro exchange rates follow a martingale? Some out-of-sample evidence. *Journal of Banking & Finance* 32, 729–740.

Kolm, P. N., Tütüncü, R. and Fabozzi, F. J., 2014. 60 years of portfolio optimization: Practical challenges and current trends. *European Journal of Operational Research* 234, 356–371.

Laloux, L., Cizeau, P., Bouchaud, J.-P. and Potters, M., 1999. Noise dressing of financial correlation matrices. *Physical Review Letters* 83, 1467.

Laloux, L., Cizeau, P., Bouchaud, J.-P. and Potters, M., 2000. Random matrix theory and financial correlations. *International Journal of Theoretical and Applied Finance*, 3, Issue 03, July 2000.

Leahy, M. P., 1996. The dollar as an official reserve currency under EMU. *Open Economies Review* 7, 371–390.

Lo, A. W. and MacKinlay, A. C., 1989. The size and power of the variance ratio test in finite samples: A Monte Carlo investigation. *Journal of Econometrics* 40, 203–238.

Markowitz, H., 1952. Portfolio selection. *The Journal of Finance* 7, 77–91.

Markowitz, H., 2014. Mean-variance approximations to expected utility. *European Journal of Operational Research* 234, 346–355.

Meese, R. A. and Rogoff, K., 1983. Empirical exchange rate models of the seventies: Do they fit out of sample? *Journal of International Economics* 14, 3–24.

Mishkin, F. S., 2004. Can inflation targeting work in emerging market countries? NBER Working Paper No. 10646. July 2004, JEL No. E5, F3.

Mishkin, F. S. and Savastano, M. A., 2001. Monetary policy strategies for Latin America. *Journal of Development Economics* 66, 415–444.

Pafka, S. and Kondor, I., 2003. Noisy covariance matrices and portfolio optimization II. *Physica* A 319, 487–494.

Pafka, S. and Kondor, I., 2004. Estimated correlation matrices and portfolio optimization. *Physica* A 343, 623–634.

Papaioannou, E., Portes, R. and Siourounis, G., 2006. Optimal currency weights in international reserves: The impact of the euro and the prospects for the dollar. *Journal of the Japanese and International Economies* 20, 508–547.

Plerou, V., Gopikrishnan, P., Rosenow, B., Amaral, L. A. N. and Stanley, H. E. 1999. Universal and non-universal properties of cross correlations in financial time series. *Physical Review Letters* 83, 1471.

Plerou, V., Gopikrishnan, P., Rosenow, B., Amaral, L. A. N. and Stanley, H. E. 2000. Econophysics: Financial time series from a statistical physics point of view. *Physica* A 279, 443–456.

Plerou, V., Gopikrishnan, P., Rosenow, B., Amaral, L. A. N. and Stanley, H. E. 2001. Collective behavior of stock price movements – A random matrix theory approach. *Physica* A 299, 175–180.

Proaño, C. R. 2011. Exchange rate determination, macroeconomic dynamics and stability under heterogeneous behavioral FX expectations. *Journal of Economic Behavior & Organization* 77, 177–188.

Proaño, C. R., 2013. Monetary policy rules and macroeconomic stabilization in small open economies under behavioral FX trading: Insights from numerical simulations. *The Manchester School* 81, 992–1011.

Putnam, B. H., 2004. Thoughts on investment guidelines for institutions with special liquidity and capital preservation requirements. In: Bernadell, C., Cardon, P., Coche, J., Diebold, F. X. and Manganelli, S., 2004. *Risk Management for Central Bank FX*. European Central Bank, Frankfurt, Germany.

Ramaswamy, S., 1999. Reserve currency allocation: An alternative methodology. BIS Working Papers No. 72, August 1999.

Rodrik, D., 2006. The social cost of FX reserves. NBER Working Paper No. 11952, January 2006, JEL No.F3.

Sharifi, S., Crane, M., Shamaie, A. and Ruskin, H., 2004. Random matrix theory for portfolio optimization: A stability approach. *Physica* A 335, 629–643.

Soesmanto, T., Selvanath, E. A. and Selvanath, S., 2015. Analysis of the management of currency composition of foreign exchange reserves in Australia. *Economic Analysis and Policy* 47, 82–89.

Tobin, J., 1958. Liquidity preference as behavior towards risk. *The Review of Economic Studies* 25, 65–86.

Truman, E. M. and Wong, A., 2006. The case for an international reserve diversification standard. Institute for International Economics, Working Paper Series May 2006 – WP 06-2.

Wooldridge, P. D. 2006. The changing composition of official reserves. *BIS Quarterly Review*, September 2006.

Yilmaz, K., 2003. Martingale property of exchange rates and Central Bank interventions. *Journal of Business & Economic Statistics* 21, 383–395.

10 Search frictions and the long-run effects of labor-market policies

Giuseppe Ciccarone, Francesco Giuli, and Enrico Marchetti

Introduction

The recent literature on dynamic stochastic general equilibrium models has been characterized by the attempt to overcome their limited ability to match a number of stylized facts characterizing the labor-market dynamic behavior, including in particular the cyclical volatilities of labor-market variables. The debate, originally started by Shimer (2005a), tried to offer solutions to this problem ranging from the inclusion of some form of wage rigidity (Shimer, 2005b) to the adoption of particular calibrations (Hagedorn and Manovskii, 2008). We contributed to the subject matter by demonstrating that the presence of undeclared work (UDW)[1] may improve the ability of real business cycle (RBC) models with search frictions to match the empirical volatilities of labor-market variables (Ciccarone, Giuli and Marchetti, 2015). More in particular, we showed that a greater size of UDW implies lower average employment, higher volatility of employment, and lower volatility of regular wages.

In this literature, dominant attention has been placed on the dynamic effects produced on the economic variables by shocks affecting technology, preferences, and interest rates. Less emphasis has instead been placed on the attempt to quantify and compare the relative long-run effects of the different types of economic policies on output and labor-market variables. This is somehow surprising, as the need for a thorough long-run effectiveness evaluation of policy measures is widely recognized. This shortcoming motivates our aim to start filling the evaluation gap by assessing the relative effects on the equilibrium values of the main economic variables of different policy measures affecting the labor-market structural parameters and the long-run values of some technological variables in a one-sector RBC model with search frictions, in a labor market characterized by the presence of UDW and linear costs of vacancy posting.

More in particular, we analyze the effects on steady-state income, employment/unemployment, regular hours, regular wages, and labor-market tightness of policy measures affecting the efficiency of the matching technology, the relative productivity of regular hours worked, the fiscal burden on employment, the cost of job-vacancy posting, and the sanctions applied to the firms that are caught employing UDW. Even though we concentrate our attention on the long-run effects of the different types of policies, and hence on the stationary results of the model, we also pay attention to the dynamic behavior of the main variables in order to provide a sound benchmark calibration of the model on the US economy.

The main conclusion we reach through this analysis is that the most effective reforms are those affecting the efficiency of the matching technology and the productivity of regular work, even though all the measures affecting the modeling elements listed above are able to produce positive effects on output, employment, and the regular wage. The policy suggestion provided by our experiments is hence to introduce reforms able to increase the efficiency and the effectiveness of public employment services, in terms of enhanced job matching ability and tailored programs for the unemployed, to favor competition between public and private entities in the market for matching services, and to improve the quality of the education and training system.

The chapter is organized as follows. In the next section we describe the basic elements of the model economy and the macroeconomic equilibrium. In the next section we present the stationary state of the model and illustrate our parameterization strategy. Then we carry out a sensitivity analysis able to assess the way in which different policy measures affect the long-run values of output and the main labor-market variables. In the final section we present the conclusions.

The model economy

The economy is described by a dynamic stochastic general equilibrium model with search and matching frictions in the labor market which draws on Ciccarone *et al.* (2015). Households own firms and are composed of a continuum of individual members/workers who supply the labor input, consume, and erogate the funds for investments. Firms produce a final good using physical capital (homogeneous with output) and labor input, which is split into an extensive margin (employment) and an intensive one (hours worked). The government collects taxes and provides both unemployment benefits and wasteful expenditure.

Search and matching

Search and matching frictions in the labor market may prevent some unemployed workers from finding jobs in every period and some posted job vacancies from being filled. We assume that in every time period all the unemployed workers passively search for a job[2] and that the number of new matches (M_t) between unemployed job seekers ($U_{S,t}$) and vacancies posted by firms (V_t) is determined by a standard Cobb–Douglas matching function (e.g., Shimer, 2005a)

$$M_t = M(V_t, U_{S,t}) = \eta(V_t)^{\xi}(U_{S,t})^{1-\xi} \tag{10.1}$$

where $\eta > 0$ represents the efficiency of the matching process and $\xi \in (0; 1)$ is the elasticity of the matching function with respect to V_t. It follows that $q_t = M_t/V_t$ is the vacancy-filling rate and $p_t = M_t/U_{S,t}$ is the searchers' job-finding rate. Furthermore, by defining as $\theta_t = V_t/U_{S,t}$ the aggregate labor-market tightness (from the viewpoint of firms), it follows that $p_t = \theta_t q_t$: if the labor-market tightness increases, unemployed searchers are more likely to find a job and firms find it more difficult to fill a vacancy. The quantities p_t, q_t, and θ_t are exogenous for the individual agents. Aggregate hiring by firms, together with the exogenous destruction of the existing jobs at the end of any given period, determines the dynamics of total employment N_t

$$N_{t+1} = (1 - \delta) N_t + (1 - N_t) p_t \tag{10.2}$$

where δ denotes the exogenous probability of separation and the total population of household members is normalized to 1. The process of matching and separation depicted by (10.1) and (10.2) implies that all workers matching in time t become productive in time $t + 1$, without the possibility for them to separate from the firm in the interval which elapses between time t and time $t + 1$. It follows that the number of searchers coincides with U_t, the total unemployed workers

$$U_{S,t} = U_t = 1 - N_t.$$

When matched with a firm, each worker can erogate two types of working services, so that the total working time is split into regular and undeclared hours worked, which are used to evade distortionary taxes levied by the government on households' regular income flows and on regular labor costs borne by firms. The government tackles tax evasion through random controls on firms and fines for those caught evading. Collected taxes are balanced (in expected terms) in each period with an amount of wasteful public expenditures.

After matching occurs, firms produce the final good using a production technology which includes stochastic shocks to both total factor productivity (TFP) and the productivity of regular hours. The markets for this good and for the capital stock are assumed to be competitive.

Households

As the possibility for workers to experience unemployment creates potential differences among employed and unemployed members, we assume that perfect insurance markets eliminate differences in workers' labor income, so as to equalize consumption across members. This is equivalent to assuming the existence of a large representative household (see Andolfatto, 1996; Merz, 1995; Thomas, 2008) whose welfare criterion is

$$\Omega_t = \mathcal{U}_t + \beta E_t \Omega_{t+1}, \quad \mathcal{U}_t = u(C_t) - \int_0^1 N_t^i \mathcal{V}_t^i \, di \tag{10.3}$$

where $u(C_t)$ is a strictly increasing and strictly concave function of consumption C_t, $\beta \in (0; 1)$ is the subjective discount rate, and E_t is the expectation operator (conditional on information at t). As there is a continuum of firms indexed by $i \in [0; 1]$, N_t^i represents the number of workers employed in firm i. The term

$V_t^i = V\left(h_{U,t}^i, h_{M,t}^i\right)$ is the disutility of work of the individual member/worker as a function of the amount of regular $(h_{M,t}^i)$ and undeclared hours worked $(h_{U,t}^i)$, with $\partial V_t^i / \partial h_{U,M,t}^i > 0$ and $\partial^2 V_t^i / \partial h_{U,M,t}^i \partial h_{U,M,t}^i \geq 0$.

The functions u and V_t^i are specified as follows

$$u\left(C_t\right) = \log(C_t); \quad V_t^i = B_0 \frac{\left(h_{M,t}^i + h_{U,t}^i\right)^{1+\psi}}{1+\psi} + B_1 \frac{\left(h_{U,t}^i\right)^{1+\psi}}{1+\psi} \tag{10.4}$$

with ψ, B_0, $B_1 > 0$, where ψ is the supply elasticity of hours worked, $\frac{B_0\left(h_{M,t}^i + h_{U,t}^i\right)^{1+\psi}}{1+\psi}$ represents the disutility of total hours worked and $B_1 \frac{\left(h_{U,t}^i\right)^{1+\psi}}{1+\psi}$ reflects additional disutility from UDW hours, which may be associated with the lack of social and health insurance when performing these activities, and with subjective costs due to a "social stigma."

The household's budget constraint is

$$C_t + K_{t+1} = (1 - \tau_Y)(WM_t + r_t K_t) + \delta_K K_t + (1 - N_t)b + WU_t$$
$$+ \Pi_t + (1 - \delta_K)K_t \tag{10.5}$$

where K_t is the physical capital stock, δ_K is the depreciation rate, r_t is the rate of return on capital, τ_Y is the constant tax rate on regular incomes, $\Pi_t = \int_0^1 E_t \pi_t^i \, di$ is the amount of expected profits accruing to the household (taken as given), and b represents a publicly financed unemployment insurance. By indicating with $w_{M,t}^i$ and $w_{U,t}^i$ the (hourly) wage rates for regular and undeclared hours worked paid by firm i, the terms

$$WM_t = \int_0^1 w_{M,t}^i N_t^i h_{M,t}^i \, di, \qquad WU_t = \int_0^1 w_{U,t}^i N_t^i h_{U,t}^i \, di$$

represent the two types of income the employed workers earn from regular and from undeclared hours worked (which is not subject to taxation). Output price is normalized to 1 in every period.

The household chooses C_t and K_{t+1} so as to maximize (10.3) under constraint (10.5). From the first-order conditions, the standard Euler equation is obtained

$$u'\left(C_t\right) = \beta E_t\left[u'\left(C_{t+1}\right)\left[1 + (1 - \tau_Y)r_{t+1}\right]\right]. \tag{10.6}$$

The increase in the household's welfare due to a marginal increase of employment in firm i at time t reads:

$$\frac{\partial \Omega_t}{\partial N_t^i} = \frac{\partial \mathcal{U}_t}{\partial N_t^i} + \beta E_t \frac{\partial \Omega_{t+1}}{\partial N_t^i}.$$

By making use of (10.5) and taking into account (10.2), we obtain

$$\frac{\partial \Omega_t}{\partial N_t^i} = u'(C_t)\left[(1-\tau_Y)w_{M,t}^i h_{M,t}^i + w_{U,t}^i h_{U,t}^i - b\right] - \mathcal{V}_t^i +$$

$$- \beta E_t D_{t+1} + (1-\delta)\beta E_t \frac{\partial \Omega_{t+1}}{\partial N_{t+1}^i}; \tag{10.7}$$

$$E_t D_{t+1} = E_t \int_0^1 p_t \zeta_t^j \left(\frac{\partial \Omega_{t+1}}{\partial N_{t+1}^j}\right) dj$$

where $\zeta_t^j = V_t^j / V_t$ and $p_t \zeta_t^j$ is the probability of finding a new job in firm $j \in [0; 1]$ posting vacancies V_t^j. The contribution of an employed member to the household's welfare is given by incomes from regular and undeclared hours worked minus the foregone benefit, all measured in utility units, and minus the disutility of work $\mathcal{V}_t^i$. This quantity is increased by the continuation value of the same job (conditional on non-separation), $(1-\delta)\beta E_t(\partial \Omega_{t+1}/\partial N_{t+1}^i)$, and is reduced by the value the same worker would contribute to the household if they searched for another job, $\beta E_t D_{t+1}$.

Firms

The individual firm i produces the homogeneous output Y_t^i by combining the "extensive" inputs K_t^i, N_t^i with regular and undeclared hours worked through the constant returns to scale technology

$$Y_t^i = A_t (K_t^i)^\alpha \left(N_t^i H_t^i\right)^{1-\alpha} \text{ with } H_t^i = (1-\omega)\vartheta_t h_{M,t}^i + \omega h_{U,t}^i \tag{10.8}$$

where $\alpha, \omega \in (0; 1)$, A_t is a stochastic variable capturing common (TFP) technology shocks, and ϑ_t is a stochastic variable capturing shocks hitting only regular hours. The stochastic processes of A_t and ϑ_t are AR(1) in log; $N_t^i H_t^i$ is the effective labor input; and the parameter ω differentiates the production shares pertaining to the two types of hours and it also allows for possible differences in their marginal productivities.

The firm sustains a job posting cost, which is a linear function of the amount of posted vacancies V_t^i

$$\kappa V_t^i; \qquad \kappa > 0. \tag{10.9}$$

As firms are assumed to be sufficiently large, δ and q_t represent the fraction of workers that are separated from the firm and the fraction of vacancies that are filled in period t (Thomas, 2008). The evolution of employment in firm i is then

$$N_{t+1}^i = (1-\delta)N_t^i + q_t V_t^i. \tag{10.10}$$

Firms try to evade taxes by using UDW, but if they are detected (with exogenous probability p_D) they must pay the constant statutory tax rate on labor, τ_N, augmented by the surcharge factor, $s_D > 1$ (Busato *et al.*, 2011), obtaining profits

$$\pi^i_{D,t} = Y^i_t - (1 + \tau_N)w^i_{M,t}N^i_t h^i_{M,t} - (1 + s_D\tau_N)w^i_{U,t}N^i_t h^i_{U,t} - (r_t + \delta_K) K^i_t - \kappa V^i_t.$$

Firms not detected evading (with probability $1 - p_D$) obtain instead profits

$$\pi^i_{ND,t} = Y^i_t - (1 + \tau_N)w^i_{M,t}N^i_t h^i_{M,t} - w_{U,t}N_t h^i_{U,t} - (r_t + \delta_K) K^i_t - \kappa V^i_t.$$

The expected profit of a generic firm i is then equal to

$$E_t\pi^i_t = Y^i_t - (1 + \tau_N)w^i_{M,t}N^i_t h^i_{M,t} - (1 + p_D s_D \tau_N)w^i_{U,t}N^i_t h^i_{U,t}$$
$$- (r_t + \delta_K) K^i_t - \kappa V^i_t. \tag{10.11}$$

At time t, firm i chooses K^i_t and V^i_t so as to maximize its value F^i_t

$$F^i_t = E_t\pi^i_t + E_t\tilde{\beta}_{t,t+1} F^i_{t+1}$$

subject to (10.8) and (10.10), where $\tilde{\beta}_{t,t+s} = \beta^s u'(C_{t+s})/u'(C_t) = \beta^s C_t/C_{t+s}$ is the adjusted discount factor of the firm. From the solution of this problem, the demand for capital is obtained

$$\frac{\partial Y^i_t}{\partial K^i_t} = r_t + \delta_K. \tag{10.12}$$

Given (10.12), the capital–labor ratio, $\frac{K^i_t}{N^i_t H^i_t}$, is the same across all firms, due to constant returns to scale in production (see (10.8)) and to the competitive equilibrium in the rental capital market. This implies that the marginal product of the effective labor input, $ML_t = \frac{\partial Y^i_t}{\partial\left(N^i_t H^i_t\right)}$, is equal for all i.

The first-order condition with respect to posted vacancies is

$$\kappa = E_t\tilde{\beta}_{t,t+1} \frac{\partial F^i_{t+1}}{\partial N^i_{t+1}} \frac{\partial N^i_{t+1}}{\partial V^i_t}$$

and, by using (10.10), it reduces to

$$\frac{\kappa}{q_t} = E_t\tilde{\beta}_{t,t+1} \frac{\partial F^i_{t+1}}{\partial N^i_{t+1}}. \tag{10.13}$$

The value of an additional worker for the firm, which is obtained by computing the derivative $\partial F^i_{t+1}/\partial N^i_{t+1}$ (from (10.10) and κV^i_t) and combining it with (10.13), turns out to be equal to the increase in productivity, net of the wage costs (both regular and UDW), plus the continuation value

$$\frac{\partial F_t^i}{\partial N_t^i} = \frac{\partial Y_t^i}{\partial N_t^i} - (1 + \tau_N)w_{M,t}^i h_{M,t}^i - (1 + p_D s_D \tau_N)w_{U,t}^i h_{U,t}^i$$

$$+ (1 - \delta) E_t \tilde{\beta}_{t,t+1} \frac{\partial F_{t+1}^i}{\partial N_{t+1}^i}. \tag{10.14}$$

By using the first-order condition (10.13), it is then possible to compute the firm's job-creation condition[3]

$$\frac{\kappa}{q_t} = E_t \tilde{\beta}_{t,t+1} \left[\begin{array}{c} \frac{\partial Y_{t+1}^i}{\partial N_{t+1}^i} - (1 + \tau_N)w_{M,t+1}^i h_{M,t+1}^i \\ -(1 + p_D s_D \tau_N)w_{U,t+1}^i h_{U,t+1}^i + (1 - \delta)\frac{\kappa}{q_{t+1}} \end{array} \right]. \tag{10.15}$$

This equation clarifies that the condition to post an additional vacancy at time t equates the expected cost of an open vacancy to the firm's discounted stream of future earnings (net of the costs of hours worked) and of future savings in the hiring process.

Wages and the intensive margin

A successful match generates a rent that is shared between the worker's household and the firm through a decentralized and efficient bargaining, in which the Nash product of the surpluses is $(S_t^{W,i})^d (S_t^{F,i})^{1-d}$ and where $d \in (0; 1)$ is the bargaining power of the worker (e.g., Thomas, 2008; Trigari, 2009).

By shifting the value of a match for the household, $S_t^{W,i} = (\partial \Omega_t / \partial N_t^i) / u'(C_t) = (\partial \Omega_t / \partial N_t^i) C_t$, one period ahead and using (10.7), we obtain

$$S_t^{W,i} = (1 - \tau_Y) w_{M,t}^i h_{M,t}^i + w_{U,t}^i h_{U,t}^i - b - C_t \mathcal{V}_t^i - E_t \tilde{\beta}_{t,t+1} D_{t+1}$$

$$+ (1 - \delta) E_t \tilde{\beta}_{t,t+1} S_{t+1}^{W,i}. \tag{10.16}$$

We also know the value of a match for firm i is

$$S_t^{F,i} = \frac{\partial F_t^i}{\partial N_t^i} = \frac{\partial Y_t^i}{\partial N_t^i} - (1 + \tau_N)w_{M,t}^i h_{M,t}^i +$$

$$- (1 + p_D s_D \tau_N)w_{U,t}^i h_{U,t}^i + (1 - \delta) E_t \tilde{\beta}_{t,t+1} S_{t+1}^{F,i}. \tag{10.17}$$

We assume that wages are renegotiated in every period and that, at time t, the variables $[w_{M,t}^i, w_U^i, h_{M,t}^i, h_{U,t}^i]$ are such that the individual bargaining equilibrium satisfies the following three properties. First, hours $h_{M,t}^i$, $h_{U,t}^i$ are privately efficient. Second, the regular wage $w_{M,t}^i$ has no allocative effect on the same hours, so that it maintains the role of the "distributive" variable transferring units of wealth among agents. Finally, the wage $w_{U,t}^i$ is determined so as to bring about the privately efficient allocation of hours.

This equilibrium solution can be obtained in the following way.

i   For a given $w_{U,t}^i$, hours and regular wage solve the Nash bargaining problem

$$\max_{w_{M,t}^i, h_{M,t}^i, h_{U,t}^i} (S_t^{W,i})^d (S_t^{F,i})^{1-d}. \tag{10.18}$$

ii   The UDW wage equates the household's marginal rate of substitution between $h_{U,t}^i$ and consumption, on the one hand, with the marginal productivity of $h_{U,t}^i$ of the additional worker, on the other

$$MRS_{U,t}^i = w_{U,t}^i = \frac{(1-\alpha)}{(1+p_D s_D \tau_N)} MP_{U,t}^i \tag{10.19}$$

where $MRS_{U,t}^i = (\partial V_t^i / \partial h_{U,t}^i)/u'(C_t)$ and $MP_{U,t}^i = \omega ML_t$.

It can be shown (see Ciccarone *et al.*, 2015)that the resulting equilibrium values for $[w_{M,t}^i, h_{M,t}^i, h_{U,t}^i]$ are given by these equations

$$MRS_{M,t}^i = \frac{(1-\tau_Y)(1-\alpha)}{(1+\tau_N)} MP_{M,t}^i; \tag{10.20}$$

$$MRS_{U,t}^i = \frac{(1-\alpha)}{(1+p_D s_D \tau_N)} MP_{U,t}^i; \tag{10.21}$$

$$w_{M,t}^i = \frac{d}{h_{M,t}^i (1+\tau_N)} \left(\frac{\partial Y_t^i}{\partial N_t^i} - (1+p_D s_D \tau_N) w_{U,t}^i h_{U,t}^i \right)$$
$$- \frac{(1-d)}{h_{M,t}^i (1-\tau_Y)} \left(w_{U,t}^i h_{U,t}^i - b - C_t V_t^i - E_t \tilde{\beta}_{t,t+1} D_{t+1} \right)$$

where $MRS_{M,t}^i = (\partial V_t^i / \partial h_{M,t}^i)/u'(C_t)$ and $MP_{M,t}^i = \vartheta_t (1-\omega) ML_t$.

Given this bargaining solution, and under competitive equilibrium in the markets for capital and output, individual behaviors translate into aggregate relations. As $\partial Y_t / \partial N_t$, $h_{M,t}$, $h_{U,t}$, $w_{M,t}^i$ and $w_{U,t}$ are the same in all firms, index i can hence be dropped and it can be shown that $w_{M,t}$ writes as follows

$$w_{M,t} = \frac{d}{(1+\tau_N)h_{M,t}} \left(\frac{\partial Y_t}{\partial N_t} - (1+p_D s_D \tau_N) w_{U,t} h_{U,t} + \kappa \theta_t \right)$$
$$+ \frac{(1-d)}{(1-\tau_Y)h_{M,t}} (C_t V_t + b - w_{U,t} h_{U,t}). \tag{10.22}$$

The bargained regular wage is hence a weighted average of the reservation values of firms and workers. The former value is given by the sum of the marginal revenue and the variation in the vacancy posting cost net of the cost of UDW, plus the expected net present value of a non-severed match. The worker's reservation value is given by the sum of the overall disutility of work plus the foregone flow benefit from unemployment, net of what the worker earns by providing UDW. It is worth noting that, other things being equal, the regular wage is negatively related to the UDW wage, because a part of the overall disutility of work and a part of the marginal product of employment are generated by UDW, and there exists substitutability between the two types of hours.

Government and macroeconomic equilibrium

Under aggregation, the government budget constraint is equal to

$$b\left(1-N_t\right)+G_t=\tau_Y\left(w_{M,t}N_t h_{M,t}+r_t K_t\right)+s_D p_D \tau_N w_{U,t}N_t h_{U,t}$$
$$+\tau_N w_{M,t}N_t h_{M,t} \tag{10.23}$$

where the right-hand side represents expected revenues and the left-hand side contains expenditures (unemployment benefits and wasteful expenditure, G_t). Using (10.23) together with the household's budget constraint (10.5) and firms' aggregate profits derived from (10.11), the aggregate resource constraint (expressing the equilibrium condition in the goods market) is obtained

$$C_t+K_{t+1}-\left(1-\delta_K\right)K_t+G_t=Y_t-\kappa V_t \tag{10.24}$$

where $K_{t+1}-\left(1-\delta_K\right)K_t=I_t$ is the aggregate investment.

We define the aggregate state of the economy as the vector $\mathbf{z}'=[N_t, K_t, A_t, \vartheta_t]$ and focus on a macroeconomic equilibrium in which: (i) agents maximize their welfare criterion; (ii) wages and hours worked are set according to our bargaining solution; (iii) the markets for K and Y clear; (iv) the government balances its budget; and (v) the labor market evolves according to the search and matching mechanism described above. In this equilibrium, the ratio of undeclared and regular hours, $h_{R,t}=h_{U,t}/h_{M,t}$, can be computed by dividing side by side the aggregate versions of the equations (10.20)–(10.21), and it is equal to

$$h_{R,t}=\left\{\left[\left(\frac{1+\tau_N}{\left(1-\tau_Y\right)\left(1+p_D s_D \tau_N\right)}\right)\left(\frac{\omega}{\vartheta_t\left(1-\omega\right)}\right)-1\right]\frac{B_0}{B_1}\right]^{-\frac{1}{\psi}}-1\right\}^{-1}.$$
$$\tag{10.25}$$

Equation (10.25) shows that this ratio is independent of the TFP shock A_t and the model's endogenous variables. It can be shown that the incentive to use UDW disappears (i.e., $h_{R,t}=0$) when the relative productivity of regular hours (ϑ_t) is greater than (or equal to) the threshold value $\bar{h}=\frac{\omega}{1-\omega}\left(\frac{1+\tau_N}{\left(1-\tau_Y\right)\left(1+p_D s_D \tau_N\right)}\right)$, which decreases with the deterrence parameters p_D, s_D and increases with the tax rates and the technology parameters ω and ϑ_t.[4]

Benchmark parameterization

Indicating stationary values with starred variables, the steady state of the model is described by the following equations:

$$Y^* = C^* + \delta_K K^* + G^* + \kappa V^*$$

$$r^* = \frac{\beta^{-1} - 1 + \delta_K}{1 - \tau_Y} - \delta_K$$

$$MRS_M^* = \frac{(1 - \tau_Y)(1 - \alpha)}{(1 + \tau_N)} MP_M^*$$

$$MRS_U^* = \frac{(1 - \alpha)}{(1 + p_D s_D \tau_N)} MP_U^*$$

$$w_U^* = MRS_U^*$$

$$Y^* = A^* (K^*)^\alpha \left[\vartheta^* (1 - \omega) N^* h_M^* + \omega N^* h_U^* \right]^{1-\alpha}$$

$$q^* = \eta(\theta^*)^{1-\xi}$$

$$\delta N^* = q^* V^*$$

$$\alpha \left(\frac{Y}{K} \right)^* = r^* + \delta_K$$

$$G^* = \tau_Y \left(w_M^* N^* h_M^* + r^* K^* \right) + s_D p_D \tau_N w_U^* N^* h_U^*$$
$$+ \tau_N w_M^* N^* h_M^* - b(1 - N^*)$$

$$w_M^* = \frac{d}{(1 + \tau_N) h_M^*} \left[\left(\frac{\partial Y}{\partial N} \right)^* - (1 + p_D s_D \tau_N) w_U^* h_U^* + \kappa \theta^* \right]$$
$$+ \frac{(1 - d)(C^* V^* + b - w_U^* h_U^*)}{(1 - \tau_Y) h_M^*}$$

$$\frac{\kappa}{q^*} = \frac{\beta \left[\left(\frac{\partial Y}{\partial N} \right)^* - (1 + p_D s_D \tau_N) w_U^* h_U^* - (1 + \tau_N) w_M^* h_M^* \right]}{1 - \beta(1 - \delta)}. \qquad (10.26)$$

As the system (10.26) cannot be solved in closed form, we solve it numerically by calibrating the model on the US economy at quarterly frequency and adopting the values of the model's parameters now to be specified, which also guarantee a volatility of unemployment relative to income in line with empirical evidence.[5]

In the baseline parameterization, we set the idiosyncratic productivity of regular work $\vartheta^* = 1$ and choose the conventional target $q^* = 0.71$ for the long-run vacancy-filling rate. From steady-state computations, the values of the stationary job-finding rate and the market tightness are $p^* = 0.5$ and $\theta^* = 0.72$.[6] We target the stationary unemployment rate to 11 percent (as in den Haan *et al.*, 2000 and Yashiv, 2005), and similarly to models that include the flows in and out of the labor force into the mass of searchers (Andolfatto, 1996), or that take into account a labor-leisure choice (Walsh, 2005, p. 838). As a precautionary and conservative

Table 10.1 Benchmark parameterization

Technology	$\alpha = 0.33$	$\omega = 0.459$	$\kappa = 0.07$	$\delta_K = 0.025$	
Preferences	$B_0 = 0.8$	$B_1 = 0.4$	$\psi = 1$	$\beta = 0.9881$	
Tax structure	$\tau_Y = 0.1186$	$\tau_N = 0.153$	$p_D = 0.01$	$s_D = 1.75$	
Labor market	$\xi = 0.5$	$\delta = 0.0625$	$\eta = 0.6$	$d = 0.34$	$b = 0.4102$

estimate, we target the ratio of UDW income over total output, $S_U^* = \frac{w_U^* N^* h_U^*}{Y^*} = 8.4$ percent, that is, the lowest figure in the range between 8.4 percent and 8.8 percent estimated by Schneider *et al.* (2010) for the period 1996–2007.[7]

We fix most of the model's parameters in accordance with various sources of independent empirical evidence and with the existing literature. Table 10.1 summarizes our benchmark parameterization.

As for the parameters that are more closely related to tax evasion and UDW, we adopt the values suggested by the existing literature. For the calibration of the surcharge factor, we follow Busato *et al.* (2011) and Joulfaian and Rider (1998) who adopt a value of 1.75 for s_D, based on the Internal Revenue Service Public Announcement Notice 97-24. Existing empirical studies on tax evasion agree on very small values for the estimated probability of auditing and detection for developed countries, which should range between 0.01 and 0.03 (see, e.g., Andreoni *et al.*, 1998). We choose the lowest figure, but results would not significantly change if we considered slightly higher values. As for the average long-run levels of taxation, the effective income tax rate τ_Y is taken from the Effective Tax Rates, 1979–1997, Table H-1a, prepared by the Congressional Budget Office, and the statutory tax rate on labor τ_N is calculated from the Social Security Administration data from the years 1990s onwards.[8]

As for preferences and technology, we choose the elasticity parameter of work disutility, $\psi = 1$, which is in line with the estimates of Kimball and Shapiro (2008). The values of β, α, and δ_K are standard in calibration exercises for the US economy. The values $\omega = 0.459$[9] and $\vartheta^* = 1$, together with those of the disutility parameters $B_0 = 0.8$ and $B_1 = 0.4$, are set so as to match the target values of the ratio of UDW income over total output $S_U^* = 8.4$ percent and of the unemployment rate $U^* = 0.11$.

As for the labor market's parameters, the value of ξ is that proposed by Petrongolo and Pissarides (2001). The matching efficiency parameter, $\eta = 0.6$, allows us to match, in steady-state computations, the targeted values of $q^* = 0.71$. The separation rate is fixed according to the value used in Costain and Reiter (2008), who calibrate an annual job loss rate of 25 percent, so as to obtain $\delta = 0.0625$ at quarterly frequency. The chosen values of ξ and δ imply the stationary value $p^* = 0.5$. For the calibration of the bargaining power parameter d, we focus on the contribution of Ciccarone *et al.* (2013), who develop a framework in which the Nash bargaining over the surpluses (10.17) and (10.16) takes into account the presence of elements related to Kahneman and Tverski's (1979) prospect theory. Based on this framework and by resorting to the existing experimental evidence on the loss aversion parameters of workers and firms, they propose a range of values for d between 0.34 and 0.39. We choose a value close to the lower bound of this range: $d = 0.3$.

We set κ to target a stationary value of the ratio $\frac{kV^*}{Y^*}$ close to 1 percent (Walsh, 2005). As for b, we focus on the model's replacement rate, f_Q^*. In a model with only the extensive margin, this variable is equal to the stationary ratio b/w^*. More generally, the parameter b should, however, also include a number of other elements, such as heterogeneity of preferences and workers' productivity, or home production (Mortensen and Nagypal, 2007; Hagedorn and Manovskii, 2008, p. 1696; Hall, 2008). As our model takes into account both the intensive and the extensive margin, together with a UDW income, our replacement rate is given by the ratio between the steady-state flow value of unemployment to the worker, which corresponds to the minimum value of the wage they are willing to accept in the Nash bargaining $\left(Q_N^* = C^*V^* + b - w_U^*h_U^*\right)$ and the steady-state flow value of their contribution to the labor match, which corresponds to the maximum value of the wage the firm is willing to grant $\left(Q_D^* = \left(\frac{\partial Y}{\partial N}\right)^* - (1 + p_{DS}s_D\tau_N)w_U^*h_U^*\right)$, corrected by the adjustment for the two tax rates $\left(\frac{1+\tau_N}{1-\tau_Y}\right)$. We hence choose $b = 0.4102$ so as to obtain a replacement rate $f_Q^* = 0.94$, which is in the range of values included between 0.723, that is the estimate provided by Gertler *et al.* (2008) in a model without the intensive margin,[10] and 0.955, which is the value set by Hagedorn and Manovskii (2008).

Policy experiments

As already clarified in the introduction, the main aim of this contribution is to provide a preliminary assessment of the long-run effects of labor-market policies on output and labor-market variables. To this aim, in this section we study the way their stationary equilibrium values change following policy reforms that affect five parameters which characterize the labor market of our model economy:

1   the efficiency of the matching technology, η;
2   the productivity of regular hours worked, ϑ^*;
3   the fiscal burden on employment, τ_N;
4   the cost of job-vacancy posting, κ;
5   the penalty rate the state applies to firms caught using undeclared work, s_D.

We carry out this test by comparing the model's steady-state equilibrium obtained with the benchmark parameterization with that obtained under different values of the parameters listed above. More specifically, besides output, we focus on the effects produced on steady-state employment/unemployment, regular hours, regular wages, and labor-market tightness.

Increase the efficiency of the job matching technology

The first experiment we carry out explores the effects produced in our model economy by an increase in the efficiency of the job matching technology, expressed

Table 10.2 Effects of higher matching efficiency η

	Y^*	U^*	N^*	h^*_M	w^*_M	θ^*
$\eta = 0.6$ (benchmark)	1.1146	0.1095	0.8905	0.6812	0.9241	0.7183
$\eta = 0.7$	1.1269	0.0961	0.9039	0.6786	0.9255	0.7045
$\eta = 0.8$	1.1365	0.0858	0.9142	0.6766	0.9266	0.6930
$\eta = 0.9$	1.1441	0.0775	0.9225	0.6751	0.9274	0.6833
$\eta = 1.0$	1.1504	0.0707	0.9293	0.6738	0.9280	0.6749
$\eta = 2.0$	1.1806	0.0379	0.9621	0.6679	0.9308	0.6298
$\eta = 2.5$	1.1871	0.0308	0.9692	0.6666	0.9314	0.6188
$\eta = 3.0$	1.1915	0.0260	0.9740	0.6658	0.9317	0.6111
Effect	↑↑	↓↓	↑↑	↓	↑	↓

Note: The second row shows the benchmark values of selected steady state variables; the other ones contain the values generated by the model when η is progressively increased above the benchmark value.

by the parameter η. This innovation may be obtained through policy measures aiming, for example, at improving the organization of the public employment services and/or the workers there employed. Matching efficiency may also be fostered by targeting the training of unemployed workers to firms' needs, so as to shrink the skill mismatch, or by introducing/enhancing competition in the market for matching services by allowing/favoring the participation of private entities providing services to workers and firms together with public employment services. The results of this experiment are summarized in Table 10.2.[11]

Changes in the efficiency of the matching technology have a strong positive effect on stationary output and employment, with the unemployment rate falling from 11 percent to 7 percent as η is increased from 0.6 to 1.0. The enhanced matching efficiency generates more matches for the same number of vacancies posted by firms, thus reducing the steady-state value of vacancies and expanding N^*. This fall in vacancies, which is sharper than the fall in the number of searchers U^* produced by the employment increase, causes the labor-market tightness to decrease. It should be noted that the incentive to hire allows firms to increase output through increases in employment and with a slight reduction in the intensive margin. As the increase in Y^* is sharper than the increase in N^*, the overall productivity of employment $\partial Y^*/\partial N^*$ goes up, while the fall in undeclared hours worked (not shown in Table 10.2) reduces the cost of UDW in (10.22), producing a moderate increase in the bargained wage.

Favor the productivity of declared work

The second sensitivity analysis we wish to perform is on the idiosyncratic productivity of regular work ϑ^*, which in real word situations can be persistently affected by improvements in the education system and by several active labor-market policies, from general training to improved tailored services to the unemployed offered by employment centers. The results of this experiment are shown in Table 10.3.

Table 10.3 Effects of higher productivity ϑ^*

	Y^*	U^*	N^*	h_M^*	w_M^*	θ^*
$\vartheta^* = 1$	1.1146	0.1095	0.8905	0.6812	0.9241	0.7183
(benchmark)						
$\vartheta^* = 1.1$	1.3126	0.0681	0.9319	0.8495	0.9447	2.0293
$\vartheta^* = 1.2$	1.5041	0.0514	0.9486	0.9780	0.9935	3.6926
$\vartheta^* = 1.3$	1.6986	0.0422	0.9578	1.0745	1.0555	5.5785
$\vartheta^* = 1.4$	1.8970	0.0364	0.9636	1.1471	1.1246	7.6205
$\vartheta^* = 1.5$	2.0986	0.0322	0.9678	1.2023	1.1981	9.7768
$\vartheta^* = 2.0$	3.1358	0.0220	0.9780	1.3426	1.5943	21.5181
$\vartheta^* = 2.5$	4.1971	0.0175	0.9825	1.3941	2.0091	34.0079
Effect	↑↑	↓↓	↑↑	↑↑	↑	↑↑

Note: The second row replicates the corresponding row of Table 10.2; the other ones contain the values generated by the model when ϑ^* is progressively increased above the benchmark value.

This evidence shows that policies able to increase the efficiency of declared work are very effective in expanding stationary output: if the efficiency of declared work is doubled, output increases by almost three times (from 1.11 to 3.14). The policy measure is also able to substantially increase employment and the declared hours worked, and to curb unemployment. The main explanation for these results is related to the ability of an increase in the productivity of declared work to alter the optimal proportion between regular and undeclared labor, and to induce an immediate increase in the overall productivity of employment $\partial Y^*/\partial N^*$,[12] which directly translates into an incentive for firms to hire more workers and to expand output. The augmented productivity of N^* and the consequent fall in the number of searchers U^* raises the labor-market tightness and increases the value of a match, as well as the bargained wage.

Reduce the tax burden on labor

The reduction of labor costs obtained through tax cuts able to reduce the fiscal burden on employment has been frequently envisaged as a policy measure able to favor the growth of income and employment. In order to elaborate on this intuition, we progressively decrease the stationary value of the labor tax rate, τ_N^*, below the benchmark calibration and consider the effects of this intervention in our model economy. The results of this test are summarized in Table 10.4.

The ability of reductions in the tax burden on labor to increase stationary output, employment, and declared hours worked is confirmed by this experiment. The policies affecting this parameter are, however, only mildly effective: the tax rate must be reduced to more than one-third of the benchmark value in order to cut stationary unemployment from 11 percent to 7 percent of the workforce. These adjustments are triggered by the reduction in labor costs, which has an impact on both the extensive and the intensive margin. As for the extensive margin, a fall in the overall cost of labor, $(1 + \tau_N)w_M Nh_M + (1 + p_D s_D \tau_N)w_U Nh_U$, fosters the hiring process and leads to an increase in stationary employment N^*. The

Table 10.4 Effects of lower labor tax rates τ_N^*

	Y^*	U^*	N^*	h_M^*	w_M^*	θ^*
$\tau_N^* = 0.153$ (benchmark)	1.1146	0.1095	0.8905	0.6812	0.9241	0.7183
$\tau_N^* = 0.14$	1.1287	0.1016	0.8984	0.7024	0.9247	0.8485
$\tau_N^* = 0.13$	1.1386	0.0964	0.9036	0.7187	0.9256	0.9537
$\tau_N^* = 0.12$	1.1479	0.0918	0.9082	0.7351	0.9268	1.0629
$\tau_N^* = 0.11$	1.1567	0.0877	0.9123	0.7516	0.9284	1.1756
$\tau_N^* = 0.10$	1.1649	0.0840	0.9160	0.7680	0.9303	1.2917
$\tau_N^* = 0.08$	1.1800	0.0776	0.9224	0.8009	0.9351	1.5325
$\tau_N^* = 0.05$	1.2001	0.0700	0.9300	0.8500	0.9444	1.9131
Effect	↑	↓	↑	↑	↑	↑↑

Note: The second row replicates the corresponding row of Table 10.2; the other lines show the values of the stationary variables corresponding to the tax cuts.

consequent reduction in the number of searchers raises the labor-market tightness, and the bargained wage increases. As for the intensive margin, the lower tax rate modifies the relative allocation of regular and undeclared labor services: as the impact of a change in τ_N^* on the labor cost is stronger in the case of regular labor services than in the case of undeclared ones, because it also reduces the incentive to evade taxes, the firms will increase their use of regular hours worked.[13]

Reduce the cost of vacancy posting

Another set of policy measures which have been widely employed in recent years aim at fostering output and employment growth by reducing the cost of vacancy posting. A decrease in this parameter may be produced, for example, by favoring ICT innovation in job posting,including electronic job advertisements, or by helping firms to access labor-market portals[14] and placement services offered by universities[15] and other entities. The quantitative effects produced in our model economy by a reduction of κ are reported in Table 10.5.

Table 10.5 shows that a lower cost of vacancy posting increases output and employment, with the unemployment rate falling from 11 percent to 9.5 percent as κ is reduced from 0.07 to 0.05. The fall in κ progressively induces firms to generate the higher output by expanding jobs and reducing hours worked. The increase in the number of vacancies adds to the fall in the number of searchers to raise the labor-market tightness, which puts upward pressure on the bargained wage.

Increase the penalty rate on UDW

In our final experiment, we study the effects of a progressive increase above the benchmark value of the penalty rate the state applies to firms caught underground, s_D. This parameter is fully in the hands of the public authorities and so it can be

Table 10.5 Effects of lower vacancy-posting cost κ

	Y^*	U^*	N^*	h_M^*	w_M^*	θ^*
$\kappa = 0.07$ (benchmark)	1.1146	0.1095	0.8905	0.6812	0.9241	0.7183
$\kappa = 0.06$	1.1209	0.1026	0.8974	0.6799	0.9249	0.8299
$\kappa = 0.05$	1.1280	0.0950	0.9050	0.6784	0.9256	0.9846
$\kappa = 0.04$	1.1360	0.0864	0.9136	0.6767	0.9265	1.2139
$\kappa = 0.03$	1.1453	0.0763	0.9237	0.6748	0.9275	1.5909
$\kappa = 0.02$	1.1567	0.0639	0.9361	0.6725	0.9286	2.3317
$\kappa = 0.01$	1.1724	0.0468	0.9532	0.6695	0.9301	4.5002
Effect	↑	↓↓	↑↑	↓	↑	↑↑

Note: The second row replicates the corresponding row of Table 10.2; the other ones contain the values generated by the model when κ is progressively decreased below the benchmark value.

Table 10.6 Effects of a higher surcharge s_D

	Y^*	U^*	N^*	h_M^*	w_M^*	θ^*
$s_D = 1.75$	1.1146	0.1095	0.8905	0.6812	0.9241	0.7183
$s_D = 1.8$	1.1146	0.1095	0.8905	0.6813	0.9241	0.7183
$s_D = 1.9$	1.1147	0.1095	0.8905	0.6816	0.9239	0.7182
$s_D = 2.0$	1.1147	0.1095	0.8905	0.6819	0.9238	0.7182
$s_D = 3.0$	1.1154	0.1095	0.8905	0.6849	0.9225	0.7180
$s_D = 4.0$	1.1161	0.1095	0.8905	0.6879	0.9213	0.7179
$s_D = 5.0$	1.1167	0.1095	0.8905	0.6909	0.9200	0.7177
$s_D = 9.0$	1.1194	0.1095	0.8905	0.7026	0.9152	0.7175
$s_D = 18$	1.1251	0.1094	0.8906	0.7284	0.9050	0.7170
Effect	↑	–	–	↓↓	↓↓	↓

Note: The second row replicates the corresponding row of Table 10.2; the other rows contain the values of the same variables obtained by increasing s_D above the benchmark value.

directly modified through legislative actions. The results of this experiment are shown in Table 10.6.

Table 10.6 shows that an increase in the penalty rates on UDW mildly raises the stationary value of output. This is not produced by an increase in employment (the extensive labor margin), but rather by an increase in declared hours worked (the intensive margin). Stationary unemployment hence remains almost stable. This is due to the fact that the rise in income is small and it is hence convenient for firms to increase the declared intensive margin—which becomes relatively cheaper than undeclared hours worked as the rise in the fines paid by firms following s_D pushes up the expected cost of UDW—rather than increasing the costly posting required to increase employment. At the same time, the higher productivity of the declared hours worked increases the firm's profit, thus raising the value of a match and hence of the bargained wage. Even though the very limited increase which is recorded in the extensive labor margin somewhat reduces the number of searchers, posting activity increases slightly more sharply and this lowers the labor-market tightness.

Conclusions

In this chapter we made a first step toward the identification of the quantitative effects of different policy measures affecting the labor market on long-run employment/unemployment, regular hours, regular wages, and labor-market tightness. By comparing the model's steady-state equilibrium under a benchmark parameterization with the equilibria obtained by changing some key parameters' values, we showed that these effects are differentiated, with some policy measures affecting output and employment more sharply, and others affecting the intensive labor margin more than the extensive one.

The general intuition for the differentiated consequences of the five sets of policy approaches relies upon the different channels through which they propagate their effects in the economy and on the different economic incentives they affect. Basically, whereas some measures positively affect firms' costs—as is the case with a higher penalty rate, a lower cost of job-vacancy posting, and a lower tax burden on labor—some other measures more directly affect employment and the activity level by making the economy more productive, as in the case of enhanced productivity of regular hours worked, or by increasing the efficiency of the economy's institutions, such as that affecting the matching technology.

Enhanced matching efficiency expands employment at the expense of hours worked, because it allows us to reduce the number of costly vacancies in relation to successful labor matches. This contrasts to the fall in the number of searchers produced by the employment increase and causes the labor-market tightness to decrease. In spite of this outcome, the fall in undeclared hours worked reduces the cost of the undeclared wage bill and produces a moderate increase in the bargained wage. Policies able to increase the efficiency of regular hours worked alter instead the optimal proportion between regular and undeclared labor and increases the overall productivity of employment, which induces firms to hire more workers and expand output. Such augmented productivity and the fall in the number of searchers raises the labor-market tightness and increases the bargained wage.

Moving to policies acting through indirect cost channels, in the case of reductions in the tax rate on labor, the main impact is twofold. On the one hand, a lower fiscal burden on employment decreases the overall labor cost and reduces firms' incentive to evade taxes and hence their convenience of using UDW in production. On the other, it stimulates production and employment via the standard cost-based mechanism: a reduction in firms' overall cost of employment stimulates the hiring of more workers and hence fosters economic activity. A lower cost of vacancy posting induces firms instead to increase output and employment by expanding jobs and reducing hours worked. The opposite outcome is generated by an increase in the penalty rates on UDW, which produces a mild rise in the stationary value of output, determined not so much by the increase in the costly extensive labor margin, but rather by that of the declared intensive margin, which becomes relatively cheaper than undeclared hours worked.

When generally interpreted, these results suggest that the attempt to foster the growth of output and employment should be primarily centered on education and training, as well as on the improvement of job matching institutions and mechanisms. It should, however, be noted that these policies, on the one side, and others such as tax cuts or increases in the penalty rate, on the other, are not equivalent in terms of their implementation costs. It is trivial to observe that, for example, implementing an improved system of education and training may be more costly than adopting a more severe set of deterrence policy measures. For this reason, we aim in future work to introduce these costs into the model economy and to try to carry out a thorough welfare analysis.

Notes

1 This is a ubiquitous feature in production systems and labor markets which is particularly relevant for developed economies—see World Bank (2000).
2 The model could, however, easily incorporate a search cost, as in Andolfatto (1996).
3 Detailed calculations of all the model's equations are provided in a technical appendix available from the authors upon request.
4 Note that, given $B_1 > 0$ (so as to avoid corner solutions), if regular hours are on average more productive than undeclared ones, then the adoption of UDW at equilibrium ($h_R > 0$) requires at least one of the tax rates to be strictly positive, as shown by (10.25). This shows that in developed economies, where it is reasonable to assume $\omega < 0.5$, the rationale for UDW usage is tax evasion.
5 More specifically, in the numerical simulation we compute the percentage standard deviation of the cyclical component of unemployment, $\sigma_{\hat{U}}$, and the percentage standard deviation of the cyclical component of output, $\sigma_{\hat{Y}}$, and obtain a ratio $\frac{\sigma_{\hat{U}}}{\sigma_{\hat{Y}}} = 3.56$. The empirical value of the same ratio for the US economy, using official time series for the period 1964:1 to 2010:2, turns out to be equal to 3.92, once the procedure suggested by Yashiv (2005) is adopted. See Ciccarone *et al.* (2015) for a detailed discussion.
6 The value of p^* is in the range commonly used in the literature (e.g., 0.45 in Shimer, 2005a, b), q^* is that of den Haan *et al.* (2000) and θ^* is slightly higher than the value found by the same authors.
7 Schneider and Enste (2000) and Schneider *et al.* (2010) focus on the legal value-added creating activities that are not taxed or registered, which are broadly consistent with our definition of UDW income.
8 Available at www.ssa.gov/oact/ProgData/taxRates.html (accessed November 1, 2015).
9 This implies that undeclared hours are less productive than regular ones due to (technical and/or psychological) factors related to additional hindrances or difficulties in carrying out UDW.
10 Hall (2008) proposes instead $f_{\hat{Q}}^* = 0.7$ in a model in which utility from leisure is explicitly included.
11 In this and other experiments discussed in the following sections, the tables contain only selected values of the considered parameter. The general validity of our conclusions is, however, confirmed by the monotonicity of the results we obtain.
12 In order to verify that the overall productivity of employment increases with ϑ, consider the aggregate production function $Y = K^\alpha N^{1-\alpha} H^{1-\sigma}$, where $H = (1 - \omega) \vartheta h_M + \omega h_U$. Employment productivity is then $\partial Y / \partial N = (1 - \alpha) \frac{Y}{N}$ and its reaction to ϑ is $\frac{\partial^2 Y}{\partial N \partial \vartheta} > 0$.

13 Clearly these results depend on the assumption of wasteful public expenditure financed with τ_N and could be different, both in magnitude and direction, if G were allowed to play a role in production or in the household's welfare. This, however, complicates the analysis and is left for subsequent research.

14 A well-known example in the Italian experience is the public portal "Cliclavoro," introduced and managed by the Ministry of Labor. Details can be found at www.cliclavoro.gov.it (accessed November 1, 2015).

15 Italian examples of the types of placement services offered by universities are represented by those offered by the Sapienza University of Rome through the SOUL (Sistema Orientamento Università Lavoro) office and by its Faculty of Economics through the SOrT & Placement (Sistema Orientamento Tutorato and Placement) office. For details, visit the URLs www.jobsoul.it/ (accessed November 1, 2015).

References

Andolfatto, D. (1996). Business cycles and labor-market search. *American Economic Review* 86, 112–132.

Andreoni, J., Erard, B., and Feinstein, J. (1998). Tax compliance. *Journal of Economic Literature* 36, 818–860.

Busato, F., Chiarini, B., and Marchetti, E. (2011). Indeterminacy, underground activities and tax evasion. *Economic Modelling* 28, 831–844.

Ciccarone, G., Giuli, F., and Marchetti, E. (2013). Power or loss aversion? Reinterpreting the bargaining weights in search and matching models. *Economics Letters* 118, 375–377.

Ciccarone, G., Giuli, F., and Marchetti, E. (2015). Search frictions and labor market dynamics in a real business cycle model with undeclared work. *Economic Theory*, forthcoming, DOI 10.1007/s00199-015-0903-x.

Costain, J., and Reiter, M. (2008). Business cycles, unemployment insurance, and the calibration of matching models. *Journal of Economic Dynamics & Control* 32, 1120–1155.

Den Haan, W., Ramey, G., and Watson, J. (2000). Job destruction and propagation of shocks. *American Economic Review* 90, 482–498.

Gertler, M., Sala, L., and Trigari, A. (2008). An estimated monetary DSGE model with unemployment and staggered nominal wage bargaining. *Journal of Money, Credit and Banking* 40, 1714–1764.

Hagedorn, M., and Manovskii, I. (2008). The cyclical behavior of equilibrium unemployment and vacancies revisited. *American Economic Review* 98, 1692–1706.

Hall, R. (2008). Sources and mechanisms of cyclical fluctuations in the labor market, Stanford University, mimeo.

Joulfaian, D., and Rider, M. (1998). Differential taxation and tax evasion by small business. *National Tax Journal* 4, 675–687.

Kahneman, D. and Tversky, A. (1979). Prospect theory: An analysis of decision under risk. *Econometrica* 47(2), 263–291.

Kimball, M., and Shapiro, M. (2008). Labor supply: Are the income and substitution effects both large or small? NBER Working Paper No. 14208.

Merz, M. (1995). Search in the labor market and the real business cycle. *Journal of Monetary Economics* 36, 269–300.

Mortensen, D., and Nagypal, E. (2007). More on unemployment and vacancy fluctuations. *Review of Economic Dynamics* 10, 327–347.

Petrongolo, B., and Pissarides, C. (2001). Looking into the black box: A survey of the matching function. *Journal of Economic Literature* 39, 390–431.

Schneider, F., and Enste, D. (2000). Shadow economies: Size, causes and consequences. *Journal of Economic Literature* 38, 77–114.

Schneider, F., Buhen, A., and Montenegro, C. (2010). New estimates for the shadow economies all over the world. *International Economic Journal* 24, 443–461.

Shimer, R. (2005a). The cyclical behavior of equilibrium unemployment and vacancies. *American Economic Review* 95, 25–49.

Shimer, R. (2005b). Reassessing the ins and outs of unemployment. University of Chicago, IL, Mimeo.

Thomas, C. (2008). Search and matching frictions and optimal monetary policy. *Journal of Monetary Economics* 55, 936–956.

Trigari, A. (2009). Equilibrium unemployment, job flows, and inflation dynamics. *Journal of Money, Credit and Banking* 41, 1–33.

Walsh, C. (2005). Labor market search, sticky prices, and interest rate policies. *Review of Economic Dynamics* 8, 829–849.

World Bank (2000). The world business environment survey (WBES) 2000, Washington, DC, World Bank. http://info.worldbank.org/governance/wbes/. Accessed 2 July 2015.

Yashiv, E. (2005). Evaluating the performance of the search and matching model. *European Economic Review* 50, 909–936.

Index